THE HOMOSEXUAL(ITY) OF LAW

The Homosexual(ity) of Law is an innovative and important investigation of the legal representation of identity and sexuality. This wide-ranging and theoretical study demands that we think again about the legal regulation of sexual relations. It examines how both sense and nonsense of same-sex relations are made in law by way of 'homosexual'. It explores how the introduction of an idea of homosexuality both promotes the continued abhorrence and increased punishment of same-sex relations and makes possible reforms in the law that promote respect for these relations.

This study investigates the struggles that surround the review of the law on 'homosexuality' undertaken by the Wolfenden Committee in the 1950s and explores the peculiarities of the enactment of the term 'homosexual' into the law of England in 1967. It challenges the current understanding that 'homosexual' is either a term used to name a specific category of act or a term that is merely used to name an identity. *The Homosexual(ity) of Law* shows how 'homosexual' is a term that signifies both of these things, but it is also capable of expressing many other meanings. It explores the values that are given a voice through this new term in law. It also demonstrates that 'homosexual' in law is a reference to a complex technology of interrogation, surveillance and documentation that isolates gestures, speech and deportment and gives them meaning as 'homosexual' in law. Through an analysis of various police practices, the day-to-day decisions of the judiciary in high profile test cases and recent Parliamentary debates relating to the age of consent law reform, *The Homosexual(ity) of Law* explores the way this 'homosexual(ity)' is put to use in current legal practice.

Leslie J. Moran is Senior Lecturer in Law at the University of Lancaster.

THE
HOMOSEXUAL(ITY) OF
LAW

Leslie J. Moran

London and New York

First published 1996
by Routledge
11 New Fetter Lane, London EC4P 4EE
Simultaneously published in the USA and Canada
by Routledge
29 West 35th Street, New York, NY 10001

Routledge is an International Thomson Publishing company

© 1996 Leslie J. Moran
Typeset in Baskerville by Routledge
Printed and bound in Great Britain by
T J Press (padstow) Ltd, Padstow, Cornwall

British Library Cataloguing in Publication Data
A catalogue record for this book is available from the British Library

Library of Congress Cataloguing in Publication Data
Moran, Leslie, 1955–
The homosexual(ity) of law/ Leslie Moran.
p. cm. Includes bibliographical references and index.
1. Homosexuality – Law and legislation – Great Britain.
2. Sodomy – Great Britain. 3. Homosexuality. I. Title.
KD7976.S6M67 1996 346.4101'3 – dc20 [344.10613]
95–26467 CIP

ISBN 0–415–07952–7 (hbk)
ISBN 0–415–07953–5 (pbk)

CONTENTS

PREFACE
Outlaw

This project has had a long gestation. In undertaking it, I have had to negotiate a complex economy of silence within the institution of academic legal studies. While 'homosexuality' did appear within that institution it appeared according to a specific lexicon of the law, as buggery and gross indecency or indecent assault, as part of a project of the criminalization of the male genital body where that body was made in the law outside the law. This book engages with that agenda but in a way that radically departs from that agenda. It gives a voice to that which in law has been silenced and denied a voice through the verbosity and prolixity of the law. This is the voice of the outlaw in the law.

Being an outlaw in the law has been an important influence on this project. For much of that period, working as a man on the topic of male sexuality in general and on homosexuality in particular within academic legal studies has been to undertake work on a topic that formally did not exist. To take up that work and to pursue it within a theoretically informed and critical perspective, particularly within English legal scholarship, gave this work the status of pariah twice over. In many respects this state of affairs continues. Lesbian and gay legal scholarship is still rarely heard of within the legal academy, even though lesbian and gay scholarship is burgeoning not only elsewhere but also within it.

This project was supported by the financial assistance of the British Academy and the Nuffield Foundation. It has also been sustained by the comfort of many individuals. Peter Goodrich has in many different contexts been a long-standing source of inspiration, patience and boundless support. Costas Douzinas, Ronnie Warrington, Peter Rush and Alison Young and, more recently, Sarah Beresford, Marinos Diamantidis and Elena Loizidou provided an academic home at Lancaster. I am particularly indebted to Marinos, whose friendship and tenacity inspired me in the final stages of this project. All, in various ways, were and continue to be a source of inspiration that saved this project from abandonment and nurtured it to fruition. Tim Murphy's early encouragement helped to give life to this project. His support has been an inspiration throughout. Richard Collier has been a constant source of stimulation. Many is the time we have been forced to share the notoriety, each in different ways, of being outlaws in the legal academy. Shaun McVeigh, Alain Pottage and Carl Stychin have in different ways kept this project alive. Anne Barron has sustained me with her generosity. Ian Brownlee offered his friendship, which has been a source of comfort and strength throughout my academic life. Professor David Sugarman stimulated my work in various ways. Michael Salter provided feedback in the final stages of this project. Rob Killeen and Paul Dugmore introduced me to new ways of sustaining my research. Many others have given their time, enthusiasm and support. Particular thanks are due to Anne Bottomley, Sue Brimelow, Nicole Crockett, Ray Cox, Meryll Dean, Willie Dotson, Neil Duxbury, Robert Fildes, Nancy Hobbs, Leo Flynn, David Greenberg, Piyel Haldar, Sharon Halliwell, Didi Hermann, Derek Mcghee, Sandy and Alice Miller, Katherine O'Donovan, Fiona Macmillan, Andrew Quick, Derek Rawse and Austin Sarat. Finally, my thanks go to my parents Annie and Alex. They have provided the love and support that only they can.

1

INTRODUCTION
Brief encounters

On a Friday evening sometime in 1954, John Wolfenden, later Lord Wolfenden, on boarding the sleeper train from Liverpool to London, perused the list of fellow travellers, 'as one always does' (Wolfenden 1976: 129). He was entertained to find that one of his fellow travellers was a government minister, the Home Secretary, Sir Maxwell Fyfe. The subsequent brief encounter between these two men was described by Wolfenden in his autobiography in the following terms:

> As the train left I wrote him a note suggesting that if it would save his time next week we might have some conversation now. His detective took it to him and came back with the reply that the Home Secretary would be very glad to see me straight away.
>
> I suspect that he had been half undressed when he got my message. But he nobly put his overcoat over what was left; and so it happened that my first conversation about this whole business took place as we sat side by side on his sleeping berth. By the time I left him after Crewe and lurched back to my own compartment my head was in a fair whirl.
>
> (Wolfenden 1976: 129)

The conversation that took place between Wolfenden and Maxwell Fyfe as they sat, under the protection of the police, in various states of dress and undress, side by side in a private compartment of the train, related to homosexuality, prostitution and the law. In the course of this brief encounter, Maxwell Fyfe propositioned Wolfenden. Wolfenden was asked to act as the chairperson of a government committee to review the law and practice relating to homosexuality and prostitution. He consented to the task and the committee formally began its work on 24 August 1954. On 28 August Wolfenden wrote to the Secretary to the committee, Mr W.C. Roberts. He declared that while the work was going to be difficult, 'in a queer sort of way I'm rather looking forward to it' (PRO HO 345/2).

The Wolfenden Committee worked for three years. It conclusions were published on 3 September 1957 (Wolfenden 1957). Many of the proposals relating to prostitution were enacted in the Street Offences Act 1959. Those relating to 'homosexual acts' and the law were enacted later, after much public and Parliamentary debate, in the Sexual Offences Act 1967.

1

As a result of the Wolfenden Committee and the 1967 Act, 'homosexual' became a term of formal significance within the law. This book is a study of the many brief encounters, snatched conversations, states of dress and undress, shared private moments, silences and queer experiences through which this 'homosexual' of law came into being and continues to operate within contemporary law.

This is a study that seeks to explore the many problems, complex contemporary struggles and diverse meanings that come into play with the introduction of the category of 'homosexual' into the law. The Wolfenden archive, the law reforms that followed and the legal practices that preceded, informed and post-date those events provide a rich resource through which these matters might be explored. It is a study that has significance for any politics of identity that engages with same-sex genital relations and the law.

It is first and foremost a book about the law. Its general aim is to pursue a study of the representation of same-sex genital relations in the law. Its specific objective is to undertake an analysis of the representation of these genital relations by way of this 'homosexual' of the law. In the first instance it is a study of the use of 'homosexual' in a specific legal context: the English common law.[1] Its significance, however, goes beyond the confines of that particular legal system, having a significance for any legal system within that family of laws and legal systems related to the English common law: specifically, those of Australia, Canada, Ireland, New Zealand, Scotland and the United States of America.

The study of the introduction of the 'homosexual' into law and the terms of its contemporary operation is not confined to an analysis of the important but limited parameters of the specific rules that install the 'homosexual' in the law. As I shall demonstrate, the 'homosexual' has significance in the context of a wider collection of legal rules that are formally silent on the matter of homosexuality. Nor should the significance of the 'homosexual' of law be understood only as a matter of rules. For the purpose of this study the significance of law lies in the fact that it is an important social space, a particular set of cultural practices through which meaning and order are generated and enforced. This study seeks to explore the introduction of the 'homosexual' into that specific social and cultural space. The addition of the 'homosexual' to the formal language of law brings into being and authorizes the use of a new category of object and subject through which law imagines human relations. This is a particularly important focus of the book.

HOMOSEXUALITY

As a book about the interface between same-sex genital relations and the law, this is a study that falls within a well-established tradition of a politics that defines itself by way of same-sex genital relations. Many terms have been invented and deployed to create the sense and nonsense of these relations. These include 'homosexual', 'Uranian', 'invert' and, more recently, 'gay' and 'queer'. All have been coined in order to name. As such they emblematize a claim to and a desire for autonomy

(Butler 1993: 19). Of particular interest here is the manner in which, in various ways, all produce that autonomy in relation to law.

'Homosexuality' is a term coined by a Hungarian doctor, Karl Maria Benkert (who used the pseudonym K.M. Kertbeny), in the mid-nineteenth century (Lauristen and Thornstad 1974). It was first put to use to express defiance and indignation at bigotry, ignorance and intolerance towards the male genital body in its male-to-male genital relations. It was used to imagine that body as a celebration of the present by reference to a past, by creating a huge catalogue of western cultural icons that were named homosexual: from general aspects of a venerated epoch within Greek culture[2] to specific individuals – Michelangelo, Byron, Newton, Louis XVIII and Shakespeare (to name but a few). Its connection with the juridical is not so much an afterthought as something already present at the moment of its conception. As a vehicle for the expression of defiance and indignation at bigotry, ignorance and intolerance it emerged in response to an immanent threat of criminalization. Here the juridical theme of this homosexual(ity)[3] was connected to certain ontological and aetiological imaginings. 'Homosexuality' was invented as a term that imagined this genital body by way of a specific subjectivity (ontology) with certain causes (aetiology), as an identity that is fundamental to the sense of self, natural and inborn. This conjunction between law and ontological and aetiological themes tends to take the following form. If homosexuality is fundamental to the sense of self and is innate, it cannot be regarded as punishable by rational persons who respect the laws of nature. 'Homosexuality' was thus put to work as a term that demanded a 'rational' and 'progressive' legal approach to such same-sex genital relations, or, more specifically, it was a term through which the non- or de-criminalization of those relations might be imagined. Finally, it was also a term through which this juridical Arcadia might be given a history, by specific reference to the Code Napoleon.[4]

Contemporaries of Benkert, and others that followed him, not only deployed the term 'homosexual' in the same way but also translated its themes into other contexts, inventing other terms having different inflections. For example, Karl Heinrich Ulrich, who coined the term 'Uranian',[5] produced a vast body of work that both echoed the themes articulated by Benkert and gave them a particular inflection (e.g. Ulrich 1975). Ulrich appears to have focused upon the theme of ontology. He used the term to imagine the male genital body in its male-to-male genital relations as an identity that might be explained as a woman's mind in a man's body. Likewise, we could follow the development of these themes and map further inflections and transformations into other terms such as 'inversion', which is a term closely associated with the work of Havelock Ellis (Ellis 1897, 1900). Of particular note to the concerns of this analysis is the similarity of the ontological and aetiological claims found in each of these terms and their juridical representation.

A more recent and familiar term within genital politics, one that continues to have great contemporary significance, is 'gay'. It is similar to 'homosexual' in that its significance is as a term that has been deployed as a vehicle through which, in a different time (historians have tended to locate the deployment of 'gay' as a term through which the male genital body in its male-to-male genital relations might be celebrated as a post-war development) and a different cultural context (inaugurated in the USA (Altman 1982; Young 1995),[6] disseminated through the globalization of the USA), defiance and indignation at bigotry, ignorance and intolerance towards same-sex genital relations have been expressed. Like 'homosexual' before it, 'gay' was mobilized to imagine a celebration of the present by reference to a past.[7] The Introduction to the UK Gay Liberation Manifesto provides a good example of the attribution of these themes to 'gay':

> Throughout recorded history, oppressed groups have organised to claim their rights and obtain their needs. Homosexuals, who have been oppressed by physical violence and by ideological and psychological attacks at every level of social interaction, are at last becoming angry.
>
> To you, our gay sisters and brothers, we say that you are the oppressed; we intend to show you examples of the hatred and fear with which straight society relegates us to the position and treatment of sub-humans, and to explain their basis. We will show you how we can use our righteous anger to uproot the present oppressive system with its decaying and constricting ideology, and how we, together with other oppressed groups, can start to form a new order, and a liberated lifestyle, from the alternatives which we offer.
>
> (GLF 1971)

At the same time, this particular deployment of 'gay' has a different grammar from that of 'homosexual'. It stands over against the disqualification and the negativity that is said to have become associated with 'homosexual'. More specifically, it is set up in contrast to the 'homosexual' of other homophile organizations.[8] In the UK, it set itself over against 'homosexual' in its utilization of a leftist agenda, a particular, Marxist-inspired, analytical perspective and a programme of revolutionary change (Gough and MacNair 1985; Cooper 1994). 'Gay' as a project of liberation imagines an authentic ontology that precedes the structurally determined cultural practices of oppression and repression.[9] As such it awaits liberation. As a term through which a juridical Arcadia might be imagined it is beyond the confines of the agenda of decriminalization and more firmly placed within a project of rights associated with a broader agenda of a sexualized lifestyle.

'Queer' is more recent still. Again it is a term through which the male genital body in its inter-male relations might be imagined as indignation, defiance and celebration. While queer politics defines itself against 'gay', it builds on the considerable success of a gay politics particularly in its intellectual development and institutional successes. But at the same time it is born at the limits of the success of that politics, as has been made apparent in the wake of the AIDS pandemic. As such, queer politics is born in the shadow of and in response to extreme violence: the ravages of death (Signorile 1993). It emerges in response to the sense of loss and hopelessness that AIDS has made manifest. It is connected to gay politics in that it seeks to mobilize pride but in the same instance it differs from gay in that it makes

4

pride appear in unexpected places: in death, shame (Sedgwick 1993) and in terms of vilification such as 'queer'. Like gay it is a return to direct action: Act Up and Queer Nation (Smyth 1992). In contrast to gay, it is a post-liberation politics informed by a post-structuralist critique (Fuss 1991; Butler 1990, 1993; Warner 1993) and a cynical politics of identity. As such it is an identity politics where identity is more diffuse, not just a sexualized identity but also sexualized according to the needs of race, ethnicity, age, gender and sex. Queer ontology has become fragmented and multiple. Here the problem of aetiology is at best irrelevant or at worst marginal. Queer was also born at the limits of the juridical practice of gay as symbolized in the USA in the refusal of constitutional respect for gay rights in *Bowers* v. *Hardwick* (1986). Queer imagines the juridical as a practice of confrontation, exposure, denigration, radical submission, fragmentaion, contingency (Stychen 1995). In general the juridical theme is ironic, but, like the gay agenda that preceded it, it is a demand for juridical respect and for the protection of a specific lifestyle.

So far, particular attention has been paid to the way these terms have been deployed to express defiance and indignation at bigotry, ignorance and intolerance, and to imagine a juridical Arcadia where same-sex genital relations are no longer denigrated. It is also important to place these ideas of same-sex genital relations and desires in the context of other ways of making sense of the male genital body in its male-to-male genital relations and to appreciate what has been given a voice in and through these terms, and in particular through that of 'homosexual'.

These other ideas are particularly important, as they have been used to give the term 'homosexual' a very different inflection from that outlined above. These other articulations of homosexual(ity) are particularly important in three respects. First, they draw our attention to the fact that it is wrong to conclude that terms such as 'homosexual' (and to a lesser extent 'Uranian', 'inversion' and 'gay') are univocal with respect to their various juridical, ontological or aetiological themes. As Butler has noted:

> As much as it is necessary to assert political demands through recourse to identity categories, and lay claim to the power to name oneself and determine the conditions under which that name is used, it is also impossible to sustain that kind of mastery over the trajectory of those categories within discourse.
>
> (Butler 1993: 19)

Second, as this study will demonstrate, these other ideas of the 'homosexual' have been successfully institutionalized, producing a male genital body as an object of the law in general and of its criminalization and re-criminalization in particular. Finally, they are not only other ways of making sense and nonsense of same-sex genital relations by way of the 'homosexual' but, more specifically, they are ways of making sense and nonsense of those relations against which particularly the homophile organizations of the 1950s and beyond have developed their own agenda.

Krafft-Ebing's work, *Psychopathia Sexualis* (Krafft-Ebing 1947), is of particular importance here. It illustrates other ways of making sense and nonsense of the genital body in its same-sex genital relations that are remote from those already considered. It also illustrates how, at the same time, his idea of the 'homosexual' rehearses those other different, prior and coextensive, imaginings of this body to which I have already referred. In Krafft-Ebing's scheme of things, this genital body in its same-sex genital relations is made sense and nonsense of by way of a more general category of perversion. In turn, this category is split into two sub-categories: congenital and acquired perversion. (The latter is then further distinguished into pathological and moral perversity.) Of the first category Krafft-Ebing explained that 'congenital sexual inversion occurs only in predisposed (tainted) individuals' (Krafft-Ebing 1948: 382). For Krafft-Ebing these individuals were 'homosexuals'. Thus Krafft-Ebing here deploys the term 'homosexual' as a way of imagining the genital body as a very specific body: as a congenital state.

However, there is a need for some caution here. Two preliminary points are of particular significance. First, it is important to recognize that there is a certain interchangeability of the terms 'perversion', 'inversion' and 'homosexual'.[10] Second, while Krafft-Ebing attributes a dichotomy of psychic and somatic states (the congenital and the acquired) to different terms ('homosexual' being a term that had been coined to represent only the congenital), 'homosexual' might also be used to designate the other psychic and somatic state (the acquired). Of particular importance is the way in which the conflation of congenital and acquired in the common term 'homosexual' masks the fragmentation of the ideas relating to the nature of that embodied subject (ontology) and the causes (aetiology) of that identity associated with the new use of the term. This conflation makes 'homosexual' an ambiguous term.[11]

Despite the reworking of this language of the male genital body in its male-to-male genital relations, Krafft-Ebing's writings demonstrate that the term 'homosexual' still works as a vehicle through which it might be possible to mobilize defiance and imagine a different social order. In particular it still works as a name through which a reform of the law might be staged. So this new 'homosexual' might still be deployed as a term to invoke the naturalness of abnormality.[12] Krafft-Ebing suggests that this has particular significance for law reform:

> The jurist could not consent to [a repeal of the law], if he is to remember that pederasty [which here refers to 'Sodomy in its strict sense . . . inserting the penis into the anus', p. 381] is much more frequently a disgusting vice than the result of a physical and mental infirmity; and that, moreover, many homosexuals, though driven to sexual acts with their own sex, are yet in nowise compelled to indulge in pederasty, – a sexual act which, under all circumstances, must stand as cynical, disgusting and when passive, as decidedly injurious.
>
> (Krafft-Ebing 1948: 386)

Here he draws attention to the importance of the interface between the law and the various ways of making sense and nonsense of this genital body, its desires, practices and pleasures. He suggests that law reform is at least in part the installation in law of a very specific sense and nonsense of this genital body in its relations with other bodies. In the first instance, his reform trajectory is associated only with the congenital. Within this scheme of things, homosexuality as acquired perversion might be problematic, being remote from the naturalness that grounds the claim for juridical reform.

This draws our attention to another aspect of his reform agenda. While Krafft-Ebing argues that the 'homosexual' ought not to be imagined as an object of regulation in the law, he does not elaborate the term in order that the male genital body be taken out of social regulation. For Krafft-Ebing, 'homosexual' is a term by means of which this male genital body might become a new object within a different field of regulation. The term 'homosexual' is deployed to produce this male genital body as an object of medicine in order that the genital body might be subjected to medicine as a regulatory regime.

A recognition not only of the multiplicity of meanings but also of the divergence of meanings that might be generated in a single term has particular significance for an understanding of the history of the emergence of the 'homosexual' in law. This is a particular feature of the debates generated by the Wolfenden review. It also has a more general significance. As this study will show, the 'homosexual' that becomes installed in the law is informed by these different ideas.

LAW

In the past, work on the law that has been undertaken within that particular tradition of homosexual(ity) that sought to express defiance and indignation at bigotry, ignorance and intolerance towards the genital body in its same-sex genital relations has taken the form of demands for decriminalization. This form of intervention has advocated the removal of particular categories of wrong from the law, in particular the criminal law. More recently, the focus of gay and lesbian political engagement with the law has changed. Demands have been made to add references to same-sex genital relations to the law, for the enactment of a new set of terms and categories within the law, such as 'sexual orientation', 'lesbian', 'gay' or 'homosexual'. In turn it has been argued that these new terms should be linked together with others, such as 'discrimination', 'rights' and so on (Winter-mute 1995).[13]

This study differs from these initiatives in that it is not directly concerned either with an argument that promotes the removal of terms or with demands for the addition of new terms to the law, though I hope that this study has something to contribute to an understanding and appreciation of both these approaches. The project pursued in this analysis is more closely connected to a general trend of critical legal scholarship and an emerging scholarship and genital politics that seeks to develop a critique of the law in the face of the limited nature of the success of 'homosexual rights' or 'gay rights' in particular and of law reform in general.[14] In part this has emerged in the wake of the impact of the HIV/AIDS pandemic, and more specifically out of developments that have taken place in the USA around recent civil rights activism since *Bowers* v. *Hardwick*. This scholarship has drawn attention to the peculiarities of the language of the law through which genital relations between persons of the same sex are represented within the law (Thomas 1992, 1993; Halley 1991, 1993a, 1993b). In line with this scholarship, my own study attempts to provide new insights into the peculiarities of the interface between law and same-sex genital relations. More particularly, it seeks to explore the specific characteristics of the representation of same-sex genital relations within the particular social medium of law, with a view to developing an understanding of the legal practices that generate the specific social meanings that shape, invest and are given such a persistent voice through the medium of the law. The critique that emerges is concerned with the development of an analysis of the terms of political engagement with the law.

Central to this study is a recognition of the fact that law is an idiosyncratic textual practice. As such it is a textual practice that must be performed according to specific criteria. Furthermore it is important to recognize that law is a practice that seeks to represent its own practice in a very particular way (Sarat and Kearns 1991, 1992; Moran 1995). Any attempt to understand the law and any attempt to engage with the law will have to take account of, reflect upon and participate in these peculiarities and practices.

As a literary genre or discursive formation, law is a set of practices that strive to achieve particular objectives. Law is a social textual practice that is hierarchical and authoritarian. As such it is a set of practices that seek to impose a particular and exclusive meaning on the world. These textual practices are used systematically to appropriate, privilege and secure a specific and limited set of meanings, accents and connotations. In the production of privileged meanings, the literary practices of law proceed by means of displacing and rejecting alternative and competing meanings and accents. The meanings generated in and through the law also purport to have another quality; they are monologic. Thus legal textual practice seeks to produce the language of the law as a singular and monotonous meaning both at any one time and over a period of time. It generates meaning by means of a restricted number of terms and by means of an alien use of language that often, as this study will show, resorts to archaic terms (Goodrich 1987: 3). This study not only seeks to explore the operation of these idiosyncratic requirements in the context of the representation of same-sex genital relations within the law but it also seeks to develop a critique of their operation and effect.

THE LEXICON OF THE LAW

The restricted economy of the language of the law, which I refer to as the lexicon or word-stock of the law, and the presence and persistence of archaic terms therein are of particular importance. It has special significance for a study of the representation of same-sex genital relations within the law, where archaic terms such as 'buggery' and 'sodomy' have had and continue to have great significance. It is important to recognize that, while the lexicon of law might be archaic, it provides the context for various contemporary political struggles and interventions. It provides the object of intervention. Its idiosyncrasies create the limit of representing human relations and the limit of intervention. On other occasions it creates the very possibility for new ways of representing human relations. The peculiar terms that make up the current lexicon of law stand as a resource through which human relations might be presented and re-presented, fashioned and refashioned, within and through the important and valued medium of law.

While the lexicon is impoverished and dominated by archaic terms, this is not to say that it is an inadequate, fixed or unchangeable resource. Throughout this study I shall demonstrate that the strictly limited archaic word-stock of the law is an extremely rich and important source of past, present and future meaning. This study focuses upon the mechanisms whereby these archaic terms are put to work to generate contemporary meanings and thereby fashion human relations. It seeks to demonstrate that the lexicon of law, in all its impoverishment and strangeness, is none the less a depository of terms through which contemporary human relations are produced, determined and limited in their contemporary social contexts.

The word-stock of law is also of great significance in another way. It is a rich and useful archive of the historical and social effects that produce and reproduce the meaning of human relations. In the course of this study, I exploit these aspects of law to examine the claims that are made about the generation of meaning in and through law and to develop a critique of legal practice, as a practice that seeks to limit meaning, to ensure stability and consistency, to repeat the same meaning in different contexts. This study seeks to demonstrate that this self-image of legal practice is highly problematic.

The following study will demonstrate, perhaps contrary to expectations, that the monotonous repetition of archaic terms is capable, both at any one time and over a period of time, of generating many different meanings. In developing an understanding of this aspect of the peculiar practices of the law, this study seeks to explore the law as a site of struggle over the meaning of those legal terms though which key social relations are produced, reproduced and transformed. This aspect of the study seeks to emphasize that law is a medium though which the social, political and ethical aspects of life might be fashioned and lived (Foucault 1989: 21). An engagement with the lexicon of the law, in all its peculiarities, ought to be recognized as an important means of mobilization, as a way of fashioning the present.

An important focus of this book is the effect of changes – in particular the effect of the addition of new terms, in this instance 'homosexual' – to the lexicon of the law. This raises important questions about the interface between, on the one hand, the operation of the compulsory requirements of hierarchy, authoritarianism, which are put to work to generate the persistence and uniformity of meaning in law and, on the other hand, the demands of change and novelty generated by the introduction of changes into the law. In undertaking this project, I seek to reflect not only upon the production of continuity in law but also upon the nature of those legal practices that produce a temporal image of the law in time as repetition, as precedent. My concern, finally, is to address the possibilities and limitations of an engagement with law as a means of reform.

FOUCAULT

Throughout, the analysis owes much to the work of Michel Foucault. In particular it draws upon his work on sexuality, power, discourse and genealogy. First, it is informed by Foucault's writings on the materiality and historicity of sexuality. More specifically it draws upon Foucault's insights into sexuality as will to knowledge. Here sexuality is not reducible to nature or to the realization of an inner self where that particular self is the truth of the subject. Foucault's work on the materiality of sexuality draws attention to the way in which our contemporary experience of sexuality is an effect of the development and deployment of an entire machinery or technology for producing the truth of sexuality. This is of particular importance in the context of the analysis of the deployment of homosexuality in law. It potentially problematizes the relationship between law and (homo)sexuality. Rather than it being a relationship between two separate realms of, on the one hand, a pre-existing identity and, on the other hand, laws that confine, limit and repress, this study argues that law and (homo)sexuality are more intimately connected (cf. Hunt and Wickham 1994).

In perusing this analysis, the study is connected to and informed by Foucault's work on power. Foucault outlines two models of power. The first is the juridico-discursive model of power (Foucault 1980: 78–108; 1981a: 81–91). In this scheme of things, power is thought of as something that is external to things and as a force that works upon them. It is something that might be possessed, lost, exchanged, appropriated, limited or absent. It is conceptualized in terms of domination and subordination. It is thought to work through the imposition of limits. It might be negotiated, exchanged, redistributed and secured as a social contract. Its operation is thought of in terms of overstepping boundaries and in terms of its legitimacy. Law in general is often represented in these terms. It is thought of as a manifestation of power. This model also informs understandings about the interface between law and sexuality. Here the law–sexuality relation is one of outside–inside, of power and oppression, of power and repression. It is also one of social contract, popular consensus, legitimacy and abuse of power.

In contrast to this, Foucault develops another idea of power that can be used to problematize these ways of thinking about power and more specifically of problematizing the law–sexuality relation. This second model of power might be called the power–knowledge model. In this scheme of things:

> [P]ower is not an institution, and not a structure; neither is it a certain strength we are endowed with; it is the name one attributes to a complex strategical situation in a particular society.
>
> (Foucault 1981a: 93)

Foucault further explains that, according to this model, power is always multiple, exercised from innumerable points in the interplay of non-egalitarian and mobile relations. Power is not external but immanent, being the immediate effect of divisions, inequalities and disequilibria. Power is productive. Power comes from below, being in the minutiae of social practices rather than merely in its formal grand institutions such as the State and Law (Foucault 1981a: 94–6).

I seek to demonstrate that, in this second model of power, Foucault offers a way of imagining power that has significance for understanding the interface between law, sexuality and power. This study seeks to take up some of the insights that Foucault offers with respect to this alternative model of power and to use his insights in order to develop new perspectives on the nature of law and legal practice that demonstrate that law and sexuality have an intimate relationship, rather than being two domains that ought to be understood as opposites. More specifically, this study seeks to explore the way in which the machinery or technology for producing the truth of sexuality becomes an important part of legal practice, and the way in which legal practice becomes part of the machinery or technology for producing the truth of sexuality.[15]

These particular matters are pursued specifically in that section of the study (Chapter 5) that focuses upon the analysis of the meaning of 'homosexual offences' that was undertaken by the Wolfenden Committee. It also has great significance in the context of the study of police practices. Here Foucault's work is used to develop an analysis and understanding of the policing techniques that 'detect' men who have genital relations with other men in public places, in particular in public toilets. In this section of the book (Chapters 6 and 7), I seek to use Foucault's work to develop a new analysis of the legal practices of the agents of the law. I seek to show that these legal practices are a machinery and a technology for producing not only the truth of law but also (homo)sexuality in law as truth.

My analysis of the law draws upon Foucault's work on discourse (Foucault 1970, 1981b) and genealogy (Foucault 1977). Foucault's work on discourse, particularly in his essay 'The order of discourse' (Foucault 1981b), is of significance in developing an understanding of legal practice as an idiosyncratic practice that seeks system-atically to appropriate, privilege and secure a specific and limited set of meanings, accents and connotations by means of displacing and rejecting alternative and competing meanings, connotations and accents. In 'The order of discourse', Foucault describes procedures whereby this impoverishment and monopoly of meaning might be realized. In the law these practices of exclusion impose limits upon those authorized to speak. Through the imposition of the lexicon of the law, they also restrict what might be said. They proceed by way of the deployment of certain divisions, between law (reason) made manifest in an alien and archaic language and non-law (unreason) as represented by the vernacular, popular language that is placed beyond the law in subcultural dialects. Hierarchy is also produced in the division between truth and falsity, within which law is a discourse of the absolute truth of human relations. These themes are pursued in the following study of buggery (Chapters 2, 3 and 4).

Foucault's work on genealogy also has considerable significance for the study of law. In general it is used to explore and explain how meaning is generated in law. In particular it is used in this study to develop an understanding of the generation of contemporary meanings in law. It has particular significance in the context of claims made within law that the prohibition of certain genital relations is a reflection of nature's abhorrence or a social abhorrence in law that is immemorial. Foucault's work on genealogy explores the nature of claims that celebrate an origin or proceed by way of the transhistorical nature of meaning. Claims made in law that a prohibition is a manifestation of a fundamental or an essential requirement are significant in another way. They are also claims about the nature of legal practice. In the suggestion that law is consistent at any one time and over a period of time they seek to demonstrate that in each different situation law remains the same. As such it is a claim about the nature of repetition. Foucault's work on genealogy is used in this study to problematize these claims about the nature of legal practice and, more specifically, it is used to challenge the legal assumption that repetition is the production of sameness. Foucault's work on genealogy has particular importance in the development of an analysis of the claim that tradition demands that buggery must remain as a distinctive prohibition in law and that it must be named a 'homosexual act'.

While the concern with genealogy might, in the first instance, make this study appear to be a historical investigation, my intention is not to write a book of history. The genealogical approach is concerned with the present. The historical investigations developed here aims to develop an understanding of the present meanings that are given a voice or that might be spoken in and through law by way of the term 'homosexual'.

HOMOSEXUAL AS MALE

Another important preliminary point relates to the particular characteristics of the 'homosexual' of legal discourse, introduced by way of the Sexual Offences Act 1967. In focusing upon the law's 'homosexual', the following study is not an analysis of the representation of all same-sex genital relations in law. The homosexual introduced by the 1967 Act installs a way of representing or imagining a very specific body in law. It is not an official body that is constituted merely by reference to the genital or, more specifically, the body by way of its inter-genital relations. It is a genital body that is always already sexed and gendered. This 'homosexual' of law is an image of a male genital body.

The study of this 'homosexual(ity)' of law is a study of the making of legal sense and nonsense of this male genital body in its genital relations with other male bodies. This is not to suggest that the female genital body in its genital relations with other female bodies is irrelevant to or insignificant for this study. In various ways the legal sense of this female body of the law is of considerable significance here. For example, the absence of this female body of the law from that set of legal practices (Butler 1990, 1993) called criminal law,[16] where the male genital body and male

12

genital relations have been most persistently and elaborately imagined and deployed in order to prohibit certain acts and exterminate those found to have performed them, is of particular importance. It draws attention to the fact that the practices of criminal law might also be a set of practices through which a refusal to imagine same-sex genital relations is put into effect in law. Thereby the absence of representations of this female body in law draws attention to the fact that the representation of the male body in its genital relations with other male bodies through the practices of the criminal law is neither necessary nor inevitable but more a contingent and idiosyncratic practice. Furthermore, the absence of this specific female body from the criminal law, where the female body as sexuality is represented (Edwards 1981), might suggest that while same-sex genital relations might be understood as sexuality they might also be understood as primarily gendered relations (Majury 1994).

On the other hand, the simultaneous difficulties of representing this female body through the criminal law and the obsessive production of the male genital body have another significance. The practices of criminalization that have so persistently produced this male body as an object of the law have also been implicated in other legal practices that are potentially remote from acts of criminalization. As this study will seek to show, the cultural production of this criminalized male body as an object of the law has played a significant role in attempts to imagine the genital body as a subject in law with a capacity to act in law. Thus the homosexual as an embodied object of law is implicated in the production of homosexual as an embodied subject of law. As an embodied subject of law it has been possible to resort to 'homosexual' in order to claim rights, to demand the recognition and enforcement of duties, to seek the recognition and respect of interests (Lauristen and Thornstad 1974; Foucault 1981a). Thus homosexual and gay rights are not only remote from but also have a certain proximity to those criminal practices through which this male body of law has been so obsessively produced. The silence and indifference of the criminal law to genital relations between women have produced a certain invisibility and thereby made it more difficult to achieve a representation in law of the embodied genital female as an autonomous subject with a capacity to act in law. Thereby the recognition of legal subjectivity in general and the representation of their rights, interests and duties in particular has been made more problematic (Robson 1992).

While in most instances legal practices have produced this female genital body as an absence in the context of the English criminal law (cf. Young 1990), it is important to recognize that a female genital body in its genital relations with other female bodies has been imagined in other domains of law, in particular in the context of those legal practices that produce the regulation of the family in general and motherhood in particular (Rights of Women 1984, 1986; Robson 1992: ch. 11). The demonstration of an ability to imagine this female genital body through legal practices in another place draws attention to the fact that, while criminal legal practices may have been particularly important in the fabrication of the male body, the appearance of this female genital body in law draws attention to the possibility that legal practices of representing a genital body in its genital relations with others is not peculiar to the criminal law.

Its appearance also suggests that it is important to recognize that legal practice is not a set of practices that creates singular or uniform possibilities. This female genital body draws attention to the fact that a body represented through legal practices in one domain of law may be idiosyncratic and confined to a particular site of production. It suggests that legal practice is a complex of many related but different practices, performed at many different and separate, but potentially interconnected, sites. Thus the representation of body as sex, gender and sexuality within the law occurs through the medium of these various practices at many different sites.

Finally, while the analysis and critique of the female genital body of law in its genital relations with other females might be related to an analysis of the production of the male body, an analysis of that female genital body in its female genital relations is also a very different project (Jeffreys 1994; cf. Califia 1994: introduction). To proceed to study the homosexual of the Sexual Offences Act 1967 as sex/gender neutral would be to ignore the sex/gender specifics of the particular use of that term. More generally, to proceed on the basis that the homosexual of law is a sex/gender-neutral term tends to subsume the production of the female genital body under the legal practices through which the male genital body is produced. This erases the differences between these two bodies of law. It threatens to collapse the complexity of their production into a singular practice. In turn a failure to take account of these two bodies of law violates the distinct histories of development and frustrates attempts to understand their connectedness. This book seeks to respect these differences and different histories.

THE GEOPOLITICS OF 'HOMOSEXUAL'

Finally, while the primary focus of the Wolfenden debates and the Sexual Offences Act 1967 was England and Wales, the significance of the debates and the reform of the law is not confined to that limited jurisdiction. Though the addition of 'homosexual' to the word-stock of the law by way of the 1967 Act was originally of limited geopolitical significance, the Wolfenden review was far from being a parochial event. The debates that formed and invested the review that preceded the 1967 Act were informed by European and North American sexological, psychological and psychoanalytic practices,[17] and by law-reform demands and homophile initiatives that had many geopolitically diverse sources.[18] Furthermore, the Wolfenden debates and report that preceded reform and the actual installation of 'homosexual' into the law of England and Wales in the 1967 Act have not only been repeatedly cited for and against other reform debates proximate to England and Wales (Scotland and Northern Ireland) but they have also had a wider significance. They have been deployed in struggles for and against legal change in the context of the wider family of jurisdictions that are connected to the particular legal practices of the English common law, such as Australia (Chappell

14

and Wilson 1968; Bates 1979: 621; Wotherspoon 1991; French 1993), Canada (Kinsman 1987)[19] and the USA (see, for example, Katz 1983, 1992; Altman 1971). Most recently they have been given a high profile in the decision of the Supreme Court of the USA, *Bowers* v. *Hardwick* (1986) in the dissenting opinions in favour of the application for a recognition of the right to privacy. Finally, they have also had a significance beyond this family of jurisdictions. In particular they have been cited both for and against demands for human rights, particularly in Europe under the European Convention of Human Rights (Waaldijk 1993; Tatchell 1992). As such the Wolfenden review and the 'homosexual' of law introduced in 1967 Sexual Offences Act has a significance beyond the boundaries of its original limited jurisdiction.

Though this study does not attempt either to plot the specific details of the deployment of these debates and the 1967 reforms in the context of all the common-law jurisdictions, in particular Australia, Canada, Ireland, New Zealand and the USA, or to provide a complete study of the sexual politics of the 'homosexual' of the legal practices in these different contexts, it does seek to draw upon the experience of these other legal practices, particularly those in North America, in order to develop an understanding of the idiosyncrasies and contingencies of the sexual politics of the legal practices of law. In discovering points of contact and points of divergence between these related jurisdictions, this study also seeks to draw attention to the contingency and the particular effects of a wide range of legal practices by which the many senses and nonsenses of the male genital body in its genital relations with other male bodies are made.

CHAPTER OUTLINE

The first section of this study is entitled 'The Lexicon of Law: From Buggery to Homosexual'. In general, this part of the study seeks to explore the nature of the claims that are made that link buggery to the 'homosexual'. It is also an exploration of the meanings that articulate and might be given a voice through 'buggery' and in its more recent connection with 'homosexual' through that new term in law. This analysis is undertaken in three chapters.

The analysis begins in Chapter 2 by turning to the lexicon of law. In general this chapter focuses upon a matter that absorbed considerable time and energy during the Wolfenden review, the contemporary significance of the legal category of buggery between men. The proposal to remove this category from the word-stock of law was defeated. The Committee proposed the retention of the archaic term 'buggery' in the name of tradition. Furthermore, the archaic term 'buggery' was to be joined to the new legal term 'homosexual'. In pursuing this debate, the chapter explores the terms of the debate and analyses the nature of the connection that was forged between 'buggery' and 'homosexual' in name of tradition, in the new definition of 'buggery' as a 'homosexual act' that was proposed and enacted in the Sexual Offences Act 1967.

Chapter 3 then begins an analysis of buggery. The main objective of this chapter is to develop an understanding of buggery in law as a set of legal practices through which the male genital body in its male genital relations has been imagined in law. This is pursued by way of consideration of a conundrum. From the sixteenth century the law has contained an injunction against speaking of buggery; buggery is that which is not to be named. Thereby silence has been made an essential requirement of the legal practice that seeks to represent the male genital body in its genital relations with other men by way of 'buggery'. Chapter 3 uses that injunction to silence in order to explore the nature of that legal practice of representation.

Chapter 4 then takes a slightly different focus. It pursues a genealogical analysis of buggery. This chapter uses certain legal texts (commentaries and statutes that codify and consolidate the law) to explore the meanings that at any one time and over time have been given a voice through, and given meaning to, 'buggery'. Using this data, the chapter then proceeds to challenge the claims that the condemnation (and criminalization) of buggery represents an unswerving tradition in law. This chapter explores the shifting valorization of 'buggery' through which the male body has been imagined in and through law. In undertaking this analysis, the chapter also seeks to explore the complexity of the contemporary meanings that articulate and might be given a voice through the legal practice of 'buggery'. Finally, this chapter seeks to explore the nature of the legal practices by which we experience the law as tradition.

The second section of this study is entitled 'The Homosexual(ity) of Law'. Having considered the significance of buggery, the study returns in Chapter 5 to the Wolfenden debates in order to develop an analysis of the specifics of the new term 'homosexual' that is to be introduced into the law. The Wolfenden review and the reform debates provide a rich resource, which is used to develop an analysis of this 'homosexual'. While the Wolfenden Committee offered to explain the meaning of the 'homosexual' of 'homosexual offences', this chapter argues that its conclusions are problematic. Thereafter, drawing upon the papers presented to the Wolfenden Committee and upon its own deliberations, this chapter offers a new reading of this 'homosexual'. It seeks to demonstrate that this 'homosexual' is not so much a reference to a category of acts or the truth of a subject, but more a reference to the installation of a set of technologies: 'a whole machinery for speechifying, analysing and investigating' (Foucault 1981a: 32).

Chapters 6 and 7 pursue the theme of the 'homosexual' as a reference to a set of technologies in the context of the legal practice of policing. Chapter 6 explains their general significance as a means whereby the male genital body in its genital relations with other male bodies is brought within the law. Chapter 7 seeks to undertake a detailed analysis of specific technologies of production that produce this body in law.

Chapter 8, 'The uses of homosexuality', is concerned with the deployment of the 'homosexual' in the law subsequent to the 1967 Act. It pursues this theme by means of a series of case studies relating to a range of contemporary disputes and confrontations that have involved a struggle over the use of 'homosexual' in the law. By way of a consideration of the use of 'homosexual(ity)' in various contexts,

16

where the law is silent on homosexuality, human rights, sado-masochism and law reform, the chapter explores the nature of the 'homosexual(ity)' of law after the 1967 reforms. Chapter 9 closes this study. It attempts to draw some conclusions about the 'homosexual(ity)' of law and the nature of the practice of this 'homosexual(ity)' in contemporary legal practice.

Through a study of the emergence, institutionalization and subsequent deployment of the 'homosexual' in law, this book will consider the contemporary techniques and practices through which 'homosexual' becomes installed within the law as a term by which the male genital body in its genital relations with other male bodies is to be imagined. In developing this agenda, the book aims to explore the nature of the legal enterprise in order to develop a greater appreciation of the current operation of contemporary legal practice. Thereby I hope to make a contribution that might facilitate new understandings of the limitations and possibilities of legal practices and foster new interventions at a time when new efforts are being made by a variety of individuals and organizations to reform the law.

Part I

THE LEXICON OF THE LAW

From buggery to homosexual

2

NOVELTY AS THE TRADITION OF LAW

Buggery as homosexual

A STATUTORY NEOLOGISM

'Homosexual' made its first, and to date only,[1] formal appearance in English law in the Sexual Offences Act 1967.[2] There it was put to use in a specific way. Section 1(1) declares that:

> Notwithstanding any statutory or common law provisions, but subject to the provisions of the next following section, **a homosexual act** in private shall not be an offence provided that the parties consent thereto and have attained the age of twenty-one years.[3]

Here it is used to name a new category of acts that are on the one hand in certain limited circumstances to be taken out of the calendar of criminal law and on the other hand are, in most instances, to remain criminal. In s. 1(7) the statute then goes on to explain the meaning of the 'homosexual act' in the following terms:

> For the purposes of this section a man shall be treated as doing **a homosexual act** if, and only if, he commits buggery with another man or commits an act of gross indecency with another man or is a party to the commission by a man of such an act.

These two instances record the official birth of the 'homosexual' in law. This chapter is concerned with undertaking an analysis of one particular aspect of this appearance, the juxtaposition between the new term 'homosexual' and the archaic terms 'buggery',[4] and 'gross indecency'.[5]

It is a connection that has interesting characteristics. In joining the new term 'homosexual acts' to the archaic terms 'buggery' and 'gross indecency', the new statutory definition draws attention to the fact that the introduction of the new term 'homosexual act' does not mark the beginning of the law's interest in genitally defined relations between men. 'Buggery' in particular has a long and noble history as a term through which genital relations between men have been represented in law. For example, there is evidence of 'buggery' (or 'sodomy')[6] being a term of law that included genital relations between persons of the same (mainly male) sex in England and Wales from the time of Henry de Bracton, who

21

wrote in the mid-thirteenth century (Baker 1979).[7] The modern secular legal deployment of the term 'buggery' is more recent, dating from the reign of Henry VIII in 1533–4 when Parliament passed 'An acte for the punysshement of the vice of Buggerie'. This is the first example of a formal specific reference to buggery in English law. The act declared that:

> Forasmuch as there is not yet sufficient and condigne punishment appointed and limited by the due course of the laws of the Realm for the detestable and abominable vice of buggery committed with mankind or beast; It may therefore please the King's Highness with the assent of his Lords spiritual and temporal and the Commons the present parliament assembled that it may be enacted by authority of the same, that the same offence be from henceforth adjudged felony, and such order and form of process therein to be used against the offenders as in cases of felony at the common law.
>
> (1533–4, 25 Hen. 8 c. 6)

The presence of the archaic term 'buggery' in the Sexual Offences Act 1967 is testimony to the fact that those who sought to imagine this body in the law have long been enchanted by buggery.[8]

Its presence is also testimony to another important fact. For much of this prolonged history the binary opposition of homo/heterosexual has played a relatively insignificant role in producing this male genital body in the law (Sedgwick 1991). Thus the presence of 'buggery' (and 'gross indecency') reminds us that the formal introduction of 'homosexual' into the lexicon of law heralds a new and radical departure from past practice. In the juxtaposition of 'homosexual', 'buggery' and 'gross indecency', the statute makes a connection that purports to bridge the gap that separates these disparate terms and suggests that they are one and the same. It is to the making of that connection that the analysis will now turn. The analysis will pay particular attention to the nature of the connection between 'buggery' and 'homosexual'. In part, this reflects the focus of debates provoked by the Wolfenden review. In turn, these debates and this analysis reflect the fact that buggery has a particular place in the history and contemporary practices of imagining the male genital body in its inter-male relations in law. Thus buggery (sodomy) has been described as 'the bedrock of legal discrimination against lesbians and gay men' (Cain 1993: 1587).[9]

The official connection between the 'homosexual' and 'buggery' that is to be found in the Sexual Offences Act 1967 has its origins in the deliberations of the Wolfenden Committee. The archive of these deliberations draws attention to the fact that the buggery–homosexual connection was both particularly important and particularly problematic.[10] The committee's deliberations both problematized the juxtaposition of 'homosexual' and 'buggery', and advocated its introduction in the Sexual Offences Act 1967. In general, the purpose of this chapter is to develop an analysis of that connection and thereby to promote a better understanding of its significance. In pursuing this objective I shall begin to develop an analysis of the associations that make up the considerations that create the legal sense (and nonsense) of the juxtaposition of 'buggery' and 'homosexual' in current law.

THE WOLFENDEN COMMITTEE AND THE END OF BUGGERY

Buggery troubled the members of the Wolfenden Committee throughout its deliberations. Early in the committee's review of the law and practice relating to 'homosexual offences' it was suggested, not that 'buggery' should be joined to the new term 'homosexual' and thereby modernized for the present and future law, but that 'buggery' should be taken out of the lexicon of law. Thereby buggery would cease to be a category of criminal wrong in the law of England and Wales. Buggery first appeared to the committee to be a problem because it was an archaic legal term. This, it suggested, signified that 'buggery' was a term that did not express the contemporary mores and needs of a modern social and legal order depicted in terms of public order, decency, public protection, public safety, justice and equity. Thus the committee was called upon to consider the case for the abolition of the offence of buggery.

Discussions focused upon the question of the continued need for a specific distinction between buggery, which had attached to it the exceptional maximum punishment of life imprisonment, and other offences concerned with genital relations between men: indecent assault and gross indecency. In an attempt to focus the committee's attention upon the matter, two members of the committee (the two doctors and psychiatrists on the committee), Drs Curran and Whitby, produced a paper entitled 'Buggery: Points for abolitionism as a separate offence' (PRO HO 345/3).[11]

The starting point for their analysis was that buggery had a distinctive position in the law. This was represented in various ways. It was depicted in the punishments attached to the offence of buggery. The law singled out buggery from other 'homosexual crimes' and attached to it the most extreme forms of punishment. In the past, the maximum punishment had been death by various means: burying alive, burning at the stake and death by hanging.[12] More recently, the offence had attracted and continued to attract a maximum punishment of life imprisonment. The distinctive place of buggery in law was also emphasized in the lesser penalties attached to the other major offences dealing with genital relations between men: indecent assault and gross indecency. For indecent assault the maximum term of imprisonment was ten years. For gross indecency the maximum was two years. The exceptional position of buggery within the law was also reflected in the legal practice. The most frequent sentence for buggery was between one and three years, whereas for the other offences of indecent assault and gross indecency it was under one year. In response to this state of affairs, Drs Curran and Whitby posed a question: what justification, if any, existed for the imposition of heavier penalties on those convicted of buggery compared with those found guilty of other 'homosexual offences'?

They noted that the special position of buggery within the law appeared to be based upon three major factors. First, it was said to be an expression of the particular characteristics of those who performed acts of buggery. This distinction was supposed to take many forms. In general, individuals who performed acts of buggery were more likely to be criminalistic than other criminals: more likely to have a larger number of previous convictions; more likely to have more convictions for homosexual offences; more likely to be involved in prostitution activities. The distinctive attributes of those who performed acts of buggery were also said to be reflected in the fact that they were more difficult to treat than other criminals and more likely to reoffend.[13] Homosexual offenders who performed acts of buggery were said to be more likely to limit their offending to that act. They were also said to be more likely to have criminalistic personalities: to be working in criminalistic occupations; to come from the criminalistic social and economic classes. All these factors suggest that, by the date of the Wolfenden review, buggery was an act that was to be understood in and through certain ideas about the 'type' of the subject who performed the act. Thus the exceptional status of buggery symbolized not so much a distinctive act but an exceptional and extreme pathological individual.[14]

A second perceived justification for the special status of buggery was that its elevation was the expression of an association between buggery and exceptional damage. Here the exceptional damage was said to be located in the performance of the act of buggery. It might take various forms: extreme physical damage caused by the act of buggery; a special psychological damage that might take the particular form of a future propensity to homosexual behaviour; or the 'moral damage' of the individual.

'A third and final theme by which the special distinction between buggery and other forms of prohibited genital contact between men was to be explained connected buggery to another form of damage. In this instance the particular status attributed to buggery was said to represent not so much a threat of damage to the individual himself but a danger to society as a whole. Again this might take various forms. For example, it was said to be expressed in the fact that 'the relatives of a young victim of buggery would regard this offence with more seriousness and would thus represent society's horror of it' (PRO HO 345/3). It was also said to be reflected in the capacity of buggery to weaken the moral fibre of those who indulge in it and thereby to weaken the moral order of society as a whole. Finally, the special danger to society was to be found in the performance of the physical act itself. More specifically it was located in the belief that buggery imitated heterosexual intercourse. The danger to society was said to be made apparent in the fact that some individuals, not predominantly homosexual, would come to prefer it to normal intercourse.[15]

The report by Drs Curran and Whitby then proceeded to consider the evidence of the validity of each line of argument. They found that those who were convicted of buggery in fact appeared to be less criminalistic than those found guilty of other offences. They had fewer previous convictions for all types of crime and fewer previous convictions for previous homosexual offences. They showed no significant interest in prostitution. Nor did they evidence a significant difference in social, occupational or educational levels. There was no evidence of any difference in the level of offenders found suitable for treatment and recidivism was no higher than among those convicted of other offences. Nor was there any evidence to support the suggestion that buggery was a particular physical or psychological danger to the parties taking part in the act. Finally, they found no evidence to support the conclusion that buggery was a serious threat to society. They concluded that the assembled evidence demonstrated that an act of buggery between men was neither more nor less dangerous or offensive than other prohibited acts of indecency between men. Having found no evidence to support arguments for either the perpetuation of buggery as a separate offence or for the continued attachment of an exceptional punishment to the offence, Drs Curran and Whitby concluded that buggery should no longer retain its special status in law. They proposed that buggery should be abolished as a separate offence.[16]

In the final instance, the Wolfenden Committee, in responding to this analysis, came to an interesting compromise on the future of buggery. In its proposal to reform the punishments applicable to buggery, the committee effectively proceeded on the basis that buggery should be abolished as a wrongful act separate and apart from the other offences of indecent assault and gross indecency. In defining the gravity of the offences and in prescribing the penalties to be attached, it argued that the law must focus not on the physical act but on the gravity of the act by reference to the circumstances surrounding the commission of the act, such as the age of the parties, whether the act was performed in public or in private and whether the act was performed with or without consent.

Following this line of argument the committee proposed that the maximum penalty for buggery should be fragmented as follows:

a) A maximum penalty of life imprisonment would apply to those situations where an act of buggery was performed with a male person under the age of sixteen.

b) A maximum penalty of ten years would be applicable to all acts of indecent assault. Indecent assault would not only embrace all acts of buggery or gross indecency committed against the will of the other party, whatever his age, but would also cover all acts of gross indecency committed with boys under sixteen.

c) A maximum penalty of five years would be applicable to acts of buggery or gross indecency committed by a man over twenty-one with a person of or above the age of sixteen but below the age of twenty-one, in circumstances not amounting to an indecent assault.

d) A maximum sentence of two years for acts of buggery or gross indecency committed in any other circumstances (that is by a person under twenty-one with a consenting partner of or above the age of sixteen; or by any persons in public in circumstances which do not attract the higher penalties.)

(Wolfenden 1957: 34, para. 91)

The committee explained that the retention of the maximum penalty of life imprisonment for an act of buggery with a male under 16 years of age did not so much retain the special status of buggery but erase it. The retention of life imprisonment was not a reflection of the gravity of the particular act or the sex or gender of the other party. The severity of the penalty in the first instance was to reflect the age of the person against whom the act was committed. In that way it echoed the severity of punishment meted out in the context of heterosexual relations with a girl under 13, where the maximum penalty is life imprisonment. The reduction, in certain circumstances, of the maximum penalty for buggery to that applicable to the offence of indecent assault (ten years' imprisonment), or gross indecency (two years), again purported not only to express the end of buggery's special status but also to herald the end of buggery as a separate offence. Finally, these proposals advocate the erasure of buggery's special status in another way: by means of an increase in the maximum penalty associated with other offences, in particular with gross indecency. In certain instances it was proposed that the penalty for gross indecency be increased from two years to five years (where the act was committed by a person over 21 with a person over 16 but below 21). Thereby the committee hoped that the equivalence of the penalty for buggery and gross indecency would mirror the fact that buggery (anal intercourse) was considered to be no more dangerous in and of itself than other forbidden genital acts between men, such as fellatio or mutual masturbation. Together these proposals appear to accept the arguments put forward by Drs Curran and Whitby that there was no evidence to support the retention of buggery as a distinctive offence attracting special penalties, and they not only offered to bring to an end buggery's exceptional position in law but also appeared to propose the abolition of buggery as a separate offence.[17]

Some support for this conclusion is to be found in a note on the topic that was prepared by Sir John Wolfenden, the Chairman of the Committee, for the other members of the committee (PRO HO 345/10, CHP/MISC/2). He comments that prior to the production of the final report, the majority of the committee supported the abolition of buggery as a separate offence attracting special penalties. This support arose from the fact that the existing special position of buggery based upon the general nature of the prohibited act was an arbitrary and inappropriate way of expressing the gravity of the act. He concluded that the majority of the committee had accepted that the gravity of the act should relate to the special circumstances in which the act was performed.[18] Thereby a wide range of circumstances could be accommodated by way of two offences: gross indecency and 'aggravated' gross indecency – i.e., acts involving 'damage' of some sort to a 'victim'. The distribution of penalties between these two offences would better reflect current practice. The complete abolition of buggery as a separate offence would get rid of the artificial division between buggery and gross indecency and thereby make the law tidier and more logical.

However, in the final instance these observations have to be read in conjunction with the decision of a majority of the committee to support the retention of buggery as a distinctive offence. Wolfenden's note provides an insight into the production of this rather contradictory state of affairs. It explains the committee's decision to retain buggery as a distinctive offence in the following terms:

> Although we (or a majority of us) see no reason to distinguish, from the point of view of the law, between buggery *per se* and other homosexual acts, there is no doubt that the very thought of buggery causes many people, including members of both Houses of Parliament, to get hot under the collar. We cannot overlook the fact that there are a great many people who believe (however much we may disagree with them) that buggery, as distinct from other forms of homosexual behaviour, has demoralizing effects not only on individuals but on nations and empires.
>
> (PRO HO345/10, CHP/MISC/2)

In the shadow of this knowledge that buggery might generate dangerous heat, he concluded that a proposal to remove buggery from the lexicon of the law would encourage a widespread campaign against the reforms as a whole. Everything, he concluded, might be lost by trying to go 'too far too fast'. The way forward, he suggested, was to advocate the retention of the distinction between buggery and the other major offences applicable to genital relations between men, but to make such proposals as to ensure that the distinction would have 'no practical effect'.

In the final proposals of reform, the committee adopted the changes to the penalties to be attached to buggery, signifying a willingness to erase buggery as a distinct offence, and at the same time advocated the retention of the term 'buggery'. Thereby the Wolfenden Committee attempted to ensure that, while buggery might be retained in the law as a distinctive offence, in practice it might have no practical effect as a distinctive offence. However, Wolfenden's suggestion that this contradictory state of affairs would have 'no practical effect' should be treated with some caution.

THE 'PRACTICAL EFFECT' OF BUGGERY

While the punishment proposals might have been drafted with a view to reducing the practical effect of buggery, the Committee had already recognized that the retention of the term 'buggery' would have significant and important 'practical effect'. Wolfenden himself had drawn attention to one major manifestation of the 'practical effects' of buggery in his suggestion that a proposal to abolish the offence of buggery would cause 'many people, including members of both Houses of Parliament, to get hot under the collar'. Buggery was retained because of this practical effect: it is a term through which violent passions might find an expression in and through the law.

The practical effects had also been considered in some detail in coming to the conclusion that buggery should be retained as a separate offence. During those discussions it was accepted that buggery could still be deployed to represent certain contemporary values and needs. First, buggery might still depict a particular revulsion that many associated with a specific practice. Second, it could still represent the belief that buggery was an act of coition that simulated more nearly than any other homosexual act the normal[19] act of heterosexual intercourse.[20] Finally, buggery could still symbolize a relationship between the past of 'buggery' and its present and future use. It was said to represent 'the wisdom of our forefathers' (PRO HO 345/4: 6). This is a symbolic dimension of 'buggery' that has particular significance.

Its continued use in the new law in its connection with 'homosexual' would represent not so much a break with the past as it would be the embodiment of that past for the present and for the future. Here the practical effect of buggery was to symbolize the new law as the manifestation of 'a long and weighty tradition' (Wolfenden 1957: 33, para. 88). The majority decision to reassert the exceptional status of buggery, expressed through the continued distinction between buggery and the other offences that related to genital contact between men, was not so much the retention of an archaic and obscure category of wrong that would be of 'no practical effect' but a decision to deploy that archaic term for a present and future in law that would generate very specific practical effects. Thus at the same time as its distinct position was to be erased, its exceptional status was to be put to use as a term in law through which a contemporary male genital body might be represented in the law according to particular cultural values and attributes. In arguing for the retention of buggery and in the enactment of the juxtaposition of 'buggery' and 'homosexual', buggery was to be given a modern function. It was to be retained as a symbol through which contemporary mores and contemporary fears and anxieties might be articulated in the terms of public order, decency, public protection, public safety, justice and equity.

'OF NO PRACTICAL EFFECT': BUGGERY IN AND BEYOND 1967

From buggery to buggeries

The Sexual Offences Act 1967 enacted many of the proposals made by the Wolfenden Committee. In particular, s. 3 of the Act revised the punishments for homosexual acts. In line with the Wolfenden proposals, the section limits the availability of the extreme punishment of life imprisonment for buggery and in some instances it equates the punishments that may be imposed in the context of buggery with those applicable to gross indecency.[21] At the same time, the Act in general and s. 3 in particular retain the distinction between buggery and the lesser offence of gross indecency (and indecent assault). However, rather than this resulting either in the disappearance of buggery or in the erasure of the practical effect of buggery, it appears to have given rise to a rather different state of legal affairs.

The question of the impact of s. 3 upon the offence of buggery subsequent to the 1967 reforms was considered by the House of Lords in the case of *R.* v. *Courtie*

(1984), a very rare instance of an appeal against sentence before the final court of appeal, the House of Lords. Courtie had been charged with, and pleaded guilty to, an offence of buggery contrary to s. 12(1) of the Sexual Offences Act 1956. The particulars of the offence read as follows:

[O]n the 6th day of February 1982 [Courtie] committed buggery with [the complainant], a male person under the age of twenty-one years, namely of the age of nineteen years.

The criminal charge focused upon the age of the party with whom Courtie had performed the act of buggery. In presenting the prosecution's version of the facts, counsel for the Crown included statements that went beyond this focus. Counsel not only indicated that the act of buggery had also been performed with a person under the then 'age of consent' but also suggested that the act of buggery had been performed without the consent of the complainant. Towards the end of the presentation, counsel for the Crown asked to formalize this addendum in a request to add another offence to the count. The new count would have charged Courtie with the offence of buggery without consent against a person between 16 and 21. The trial judge refused this request. Subsequent remarks made by the trial court judge in sentencing Courtie, however, suggested that the sentence passed against him was based upon the more serious offence of buggery without consent, with which he had not been charged. Courtie appealed against the sentence.

Lord Diplock gave judgment for the House. The basic principle determining the matter, he concluded, was that an accused person cannot be convicted of any offence with which he is charged unless it has been established by the prosecution that each one of the factual ingredients that are included in the legal definition of that specific offence was present in the case that has been brought against him by the prosecution. While a person might be found guilty of a lesser offence than the offence charged, where the ingredients of that lesser offence were contained in the more serious offence, a person could not be found guilty of an offence that was more serious than the offence charged. If a person was to be found guilty of a more serious offence he would have to be specifically charged with that offence. Therefore it was of fundamental importance to determine the relationship between a charge referring to a consensual act of buggery where one of the parties was 19 years of age and an act of buggery without consent where one of the parties was under 21.

In order to answer the question of the relationship between these two instances of buggery, Lord Diplock turned to s. 3 of the Sexual Offences Act 1967, which imposed different penalties in these two different situations. Section 3 dictated that the first situation might attract a maximum sentence of five years' imprisonment while the second might attract a maximum penalty of ten years' imprisonment. Lord Diplock concluded that the different sentences were of particular significance. Where a statute provides that the maximum punishment will vary, depending upon the presence of a particular factual ingredient, Parliament has created two (or more) distinct offences. Lord Diplock concluded that, when this principle was applied to s. 3 of the Sexual Offences Act 1967, buggery between two men was no longer a single offence. Parliament had created several specific offences of buggery between men. The first was 'the life offence' of buggery with a male person under the age of 16, whether committed in public or private and with or without the person's consent. The second offence of buggery was 'the ten-year offence', committed with a male person aged 16 years or over, without his consent, whether committed in private or in public. The third was 'the five-year offence' of buggery, where the accused is an adult and the other male party is 16 to 20 years old and consented to the act. The final offence of buggery is 'the two-year offence', where both parties are over 21 but the consensual act is committed otherwise than in private (*Courtie* 1984: 744g). Their Lordships concluded that the judge had proceeded to sentence Courtie on the basis of an offence more serious than the one with which he had been charged. The House of Lords granted Courtie's appeal.

Lord Diplock's conclusions on the law are of particular interest in that they raise serious doubts about the validity of Sir John Wolfenden's conclusions that the committee's reform proposals relating to punishment, as enacted in the 1967 Act, would have 'no practical effect'. Lord Diplock's observations suggest that the juxtaposition of the decision to retain buggery and the decision to fragment the penalties applicable to it in the name of erasing its significance as a distinct offence has had a dramatic effect. Rather than producing the insignificance or disappearance of buggery, the reforms have been interpreted as an amplification of the presence of buggery in the law, creating four different offences of buggery where only one[22] existed prior to the 1967 Act. When placed in the context of the anxieties and fears that might be given a voice and a legitimacy in and through the law, the case of *R. v. Courtie* suggests that the 1967 reforms appear to increase the profile of buggery and might be read as the institutionalized amplification of its usefulness and an amplification of its potential effects.

Tradition: enacting a consciousness of time

A second effect of the Wolfenden Committee's decision to retain the offence of buggery is found in the terms of the 1967 Sexual Offences Act. Following the Wolfenden Committee's recommendations, the Act not only retains the term 'buggery' but installs in the law an official definition of 'homosexual' that connects it to buggery. The deliberations of the Wolfenden Committee draw attention to the fact that in making this connection the Act produces particular effects. It formally connects the values and attributes associated with buggery to the new legal term, 'homosexual'. This connection is made in the name of tradition. This is of particular significance for those who seek to address and mobilize the 'homosexual' in law.

Tradition gives a particular authenticity to the new term 'homosexual' and a specific legitimacy to the buggery–homosexual relation. The gap that separates the archaic 'buggery' and the novel 'homosexual' becomes produced as an intimate connection, a resemblance having a very special quality. It is an affiliation produced by way of a particular temporality. Tradition invests the proximity of the two terms with a particular consciousness of contemporary time (a now time; Habermas 1990: 13) and a present future by reference to the present of the past (Ricoeur 1991: 340). The temporality of the connection is a now time as immemorial, a time out of mind, an endless repetition of the same, metahistory (Foucault 1977; Goodrich 1990, 1992). Tradition is also a contiguity that is staged as ahistory (Derrida 1987).

It also invokes an experience of temporality as a particular space. The connection between 'buggery' and 'homosexual' is made to appear within an epistemological space (a site of knowing but not self-knowing) that is always already exhaustively mapped. It is a connection made in the image of a particular epistemological trajectory; as the expression of an uninterrupted flow from the source, the manifestation of a single direction, a straight path.

The use of tradition to cement the connection between 'homosexual' and buggery is an operation that situates the proximity within a consciousness of time in law, as linearity, continuity, unity, orthodoxy, a monotonous repetition, the endless unfolding of the same, an indefinite but always already closed teleology. As a synonym of 'buggery', the novelty of 'homosexual' is erased. The nobility that once was and continues to be 'buggery' might be reborn as 'homosexual'.

The connection between 'buggery' and the new 'homosexual' of law made in the name of the past and of the preservation of the past in the present was ultimately enacted by Parliament in the Sexual Offences Act 1967. Not only does 'homosexual act' institute a way of imagining a male genital body in its genital relations with other male bodies in law as a series of forbidden acts; it also draws attention to the fact that the use of the category of homosexual act installs a way of endowing that body in law with particular values and attributes, a particular history and a particular legitimacy, by way of a particular temporality.[23]

I shall next explore some of the themes and values that are transferred to the 'homosexual' through this temporality and proximity with 'buggery'. During the long history of the special position of 'buggery', its secular use spanning at least four centuries, this archaic term has symbolized and legitimated practices of official terror that have embodied fear and given voice to hatred in and through the practice of law. Chapter 3 will explore the practices of law that work to produce that violence and fear against the male genital body in law. Chapter 4 will explore a wider catalogue of values by which sense and nonsense of buggery as an image of the male genital body in its male genital relations has been made in law. Taken together, Chapters 3 and 4 have a further objective. They seek to problematize the claims of tradition and durability that are put to work in order to make sense and nonsense of the association between 'buggery' and 'homosexual' formally proposed by the Wolfenden Committee, and finally installed in the law with the enactment of the Sexual Offences Act 1967. These two chapters seek to challenge the myths and solemnities of the origin of buggery in the statute of Henry VIII as source of the present and the belief in the durability of buggery as the monotonous and timeless extension of that original Act. In place of the endless repetition of the same, the analysis endeavours rather to draw attention to the vicissitudes of buggery within the common law of the UK, and so seeks to problematize the claims of tradition.

3

BUGGERY
A short history of silence[1]

Anyone attempting to explore the meanings that are produced and deployed by way of legal textual practices of buggery has to solve a riddle.[2] The riddle relates to a requirement that has had considerable durability in the Common Law. In order to speak of buggery within that legal tradition, the speaker had to proceed according to a command to remain silent.[3] This injunction to silence was neither demanded by the letter of the statute of Henry VIII that introduced the secular offence of buggery in the regnal year 1533–4, nor was it a requirement of the statute of Elizabeth I that in 1562 enacted the offence of buggery in perpetuity (see Smith 1991: 45–53). It is referred to in the early seventeenth-century writings of the judge and eminent legal scholar, Sir Edward Coke. In *The Third Part of the Institutes of the Laws of England* (Coke 1628),[4] in Chapter 10, entitled 'Of Buggery or Sodomy',[5] Coke commented that if buggery is to appear in the law then it must be described by the words 'not to be named amongst Christians' (*inter christianos non nominandum*). The requirement that the indictment, the formal written accusation required in order to initiate formal legal proceedings, must contain this injunction to silence gives rise to a strange state of affairs in law. The legal formula by which buggery was to appear in the law (through the indictment) demanded that the wrongful act be named by way of a silence.

The injunction to silence would appear to pose particular problems for those who seek to resort to the term 'buggery' in law. As a general rule, legal practice requires that an indictment must clearly name the wrong. Compliance with the injunction that buggery is 'not to be named' threatens to make that naming impossible and thereby threatens to undermine the operation of law. The history of buggery in law does not demonstrate, however, the impossibility of deploying the term 'buggery' but rather shows that 'buggery' has been the primary term through which the male genital body in its genital relations with other male bodies has been most persistently and painstakingly represented in law.

This chapter is concerned with an analysis of the history of the practice of that silence in the production of this body in law. It also seeks to use the injunction to silence as a tool through which to develop an understanding of the idiosyncrasies of law, particularly those connected to the impoverished nature of the lexicon of the law. Focusing upon case reports, the writings of legal commentators and popular reports of trials, the first section of the chapter explores the past of the English Common Law tradition in order to develop an insight into the nature of the legal silence that allows the male genital body in its genital relations with other male bodies to be so intricately imagined. In pursuing this analysis I shall explore the complex and contradictory effects of this particular practice of silence, focusing upon the way in which the legal silence at the same time gives rise to a prodigious production of speech about buggery and also generates and enforces a great scarcity of speech about buggery. The injunction to silence will also form the basis of an exploration of some of the meanings that might be produced and given a voice through the deployment of 'buggery' in law. The analysis will then shift to consider the legal practices of silence in the more recent past. Finally, I explore the wider cultural significance of the economy of silence that is generated by way of this injunction. The chapter will explore the way in which this economy of silence provides the context for debate and engagement, producing both its possibility and its limit. This line of analysis is pursued by way of a series of recent engagements with interventions in the law. First it will be considered in the context of the government-inspired review of 'homosexual offences' undertaken by the Wolfenden Committee. Particular attention will be paid to the way in which silence structured the operation of the Wolfenden Committee, its manifestation in certain themes of the debate, as evidenced in its discussions relating to blackmail, and finally in its proposals to decriminalize certain genital relations between men. The committee proposed that these relations should be placed in a new silence, which it named 'in private'. The analysis will consider the nature of this silence that was enacted and installed, in response to this proposal, by way of the 1967 Sexual Offences Act. The chapter will then consider two more recent instances of an engagement with silence. The first relates to the invocation of silence during the course of the parliamentary debates to reduce the 'age of consent' for genital relations between men in the UK, which took place in 1994. The second and final example deals with the relationship between the silence of the law and the politics and practices of 'outing', which seeks to 'shatter the conspiracy of silence' (Johansson and Percy 1994).

THE LEGAL PRACTICE OF BUGGERY

An early example of the practice of this legal silence is to be found in a report of the proceedings against Mervyn Lord Audley, Earl of Castlehaven, in 1631 (*Audley* 1631: 402; Bingham 1971). The proceedings involve three indictments. The first indictment against Lord Audley was for rape against his wife, Martini Audley, Countess of Castlehaven. The remaining two indictments were for 'Sodomy' with Florence Fitz-patrick, a male servant. Both sodomy indictments were presented in similar terms. The first reads as follows:

> Jurors for the Sovereign King superior divinity made present, that Mervin Lord Audley not long ago of Fountell Gifford in the county of Wiltshire,

deviating before the eye of God, did without restraint turn away and deviate from the order of nature, and did disturb and arouse and incite diabolical activity from far away, did on the first day of June in the sixth year of the reign of Charles in the neighbourhood of Fountell Gifford in the county of Wiltshire in the dwelling house of Mervin Lord Audley did in that place go with (force and) arms against Florence Fitz-patrick yeoman and to the same purpose and on that date and in that place did against Florence Fitz-patrick, diabolically feloniously and against the natural order of venereal habits have carnal knowledge of Florence Fitz-patrick, against morality, called sodomy detestable and abominable that the English call buggery (not to be named amongst Christians) and at that time and in that place with Florence Fitz-patrick diabolically, feloniously and against nature did commit and perpetrate and offend before the lofty bold and generous God and what is more did so act to the disgrace and dishonour of the whole of human kind and against the peace of the King and the law of the land and against all dignity and against the measure of authority brought forth.

(*Audley* 1631: 407)[6]

An interesting feature of this indictment is the way it both rehearses the demand for silence and proceeds, despite the command, to name the wrong in some detail.[7] The success of the indictment suggests that the injunction to silence does not operate as a command that demands an absolute silence and thereby operates as the limit of legal discourse. The injunction to silence found in this lengthy indictment appears to operate as an element that works alongside and in relation to a requirement to speak of such things (Foucault 1981a: 27; Bell 1993: 79; Sinfield 1994: ch.1).

If the injunction to silence does not work as an absolute prohibition on the production of buggery within the text of the law, then perhaps it was a prohibition relating to the further dissemination of references to genital relations between men in general and the dissemination of the legal text of buggery in particular. However, as others have noted (Bray 1982; Hallam 1993; Smith 1991), the injunction to silence does not seem to work in general to prohibit references to genital relations between men in other contexts. With regard to the matter of the dissemination of the legal text of buggery, Lord Audley's case has particular significance. While the case does not appear in the many scholarly legal writings that provide commentary upon the legal practice of buggery, reports of the Lord Audley case were, over the next hundred years, widely disseminated. Variations on the text of the court proceedings were the subject of popular pamphlets published in 1642, 1679, 1699, 1708 and 1710 (Audley 1642, 1679, 1699, 1708 and 1710).[8] Later in the eighteenth century, the legal text of buggery was widely disseminated through the publication of popular pamphlets that reported selected proceedings of the Old Bailey (*Select Trials* 1742) and through special pamphlets dedicated to specific buggery trials (Trumbach 1986). The wide dissemination of the Lord Audley case seems to suggest that the injunction to silence in the law marks the absolute limit of the production of buggery neither within the law nor outside the law. On the contrary, the repeated publication of the detail of the Lord Audley proceedings would appear to provide further evidence to support the conclusion that the injunction to silence is closely connected to a certain requirement to speak of buggery.

The writings of Sir William Blackstone, one of the most noted and respected eighteenth-century commentators on the common law, demonstrates various characteristics of this juxtaposition between the injunction to silence and the requirement to speak. Buggery is addressed in his *Commentaries on the Law of England* (Blackstone 1769), a widely disseminated and influential text throughout the Common Law world (Alshuler 1994). It appears in Chapter 15 (Offences Against the Person) section IV, of the fourth volume of the *Commentaries* (Blackstone 1769 [1979]: 215). There, Blackstone refers to the offence of buggery, not by resort to the word 'buggery' but by means of the title, 'the infamous crime against nature'. Having explained the need for the offence to be strictly and impartially proved he continues:

> I will not act so disagreeable a part, to my readers as well as myself, as to dwell any longer upon a subject, the very mention of which is a disgrace to human nature.
>
> (Blackstone 1769 [1979]: 215)

The practice of silence in this text is of interest in various ways. First, the injunction to silence takes the form of the absence of the word 'buggery' from Blackstone's text. However, that which is made present in law by way of 'buggery' is far from absent in this text. In Blackstone's text the injunction to silence, as symbolized in the absence of 'buggery', generates other terms to name the forbidden act. Thus, in this instance, buggery appears by way of a euphemism, 'the infamous crime against nature'. Blackstone's obedience to the command to be silent appears not to create the impossibility of the representation of the male genital body, by way of a wrongful act in the law, but rather emphasizes that the command to silence is more a prerequisite for its representation in the law. Compliance with the command creates the possibility of producing substitute names for that which is not to be named.

The injunction to silence has another manifestation in Blackstone's text. It is rehearsed in Blackstone's modesty and restraint, 'I will not act so disagreeable a part...'. In this eighteenth-century setting, the invocation of silence is presented as a practice that exhibits the English law's respect for delicacy or verbal decency. Here silence informs the ritual presentation of the law in general, and commentary on the law in particular, producing it as a sanitized public speech.

Blackstone's text also demonstrates that the silence of law has another symbolic significance. Blackstone provides an example of this in his comment that 'the very mention of which [buggery] is a disgrace to human nature' (Blackstone 1769 [1979]: 215). Here silence is rehearsed in the phrase, 'the very mention'. To break that silence in the act of naming is to threaten to unleash a great danger, which takes the form of a fall from grace. More specifically, the injunction to silence connected to buggery represents that danger in a very particular way: as a fall into silence. By way of legal command, buggery is not only unsayable, instituted as that which must remain unsaid, but it is also presented as that which might generate the ultimate silence if ever spoken: the fall from grace. Here the command to silence symbolizes buggery in law as that which is always already outside language, and thereby outside the law (Bray 1982).[9] Thereby the iteration of buggery is made a diabolical event. Through the injunction to silence, buggery in law is produced as a symbol of an exorbitant power (Kristeva 1982: 1).

But it must not be forgotten that the injunction to silence has a double significance. On the one hand, it purports to render the naming of buggery impossible. On the other hand, at the same time, it is not the absolute limit of legal discourse; it is a requirement to speak of such things. As such, the legal practice of silence marks a place in law and gives a voice in the law to a whole chain of associations that connect to buggery and produce through buggery a certain fear, dread and panic. The injunction to silence is also intimately connected with the (re)production of these themes. Through silence, buggery in law is made not only that which is always already banished from the law but also that which always already challenges from its place of banishment. The silence of the law marks the production of an assumption that, both outside and inside, buggery is an ever-present danger that threatens to destroy (Fuss 1991; Butler 1990, 1991). In turn, this silence in law also marks the place of a demand for a vigilance that seeks to generate buggery in law as a particular experience: as that which must be unsaid and remain unsayable.

Blackstone's text demonstrates that, in spite of the injunction to silence and in the knowledge of the dangers that threaten to engulf not only the speaker and the reader but also humanity in general, this legal practice of silence does not function (now beyond the context of the formal indictment, in the context of legal scholarship and commentary) as a device that produces the limit of legal discourse on buggery. Blackstone not only proceeds to name that which is not to be named but also continues to set out the detail of the offence. He proceeds to provide a commentary on the same, dealing with aspects of its history, giving examples of its use. His commentary further demonstrates that, by the late eighteenth century, the legal practice of silence continued to be conjoined with the necessity of overcoming hesitation. As such he speaks in a manner that is not determined by the requirements that might reduce buggery to silence. His hesitation rehearses the danger that is associated with buggery. In addition he demonstrates a need to speak publicly of buggery and to subject his audience to it even if, through his preliminary declarations, he seeks to preserve the injunction that condemns it to silence for both himself and his audience. In the juxtaposition of the injunction to silence and a command to speak the ritual invocation of the injunction to silence in the law appears not only to call forth the horrors that are associated with buggery but also to protect those that speak of such things in the law. Here legal practice represents itself as a heroic practice of a certain civility and the legal practitioner as a hero who might fight the good fight against evil and appear untainted and victorious.

37

NAMING THE UNNAMABLE

While Blackstone's euphemism, 'the infamous crime against nature', might suggest that the legal practice of silence licenses a proliferation of ways of speaking in law of the male genital body in its genital relations to other male bodies, a more recent case draws attention to the problematic nature of this licence to proliferate the names of the unnamable.[10] In *R. v. Rowed and another* (1842), the indictment against Rowed contained several counts that purported to describe a series of similar illegal acts performed by the accused in Kensington Gardens. The first count of the indictment read as follows:

> ...being persons of nasty, wicked, filthy, lewd, beastly and unnatural dispositions, and wholly lost to all sense of decency and good manners, heretofore, to wit on, ... with force and arms at —— in a certain open and public place there, called Kensington Gardens, frequented by divers of the liege subjects of our lady the Queen, unlawfully and wickedly did meet together for the purpose and with the intent of committing and perpetrating with each other, openly lewdly and indecently, in the said public place, divers nasty, wicked, filthy, lewd, beastly, unnatural and sodomitical practices; and then and there unlawfully, wickedly, openly, lewdly and indecently did commit and perpetrate with each other, in the sight and view of divers of the liege subjects of our said lady the Queen, in the said public place there passing and being, divers such practices as aforesaid to the great scandal and disgrace of mankind in contempt... to the evil example... and against the peace.

Of particular interest are the objections raised by counsel for the accused against this and the other charges, written in almost identical terms. The objections all related to the terms of the charges contained in the indictment. It was argued, first, that the charges failed clearly to name the unlawful act and, second, that the language used did not have legal meaning. The acts that were the object of the law's concern were described in the charges only by general epithets – 'nasty, wicked, filthy, lewd, beastly, unnatural' – none of which described the prohibited act. The mere addition of the word 'practices' did not adequately describe the proscribed act. Finally, it was argued that the formal accusation (the indictment) failed, as the phrase 'sodomitical practices' was not a term known to the law. The indictment, counsel argued, must satisfy the requirements of precision and must include certain words and phrases, such as '*peccatum illud horribile, inter christianos non nominandum*', in order for the matter to 'judicially appear' (*Rowed* 1842: 182).

In agreeing to bar judgment (after an initial finding of guilt by the trial court jury), the judges, with some reluctance, accepted the arguments presented by counsel for the accused. The judges concluded that there were several valid objections to the formula used in the indictment. First, they objected to the novelty of the formula of words used in the indictment. They could find no evidence either that indictments written in this form had ever been successful or that it was written according to precedents that had been used over a long course of time. Second, they found that the epithets – 'nasty, wicked, filthy, lewd, beastly, unnatural' – were not connected to a term that had specific legal significance, and thereby they were not connected to a term that juridically expressed the proscribed act. The court concluded that the language of the indictment did not embody a legal view.

In the context of the legal injunction to silence, the absence of any particular criticism of the immense verbosity of the counts in the indictment *per se* is of particular interest. The judicial criticism of the indictments was not that too much was said but that too little was said. If the formal accusation was to be successful then, the judges concluded, the manifold epithets had to be joined to an additional legal term: buggery. Furthermore 'buggery' is said to have the capacity of 'shewing the intention implied by the epithets' (*Rowed* 1842: 187).

In giving their qualified approval to the verbosity of the indictment, the judges draw attention to the potential viability of the multitude of epithets. They demonstrate that silence might operate not just to promote the production of new terms but as a requirement that those new terms be spoken in a particular way. Thus these additional terms must be deployed according to the requirements of a lexicon that always already has juridical validity and by way of a certain ritual of repetition and citation of terms of law. This suggests that the proliferation of speech in law (and thereby a plenitude of meaning) takes place within the context of an economy of speech that is characterized by a restriction and scarcity of terms.

The juxtaposition of the impoverishment of the legal lexicon and the many epithets of abhorrence in this indictment is of interest in other ways. For example, the diversity of the terms used draws our attention to the determination to imagine this male genital body in many different domains, each domain being a distinct site of production: theology, morality, manners, biology, medicine, pedagogy. Each is a separate site from which to speak of the genital male body in its relations with other male bodies, with authorized speakers taking up idiosyncratic perspectives set within particular institutions. The judicial observations in *R. v. Rowed* that these epithets might appear in law when conjoined to a term of law suggests that, while the law may remain separate and distinct from these other sites of production, at the same time they are of some significance for the practice of the law.[11] On the one hand the failure in law of the epithets when used in isolation from a term drawn from the lexicon of the law draws attention to the discontinuous juxtaposition of each of these separate domains of production of the male genital body. On the other hand the ability to make these other terms appear judicially when conjoined with a term within the authorized legal lexicon draws attention to the possibility of producing a continuity between these disparate sites of production. This draws attention to the capacity of the limited lexicon of the law to accommodate the verbose representation of the male genital body in its genital relations with other male bodies in the law.

The multiplicity of epithets of abhorrence has another significance. Their presence in the law draws attention not only to the diversity of the language used to name this male genital body as buggery, but also to the interrelationship between the law and other discourses through which the male body is imagined (Moran

1989a). It is important to place the legal production of buggery in the context of these other sites of production. While each epithet is separate it is also made to connect with the others. In their connection, each term expresses a certain similarity.

In this example the legal lexicon is shown to have a compulsory quality. To be in the law the speaking subject must fulfil particular requirements. The speaking subject of law does not have the right to say everything. That subject must perform according to a particular (restricted) economy of speech (Foucault 1981b: 61). Thus in order to articulate the male genital body in its male genital relations in law, that body must be imagined by way of a strict lexical economy. Another aspect of that impoverished economy is illustrated in *R. v. Rowed*. It appears in the judicial observation that the legal term may show 'the intention implied by the epithets' (*Rowed* 1842: 187). This draws attention to the flexibility of the legal lexicon. A rich menu of different intelligibilities and unintelligibilities of this body outside the law may be given significance and a voice within the law in a conjunction with the authorized term in the legal lexicon. Thereby non-law is made law. In the context of the indictment, the single archaic legal term 'buggery' is the means through which the novel and multiple sentiments expressed through the epithets might judicially appear. It is a vehicle through which the sum of those disparate energies that are connected individually and collectively to those various epithets may be expressed in law. As such, the poverty of the legal lexicon must be recognized as the severe limit of meaning in the law and also as the means of creating the possibility of a superabundance of meaning in law.

The analysis of the juxtaposition of silence and buggery thus far has drawn attention to various important features of the legal practice of buggery. First, the injunction to silence ought not to be read as a requirement of the legal practice of buggery that stands for the imposition of an absolute limit or a total prohibition. The commentaries and cases draw attention to the way this requirement of silence appears to operate as a prerequisite for the prolix production of the male genital body in its male genital relations in law. Second, it draws attention to the fact that the injunction to silence points to certain limits of law as a discursive practice. To be in the law, the body must be represented according to these complex textual limits. This body must be represented by way of a specific and limited lexicon. While the requirement to use 'buggery' might suggest a scarcity of meaning in the law, the commentaries and cases draw attention to the fact that resort to that single term generates not a scarcity but, its opposite, a plenitude of meaning. Third, the legal practice of silence marks the place of a requirement that, as buggery, this male genital body of law must be imagined according to certain rituals of a particular civility. Finally, this silence draws attention to the fact that the legal practice of buggery has a rich symbolic function in law. It operates not only as a mark of the fear and terror but also as a means whereby that fear and terror might be invoked and experienced and brought under some sort of control. It is according to these rituals and requirements of a legal practice that this male genital body in its male genital relations as buggery might be produced as the truth in law (Foucault 1981b: 60).

SILENCE, VIOLENCE AND THE AUTHORIZED
SPEAKING SUBJECT OF LAW

The silence connected to buggery is also concerned with another matter: access to and deployment of the legal practices of buggery. This issue was addressed in a line of cases that begins in the late eighteenth century and deals with robbery. In the context of the crime of robbery the name of buggery is invoked in the first instance by the defendant in order to threaten. Here the defendant appropriates its capacity to generate violence and fear in order to extract money or property from another person. In this instance, the deployment of buggery appears not so much as a practice of representation within the law, performed by those duly authorized to speak the law, but as a practice of representation outside the law.

This use of buggery first appears as a problem before the courts in a decision reported in 1775: *R. v. Thomas Jones*. Mitchel Newman, the prosecutor, had attended the Play-house in Covent Garden, London. The law report tells us that, in his eagerness to get a good seat in a crowded theatre, Newman touched the accused's breeches with his hand. As a result the accused, Jones, followed Newman and eventually took a seat by him. A short conversation took place between the two men. (Jones asked Newman if another man, with whom Newman had spoken, was of his company.) On leaving the Play-house, Jones asked Newman if he would 'have something to drink after the heat?' Newman agreed and the two men retired to a public house in Bow Street. Having finished the drink, Jones turned towards Newman and asked him, 'what he meant by the liberties he had taken with his person in the Play-house'. (At the trial Newman informed the court that he understood this to be an imputation of sodomy.)[12] Newman denied knowledge of any such activities and left the public house. Jones followed him out to the street, where he began to make further references to the incident in the Play-house. When Newman asked what he wanted, Jones demanded money. Money was exchanged and the incident came to an end. Subsequent to that, Jones proceeded to follow Newman and, using the accusation of 'sodomy', made several further demands for money. Eventually Newman apprehended Jones and brought him before the Magistrate, Sir John Fielding. Jones was committed for trial for the offence of highway robbery.

At the trial the charge against him proved to be problematic. The proceedings were suspended while twelve judges considered whether, under the circumstances of the case, the accused had been guilty of a robbery. In the judge-made rules of the common law, robbery is defined in the following terms:

> as the stealing or taking from a person, or in the presence of another, property of any amount, with such a degree of force or terror, as to induce the party unwillingly to part with the property.

The problem that faced the court was in the fact that in this instance property had been given up not as a result of physical force or terror arising from the threat of physical violence but from a present and future violence generated by language, in particular through the invocation of the term 'sodomy'. The twelve judges had to determine whether an accusation of sodomy would amount to a force or terror sufficient to satisfy the legal requirement of the offence of robbery. They concluded that the imputation of sodomy was so alarming a suggestion that it was sufficient to satisfy the requirement of force or terror and Jones was duly sentenced to death.

While the case report provides no evidence of the reasoning behind this conclusion, the report of a decision in 1783, *R. v. Daniel Hickman*, which referred to and followed the decision in *R. v. Jones*, provides an insight into the reasoning that informed this development in the law. Again the incident in the *Hickman* case related to an accusation of sodomy:

> [the prisoner said to the prosecutor] . . . I am come for satisfaction; you know what passed the other night; you are a Sodomite; and if you do not give me satisfaction, I will go and fetch a sergeant and a file of men, and take you before a Justice; for I have been in the Black-Hole ever since I was last here, and I do not value my life.
>
> (*Hickman* 1783: 278)

Acting under this threat, the prosecutor paid money to Hickman. He explained that he 'parted with his money under an idea of preserving his character from reproach, and not from fear of personal violence'. The jury found the prisoner guilty. It also found that the prosecutor parted with his money against his will, through a fear that his character might receive an injury from the prisoner's accusation. The matter was again reserved for consideration by a special court of twelve judges.

After due consideration, the twelve judges concluded that the principle of law was that:

> whether the terror arises from real or expected violence to the person, or from a sense of injury to the character, the law makes no difference; for to most men the idea of losing their fame and reputation is equally, if not more terrific than the dread of personal injury. . . a threat to accuse a man of having committed the greatest of all crimes, is, as in the present case, a sufficient force to constitute the crime of robbery by putting in fear.
>
> (*Hickman* 1783: 77)[13]

These two cases are of interest in various ways. Both draw attention to the operation of some of the effects generated by the legal practices of the injunction to silence. Here buggery (sodomy) is shown to symbolize extreme violence and thereby to generate fear, and for that fear and danger to be deployed and experienced as acute terror and as an act of embodied violence. More specifically, they draw attention to the fact that the deployment of the name of buggery as a powerful symbol and practice of violence is by the eighteenth century thought to work upon the body in a particular way; as a threat to the integrity of the person. In the judicial acceptance that the mere naming of buggery unleashes a violence or threat of violence that may take the form of real or expected fear to the person by way of injury to his character, *Jones* and *Hickman* draw attention to the great success of the buggery–violence conjunction (Thomas 1992).

The decisions in *Jones* and *Hickman* address another issue: the question of access to the practice of silence and of naming. Thereby they address the question of access to a particular power to terrorize lawfully. In reaching the conclusion that the use of silence and the naming of buggery for the purpose of obtaining money or property may be an act of robbery, the judges demonstrate a determination to limit access to the violence and terror that might be unleashed by the use of silence and naming to particular speaking subjects (Lindgren 1984: 702; Katz 1993: 1567).[14] They demonstrate that the lexical economy of the law is intimately connected to access to the power to name and thereby access to violence and terror. The command to silence is not only concerned with the specific ways in which buggery may be spoken in the law, it is also a reference to the distribution of those authorized to speak the name and thereby produce the truth of the genital male body in its genital relations with other male bodies.

The ability to impose the violence of a penalty or to extract a charge[15] upon those subjected to the legal practices of buggery is a privilege that is to be limited to a few chosen speaking subjects who are designated by the law. The police, prosecutor, magistrate and judge are designated agents of the law with particular properties and stipulated roles. They produce the male genital body through the performance of certain rituals and the recitation of particular lexical codes and formulas of law within a closed or limited space. At the same time, it is also important to recognize that these legal practices of violence are performed by way of an economy of language and not an economy of space. There are no spatial limits to the practices of naming and violence for authorized speaking subjects. Their operations might stretch from the intimacy of the bedroom to the public convenience, from the street to the bar of the Court and on the bench.

The recognition of the buggery–violence conjunction and the monopoly over its deployment is not peculiar to the opinion of certain judges. It has also been recognized and formalized in legislation. This legislation is of particular importance as it brings buggery within the ambit of the law that we now refer to as blackmail. In 1825 an Act was introduced to amend the law relating to the offence of sending threatening letters and the offence of assault with intent to commit robbery. In order that the writing contained in the letter, or the words spoken, be interpreted as a threat, the law required that the words used had to take the form of an accusation relating to a crime punishable by death, transportation or pillory, or be an accusation relating to an infamous crime. The 1825 Act provided a list of offences that were, for the purpose of this offence, always to be taken to be infamous crimes. The category was to include not only every crime already deemed infamous but henceforth:

> every Assault with Intent to commit any Rape, or the abominable Crimes of
> Sodomy or Buggery, or either of those Crimes, and every Attempt or

Endeavour to commit any Rape, or the said abominable Crimes or either of them, and also every Solicitation, Persuasion, Threat or Menace, offered or made to any Person, whereby to move or induce such Person to commit or to permit the said abominable Crimes or either of them, shall be deemed and taken to be an infamous Crime within the Meaning of the said recited Act.

The provision was consolidated in the Larceny Act 1861. At that time it was also rewritten so that the category of 'infamous crime' was reduced to the 'abominable Crime of Buggery' (s. 46). Its continued viability was recognized in its re-enactment in the Larceny Act 1916. Finally, it was transformed and its viability modernized in English law in the creation of a new offence, blackmail, in the Theft Act 1968 (Criminal Law Revision Committee 1966; Smith 1989; Griew 1990).

TRANSLATION AND CONQUEST

The legal practices of buggery in general, and the injunction to silence in particular, produce what will be described here as a juridical economy of silence. In this section the analysis will focus upon the effects of that juridical economy of silence on the human world outside the law. As the previous analysis has suggested, within the law this economy works not to secure total silence but to secure the representation of the male body in its genital relations with other male bodies according to a specific impoverished lexicon of law (as 'buggery'), circulated and policed by authorized speakers. *Jones* and *Hickman* in their prohibition of the use of 'buggery' outside the law might suggest that beyond the context of legal practices the economy of silence takes the form of an absolute prohibition of speech.

However, there is considerable evidence in reports of proceedings against men to suggest that the law's injunction to silence does not mark the absolute limit of imagining the male genital body in its male genital relations outside the law. Examples can be found in the popular pamphlets of the eighteenth century that describe sodomy trials at the Old Bailey. They provide examples of marginal dialects generated by and for men who had genital relations with other men whereby the unnamable might be named without the experience of violence. These examples are also of interest in another way. They provide an opportunity to consider the relationship between the official lexicon of representation and the marginal vernacular of certain genital practices.

Many examples of these marginal dialects are to be found in a series of trials instigated by eighteenth-century morality vigilantes (Bahlman 1957). In the reports of these trials, we find that the men who engaged in genital relations with other men referred to themselves in particular ways, as 'mollies' and as 'mollying bitch'. They frequented particular ale houses in central London which they referred to as 'molly houses' (for example, see Bray 1982; Gilbert 1978; McIntosh 1981; Norton 1992; Radzinowicz 1947; Trumbach 1977). In sodomy proceedings against Gabriel Lawrence, Samuel Stevens, giving evidence for the prosecution, described a molly house scene of twenty to thirty men in the following terms:

... together kissing and hugging and making love (as they called it) in a very indecent manner... they used to go out by couples into another room, and when they came back they would tell what they had been doing, which in their dialect they called marrying.

(*Select Trials* 1742, Vol. 2: 362–72, Gabriel Lawrence for sodomy, April 1726)

'As they call it' and 'dialect' records the use of the familiar phrases such as 'making love' and 'marrying' to mean something other than their normal signification. Thereby these terms are relocated, now to be understood as a dangerous dialect, subject to special attention, given special significance. Other examples of the dialect are found in the trial of George Whittle for sodomy with Edward Courtney, of April 1726. Courtney described an incident at the Royal Oak at the corner of St James Square and Pall Mall:

He had a back room for mollies to drink in private betwixt that and the kitchen. There is a bed in the middle of the room for the use of the company and be married; and for that reason they call that room the Chappel. He has helped me to 2 or 3 Husbands there. One time indeed he put the Bite upon me; for Ned says he, theres a country gentleman of my acquaintance just come to Town and if you'll give him a Wedding night he'll pay you very handsomely.

(*Select Trials* 1742, Vol. 2: 369–72, George Whittle)

Again this report records the appropriation of familiar terms that relate to cross-sexual encounters, such as 'Chappel' and 'husband', and their reinvention as a code for a different set of practices. These popular pamphlets record the dialect of the molly that emerges in the shadow of the law's silence. Again the silence of the law does not in the first instance produce an absolute prohibition but gives rise to a certain proliferation of speech about these genital relations by way of a multiplicity of euphemisms.

These reports also document another aspect of this economy of silence that is to be found in the relationship between the dialect of the molly and the dialect of the law. The relationship is demonstrated in various instances. The reports show how the terms of the dialect outside the law, such as 'molly house', are translated into the terms of law's lexicon; thus 'molly house' becomes 'disorderly house' (*Select Trials* 1726, Vol. 3: 36–40, Mother Clap for Keeping a sodomitical House); 'marriage' becomes 'sodomy' or 'buggery'; 'putting his hand into my britches' becomes 'assaulting... with intent to commit... the detestable sin of sodomy' (*Select Trials* 1726, Vol. 3: 36–40, Martin Mackintosh). Each example demonstrates a process of capture and translation whereby the two dialects, of law and the genital subculture, take up a hierarchical relationship, with law the superior and molly speech the inferior. Through this hierarchical relation the molly dialect is re-imagined (re-coded) according to the authoritarian demands of the lexicon of law, and thereby silenced. This practice of translation is also a practice of capture and conquest. 'Marriage' as 'buggery' or 'sodomy' rewrites what might be an act of love and

45

affection and demands that it represent something else, for example an act of violence. In the process of translation, the law, through the impoverishment of meaning, seeks to produce the truth of these situations and scenarios according to its own specific lexical order and terms of representation.

Within this scheme of things the silence of the law would appear to have a particularly complex place. First it is a silence that is imposed beyond the law. It is this silence within which the molly dialect becomes possible. As such it is a silence that must again be understood not as the absolute limit of representation but as a force that shapes the production of representation. As such the juridical economy of silence promoted the invention of another code of representation. However, as these eighteenth-century cases demonstrate, at the same time as the silence of law is put into operation a silence that is to be absolute is produced and secured through the surveillance and regulation of social space. Here the dialect of the molly that the silence of the law helps to generate also threatens to violate the prohibition of representation. The process of translation and conquest seeks to re-establish the silence beyond the law. However, this practice of conquest and translation has an ironic twist. At the same time as it promotes a specific and impoverished representation of those practices it seeks to end, in the act of ending them the legal proceedings record their particular dialect, preserving it and disseminating it further.

SPEAKING THE LOVE THAT DARE NOT SPEAK ITS NAME

Evidence of the continued operation of this economy of silence in the nineteenth century is perhaps most famously preserved in Lord Alfred Douglas's phrase, 'The love that dare not speak its name'.[16] The economy of silence that is represented in 'The love that dare not speak its name' was at the heart of the most famous nineteenth-century struggle over the production of the male genital body in its genital relations with other male bodies: the trial(s) of Oscar Wilde.

Wilde was the subject and object of the law in three trials.[17] The first trial is of particular interest. *Wilde* v. *Queensbury* was a criminal action initiated by Wilde. These were proceedings for criminal libel. They were initiated by Wilde as a result of the delivery of a note from Lord Queensbury. In that note Lord Queensbury invoked the name sodomy: 'For Oscar Wilde posing as a somdomite [*sic*]'.

Before proceeding to analyse these proceedings in terms of the juridical economy of silence, it is necessary to set out the main ingredients of the criminal offence that was the subject of this legal action by Wilde. The criminal offence of libel has several ingredients. First, it requires the publication of a statement. Second, it requires that the statement is defamatory. A statement is defamatory if it is calculated to expose the person who is the subject of the statement to public hatred, contempt or ridicule or calculated to damage him in his trade, business, profession or calling. Furthermore, it must be a serious libel (and at the time of the Wilde trial it was thought that it must be of such a nature to provoke a breach of the peace). Malice must also be present, though it is not necessary to prove it as it will be imputed from the act of publication itself. Finally, by virtue of s. 6 of the Libel Act 1843, the law provided that a defendant might be protected from punishment by means of a plea of justification. Here a defendant must demonstrate that the statement made is true, and further that its publication is for the public benefit.[18]

In initiating the proceedings against Queensbury, Wilde took up the position of subject in the law, not only with individual rights and interests but also in this particular case with an interest that represented the wider public interest. The economy of silence is of particular importance in Wilde's criminal libel prosecution. Wilde's prosecution relied upon the relationship between sodomy (buggery) and violence. The sodomy–violence conjunction is to be found in his argument that an allegation of sodomy is defamatory. The violence is proved in its ability to generate public contempt, hatred or ridicule that will damage a person's reputation or trade. The sodomy–violence link is invoked in satisfying the need to demonstrate that the libel might provoke a breach of the peace. Wilde argued that Queensbury's resort to sodom was such an act of violence and threatened the public peace. This threat was to be located in the fact that Queensbury had invoked the name of 'sodom', and hence the name of violence outside the law. Being beyond the law, the name of 'sodom' might generate a violence that was not the law's violence (a breach of the peace). Wilde's criminal libel prosecution was an attempt to silence Queensbury and to return the violence appropriated by Queensbury to the law by means of penalizing Queensbury and re-establishing a silence beyond the law.

However, in the defence of justification, Queensbury sought to argue that his use of 'sodom' was not a resort to the name for his own personal gain (as was claimed in the context of the charge of blackmail or robbery). In this instance he argued that he invoked the name of sodom not against the law but within and for the law. As such, his defence was that his resort to 'sodom' mimicked the law and therefore was for the public good. In the plea of justification the law will allow a speaking subject, who speaks from a position beyond the law, to have access to the privilege of naming the unnamable of the law when that speaking subject mimics the truth of the lexical code of the law, and does so for the public good and not for his own personal benefit.

In order to secure the defence of justification, Queensbury had to demonstrate that the silence beyond the law had been violated. This was an important theme in the defence of justification. Queensbury had to demonstrate that, prior to Queensbury's reference to sodomy, Wilde had in some way already violated the requirements of the juridical economy of silence that appeared to demand an absolute prohibition of representation outside the law. Wilde's act of violation is formally described in Lord Queensbury's note: 'For Oscar Wilde posing as a somdomite' [*sic*]. Here Queensbury located the violation of the silence in Wilde's pose.

Much of the criminal libel proceedings were concerned with the demonstration of that pose. The reports of the proceedings draw attention to the way in which that pose was demonstrated in the court. It was done by means of an interpretation of Wilde's perhaps most public and persistent pose: his writings (Bartlett 1988; Cohen 1993; Goodman 1995; Hyde 1970, 1973). Queensbury's counsel referred to two texts: *The Picture of Dorian Gray* (Wilde 1891) and 'Phrases and philosophies for the use of the young' (Wilde 1894). With regard to the former it was argued that the text was to be understood by readers to describe relations, intimacies and passions of certain persons of sodomitical and unnatural tastes and habits (Cohen 1993: 128). Of the 'Phrases and philosophies for the use of the young' it was argued that they had a more general corrupting influence (Cohen 1993: 128, fn. 2). As neither directly described either corruption in general or sodomitical corruption in particular the issue became one of presenting these texts as particular sodomitical dialects or codes that were to be decoded in and through the law in order that they might be shown as violations of silence and at the same time re-presented according to the requirements of the truth of the male genital body in its male genital relations in the law.

Through the plea of justification, Wilde's text was first transported into a silence that is to be made beyond the law, then re-presented as a violation of that silence. Here the first silence of the law is a silence that is to operate as the absolute limit of speech. In the final instance, Queensbury succeeded in using the lexicon of the law, the name of sodomy/buggery, to translate and conquer the meaning of Wilde's texts and thereby to dictate the meaning of Wilde in the law.

As a legal subject with interests to protect, Wilde sought to deploy the juridical economy of silence that distributes the buggery/sodomy–violence relation in order to protect his name. Lord Queensbury sought to demonstrate that he merely mimicked the law and invoked the violence of the name sodomite for the public good. Through the success of this defence, Wilde's position was transformed from that of a subject in the law to an object of the law. Not only was he subjected to the violence of sodomy/buggery as the truth of his relation but in the subsequent criminal proceedings (this time through the phrase 'gross indecency') he was subjected again to the violence of the law in his incarceration.

FROM SILENCE TO PRIVACY

In this section the main focus is the impact of this juridical economy of silence upon the review and reform of the law undertaken by the Wolfenden Committee. This will be pursued by way of three themes. The first considers the interface between the economy of silence and the government command to the Wolfenden Committee to speak of homosexuality and prostitution. The second theme will focus upon the particular issue of blackmail. This matter is of importance here as it deals with the interface between silence, violence, homosexuality and the law. Furthermore it assumed considerable importance both in the course of the Wolfenden review and during the subsequent debates about law reform. Finally, consideration will be given to the Wolfenden Committee's resort to and promotion of silence in its proposals to decriminalize certain genital relations between men in private. Here consideration will be given to the relationship between silence and privacy.

In his memoirs, Sir John (later Lord) Wolfenden (1976) provides several examples of the effects of the interface between the wider cultural economy of silence and the government's command to speak of homosexuality and prostitution. For example, they appear in the following observation that:

> In those days the topics with which we were to be concerned were not mentioned in polite society. Most ordinary people had never heard of homosexuality; and of those who had the great majority regarded it with something nearer to disgust than to understanding. More of them knew about prostitution; but that knowledge was more likely to be disclaimed than paraded.
>
> (Wolfenden 1976: 132)

Wolfenden draws attention to several important points. The first is that the injunction to silence did work in some respects as an absolute prohibition. Furthermore, in his reference to prostitution and silence he draws attention to the fact that we ought not to forget that economies of silence are not unique to buggery/homosexuality. But at the same time, his comment about the differences between homosexuality and prostitution draws attention to the fact that economies of silence may operate in different ways in the contexts of different genital relations. His reference to the 'disgust' that is experienced in imagining homosexuality marks the continuing significance of violence and terror and its place in the installation of the economy of silence associated in particular with homosexuality.

Another example of the operation of this fear appears in Wolfenden's anxiety at taking on the role of chairperson to the committee. Wolfenden explained this in the following terms:

> So before I could accept this invitation there were people to be consulted. The announcement of the setting-up of the Committee and of my chairmanship of it, would probably create some stir, and we must assess in advance, as best we could, the probable consequences. My wife, of course, knew of the midnight conversation on the sleeper train.[19] But an official invitation to take the job was rather different. There were the four children to consider, one at university, the other three at school. What might they have to put up with in comment from their contemporaries if their father got involved in 'this sort of thing'? What about the university of Reading? Apart from the amount of time it would inevitably consume, would it rub off harmfully that the Vice Chancellor was busying himself with such matters? Indeed, could there be snide sniggerings about the universities in general? . . . After a fair amount of heart-searching the unanimous conclusion was that the invitation should be accepted.
>
> (Wolfenden 1976: 133)

Here Wolfenden demonstrates the contagious nature of the anxieties that might be generated by a potential violation of the economy of silence (even one authorized by the government). It might affect not only the individual but also his wife and children, institutions he worked for and others he was more generally associated with.

The economy of silence also shaped the day-to-day practices of the Wolfenden Committee. For example, Wolfenden commented that the acronym of the Committee on Homosexual Offences and Prostitution, CHOP, would be very useful as it was 'conveniently brief and uninformative [and] could bring no blush to any secretarial cheek' (Wolfenden 1976: 134). Between the members of the committee the terms 'homosexual' and 'prostitute' were replaced by euphemisms:

> The individual Huntley and Palmers I know you already have much in mind. I have had letters from 2 or 3 Huntleys who want to say something and there are indications that there may be others later on.
>
> (PRO HO 345/2, Letter from Roberts to Wolfenden 30.9.54)

'Huntley' referred to homosexuals and 'Palmer' to prostitutes (the two names coming from a well-known biscuit manufacturer, Huntley & Palmer). Here the economy of silence structures the form of communication between the participants of the committee. These examples draw attention to the way in which resort to euphemism and certain rituals of civility are put to work to manage the anxieties generated by the violence and terror of the economy of silence.

In part, the decision to undertake the review by way of a Departmental Committee was also informed by the economy of silence. To have proceeded by way of a Royal Commission would have required compliance with the tradition of publishing evidence submitted to the committee. Undertaking the review as a Departmental Committee, Wolfenden noted, allowed the committee to gather more evidence and to avoid the embarrassment of witnesses that might follow from the publication of evidence (Wolfenden 1976: 133). Witnesses giving evidence were allowed to remain anonymous. For example, important evidence on the operation of the conjunction between homosexuality and blackmail is preserved in a document entitled, 'Memorandum submitted by one of the witnesses to be heard at 2.15 p.m. on Thursday 28th July' (PRO HO 345/8, CHP/69).[20]

At the same time it is important to recognize that the Wolfenden review did transgress the boundaries of the economy of silence. The matter was discussed in correspondence between the committee's Secretary, W.C. Roberts, and Wolfenden in the following terms:

> You will remember that I told you that I was proposing to see an invert in a responsible University post to see whether, knowing now the composition of the Committee, he was still anxious to help. He called to see me last Friday, and he would be quite willing to come and talk to a small sub-committee such as you have in mind. Moreover, he has no objection to the revelation of his identity to such a sub-committee – in fact he feels that you ought to know who he is so that you may judge the better how much weight to attach to his evidence. I think he will be a useful witness; unlike so many of his particular disability he has no axe to grind – he merely feels that he has a duty to come forward and place his special knowledge at the Committee's disposal. I don't think he will be able to tell us anything of the seamier side of things because he

has been careful to steer clear of homosexual coteries (most of his friends – few of whom know of his inversion – are normals of his own standing), but nevertheless I think what he has to say will be well worth hearing. He struck me as being a very decent sort of chap (the very personification, in fact of the D.P.P.'s [Director of Public Prosecution] 'genuine homosexual').

(PRO HO 345/2, Roberts to Wolfenden 15.12.54)

What is of particular interest here are the many tactical considerations that go into the decision to break the silence. In choosing to do that by way of a particular individual with particular characteristics in a particular setting, Roberts seeks to minimize the risk and generate certain effect in speaking the name of homosexuality.

These examples illustrate some of the ways in which an economy of silence provided the context within which the Wolfenden review proceeded. It is a part of the process of review, shaping the detail of its operation, both limiting it and providing a means whereby it might not only operate but transgress the boundaries of that economy of silence.

The economy of silence was not only implicated in the process of the review, it also appeared of significance in the context of the substance of the material considered. Blackmail raised many questions about the interface between violence/terror, buggery/homosexuality and the law. It appeared as a theme in parliamentary debates that immediately preceded the government review and were implicated in generating the government's decision to stage a review of the law on 'homosexual offences'.

Various issues relating to the silences of the law were addressed during a debate in the upper legislative chamber of the UK Parliament, the House of Lords. They emerged in the course of a debate on 'Homosexual Crime'[21] and in particular in the context of a reference to the topic of blackmail. In opening the debate, Lord Winterton drew attention to the suggestion that the law as it stood was 'the blackmailer's charter' (*Hansard*, House of Lords, Vol. 187, 1953–4, col. 739).[22] In the same debate Earl Jowitt, the late Lord Chancellor, pointed out that:

When I became Attorney General, I became oppressed by the discovery that there was a much larger quantity of blackmail than I had ever realized. I have no figures – I do not suppose one can get figures in a case of this sort – but I can certainly charge my recollection to this extent. It is the fact – I do not know why it is the fact, but it is the fact – that at least 95% of the cases of blackmail which came to my knowledge arose out of homosexuality, either between adult males or between adult males and boys.

(*Hansard*, House of Lords, Vol 187, 1953–4, col. 745)

These observations draw attention not only to the viability of the conjunction of buggery/homosexuality and violence/terror but also to the ease with which this violence of the law might be seized by others and to the popularity of this appropriation.

These matters were the focus of attention of several contributors to the Wolfenden proceedings.[23] One of the most extensive presentations made to the committee on the topic of blackmail, the 'Memorandum submitted by one of the witnesses to be heard at 2.15 p.m. on Thursday 28th July' (PRO HO 345/8, CHP/69), drew the committee's attention to the ease with which the terror associated with buggery (and gross indecency) might be appropriated and the 'extreme frequency' with which it could be used to enforce payment. It described the place of blackmail in the life of a single homosexual, cataloguing a series of encounters that gave rise to the use of terror through threats of exposure joined with demands for money. It described how the refusal to respond to the demands for money was often accompanied by a type of enforced payment in the form of petty theft. A second example drew attention to the ease with which the 'sale of silence' (the blackmailer would offer to remain silent upon payment of money) might be turned into a regular business generating a regular income.

These contributions also drew attention to a close relationship between blackmail and the legal practice of buggery. This proximity was explained in the suggestion that the law as it then stood encouraged others to deploy the terror of the law through accusations of buggery. In particular the law encouraged the weak and the poor to embark upon the 'sale of silence' and thereby to embark upon a life of crime (PRO HO 345/8, CHP/69). The law was described as 'an incentive to blackmail'.

In the final report of the Wolfenden Committee, consideration was given to the proximity between blackmail and the law.[24] In the first instance this took place in the context of a consideration of the Labouchère amendment to the Criminal Law Amendment Act 1885, which, the committee noted, was frequently referred to as 'the blackmailer's charter'. The amendment had introduced a section (s. 11) creating the offence of gross indecency in the following terms:

> It shall be an offence for a man to commit an act of gross indecency with another man, whether in public or in private, or to be a party to the commission by a man of an act of gross indecency with another man, or to procure the commission by a man of an act of gross indecency with another man.

In response, the Wolfenden Committee recognized that this criminal offence did create opportunities for the blackmailer but it refused the suggestion that the proximity between law and blackmail had its roots in this 1885 reform. They existed prior to the 1885 reform. They arose by way of the fact that buggery, attempted buggery and indecent assault were already criminal offences (Wolfenden 1957: 39, para. 109).[25]

Several contributors to the review debate noted another connection between blackmail and the law. They argued that the agents of the law, particularly the police, promoted the nefarious trade of blackmail (PRO HO 345/8, CHP/68 and CHP/59). The 'Memorandum submitted by one of the witnesses to be heard at 2.15 p.m. on Thursday 28th July' (PRO HO 345/8, CHP/69) offered an example of this proximity. The case was described as an example of 'latent blackmail'. It dealt with an incident involving a town-councillor, E.F. In 1952 he sent a complaint to the police relating to the performance of their duties during a flood disaster. An inquiry into the matter officially exonerated the police. As the police inspector left the inquiry he said to E.F., 'We'll get our own back.' Six months later, eighteen charges were preferred against E.F. concerning offences against boys of the local school, which were alleged to have occurred before the police inquiry. E.F. was found guilty and sentenced to serve a five-year gaol sentence. Subsequent investigations revealed that between thirty and forty boys of the school to whom E.F. had offered 'open house' had been taken for long rides alone in a police car and grilled until 'confessions' were obtained. It was also discovered that not one boy had complained to his parents and the only boy that E.F.'s brother had subsequently been able to contact had admitted that the 'confession' was a lie. The Wolfenden witness concluded that this particular manifestation of blackmail represented a more sinister 'latent' form of blackmail, which exposed all to an accusation of homosexual acts, and so potentially placed all men at the mercy of any authority or ill-wisher.[26]

A distinctive feature of this example of blackmail is the fact that the illegitimate use of the violence of the law is carried out not by persons otherwise remote from the law but by agents of the law. While the focus of the criticism of latent blackmail appears to have been the ease with which this form of violence and terror might be (mis)used against a wide constituency of potential victims, the example reveals another important aspect of the use of the violence and terror of the law. The witness assumes a distance between the two that is far from clear.[27] The example draws attention to the proximity of the legitimate and illegitimate use of this instance of law's violence and terror in the acts of the agents of the law, in this instance the police. The threat to all men is perhaps located in the fact that the distinction between the violence and terror invoked through blackmail and the violence and terror of the law are one and the same.

The committee echoed these concerns. It found that while laws (then to be found in s. 29 of the Larceny Act 1916) enabled the agents of the law to pursue those who sought to appropriate the terror of the law for their own private use, at the same time the private use of terror might be put to another use by the agents of the law. This was addressed by way of an example:

Case I

A., aged 49, met B., aged 35, in a cinema. Afterwards they went to A.'s flat and committed buggery.

For a period of about seven years B. visited A.'s flat regularly, and the men committed buggery together on each occasion.

B. then commenced to demand money from A., from whom, in the course of about three months, he obtained £40.

A. finally complained to the police. The facts were reported to the

Director of Public Prosecutions, who advised that no action should be taken against B. for demanding money by menaces, but that both men should be charged with buggery.

Both men were thereupon charged with two offences of buggery committed with each other, and, after pleading guilty, were sentenced to nine months' imprisonment. Neither man had any previous convictions, nor were any other offences taken into consideration.

(Wolfenden 1957: 40, para. 112)

The committee noted that the agents of the law were, in this instance, able to exploit an opportunity to take up the terror of the law that had been appropriated by the blackmailer and transform the blackmailer's terror into the terror of the law. Here the agents of the law were not concerned with punishing the one who threatened to seize the violence of the law and to protect the blackmail victim but their main concern was to reappropriate the violence and terror of the law in order to make the blackmail victim a victim twice over; once as the victim of blackmail and once as the victim of the law. The ability of the police to translate the blackmailer's accusation into their own again draws attention to the proximity of the two forms of terror.[28] The committee noted that, while the terror associated with the naming of buggery, or now more generally associated with homosexuality, was not a legitimate practice exclusive to the law, its wider social usage (with or without the attendant demand for money or property) operated as a more effective form of terror precisely because of the legitimacy of the terror associated with the law and the practices of the agents of the law (Wolfenden 1957: 40, para. 111).

The dynamics of the interface between 'homosexual offences' (buggery and gross indecency) and terror in the law was given a high profile subsequent to the publication of the Wolfenden Report. In part this was due to the release in 1961 of a film, *Victim*, directed by Basil Dearden, which addressed the connection between 'homosexual offences' and the law. Blackmail was central to the film's claims for the reform of the law in line with the Wolfenden proposals. In general the story is concerned with a blackmail operation that involves making accusations of homosexual acts[29] and demanding money.

One of the blackmail incidents involves a barrister, Melville Farr. Unlike all the other blackmail victims he decides to take the matter to the police. The script explores the position of the homosexual who seeks the aid of the law. The problem is presented in the following terms in an interchange between Farr's wife Laura and Laura's brother, a fellow barrister, Scott:

SCOTT   The crime I'm talking about is blackmail. If he doesn't go to the police about this, he's covering up blackmail.

LAURA   *(slowly)* If he goes to the police, it's the end of his career – everything he's ever worked for.

SCOTT   *(quietly)* It's the end of himself if he doesn't. He can go to the police, which apparently he's reluctant to do. Or he can deal with it himself.

Oh yes, Mel's clever enough to run them down. Turn their own weapon against them. 'Do as I say, or I'll hand you over.' And what does that make him? A blackmailer. No better than they are.

LAURA   *(slowly)* You mean he can't avoid being destroyed, whatever happens?
SCOTT   Yes I do, Laura.

(Green and McCormick 1961: 75)

This draws attention to the fact that in the context of the homosexual–terror conjunction the homosexual man is always already a victim twice over: not only a victim of the blackmailer but also a victim of the law. Unlike the case considered in the Wolfenden Report, rather than being an exceptional state of affairs this double victimization is presented here as the norm.[30] Furthermore, the narrative draws attention to the proximity of the agent of the law and the blackmailer. Common to both is the threat, 'Do as I say, or I'll hand you over'.[31]

Another facet of blackmail is discussed in an exchange that takes place between the head of the blackmail practice, Miss Benham, and her assistant, the Sandy Youth. The narrative sets out the factors that motivate the blackmailer in the following terms:

The Sandy Youth looks at her with something between admiration and disgust.
SANDY YOUTH   You really are a bit odd, aren't you?
MISS BENHAM   *(immediately defensive)* What d'you mean?
SANDY YOUTH   I don't know – a sort of cross between an avenging angel and a peeping Tom.

Miss Benham turns away caught on the raw.
MISS BENHAM   It just disgusts me to see people behaving like animals, that's all.

(Green and McCormick 1961: 85)

A final comment relating to the factors that motivate the blackmailer is to be found in Miss Benham's final line as she is taken away by the arresting police officer:

MISS BENHAM   *(bitterly)* I never thought I'd live to see the ungodly in great power. And flourishing like the green bay tree.

These observations are of particular interest in the light of the fact that, at least in this context, blackmail is a practice that mimics the law's deployment of 'buggery' (and later 'homosexual') and terror. Through the proximity of black-mail and the legal use of terror, blackmail becomes a vehicle through which a critique of the terror of the law might be undertaken. The proximity suggests that the motivations that inform the act of the blackmailer are also those that inform the law and the actions of the various agents of the law.[32] The representation of the blackmailer in *Victim* draws our attention to the role of law and its agents. In the production and deployment of the buggery/homo-sexual–violence conjunction, the agents of law operate as avenging angel and peeping Tom, or as Foucault noted they operate according to the requirements of self-righteous domination and erotic pleasure (Foucault 1981a: 45).

Another important aspect of the act of blackmail described in this interchange is that the blackmailer takes up the position of the agent of the law in order to better realize the law's concerns: to unleash a terror against that which is forbidden and to punish that which is forbidden in the name of good order. This draws attention to the fact that the blackmailer is only a threat to law as she tries to usurp the terror of the law. Furthermore, while blackmailers may usurp the terror of the law for their own personal financial gain, this is not necessarily the only motivating factor behind the act of blackmail. The blackmailer also mimics the legitimate use of terror as a practice through which to produce a particular social order.

PRIVATE = SILENCE

The economy of silence is significant in another way in the Wolfenden Committee's review. It appears in the context of its proposals to decriminalize certain genital relations between men in certain limited circumstances. A key phrase in the proposals to decriminalize is 'in private'. It is by way of this phrase that the Wolfenden Committee sought to install a new silence in the law.

In coming to the conclusion that the law should install a place where the (criminal) law might no longer speak the name of buggery (or gross indecency), the binary opposition of public–private was put to work. It is a binary that has interesting characteristics. Within this scheme of things the 'public' is a realm of law's full presence. It is a space of order and decency through the law. It is also a place where the citizen is protected from what is offensive or injurious. It is presented as a place free from the exploitation and corruption of others, particularly for those who are young, or weak in body or mind, the inexperienced and those in a state of special physical, official or economic dependence. This 'public' suggests an alternative place where the law is absent, the 'private'.

The exposition of the 'public' offered here has other interesting characteristics. Of particular importance is the fact that this 'public' cannot be reduced to a geographical or spatial phenomenon. 'Public' refers to an embodied place, to the body in general as public, and in this context the genital body as a site of the full presence of the law. No matter where the spatial location, the (male genital) body as youth, as weakness, as inexperience and dependence is always a public body, always the site of law's full presence, and as such this body is the impossibility of the 'private'. At the same time, in this scheme of things the 'private' is also a question of the body.

An embodied notion of the 'private' is at work in the proposals to decriminalize certain genital relations between men. Here the body and the 'private' are connected in a particular way. The body in its intimacy and its singularity is the quintessential representation of the 'private'. More specifically the sexual as the most intimate aspect of the body is that which is most closely associated with the 'private'. It is by this chain of associations that assurance is found that this private body might exist with respect to the law. Thus the fact that the law did not criminalize all fields of sexual behaviour was taken as evidence of the limited presence of the law. While certain forms of sexual behaviour were regarded by many as sinful, morally wrong, or objectionable for reasons of conscience, or of religious or cultural tradition, and such actions may be reprobated on these grounds, they were not prohibited by the criminal law. For instance, adultery and fornication were not offences for which a person could be punished by the criminal law (Wolfenden 1957: 10, para. 14). Here the law was rendered silent. In recommending that homosexual behaviour between adults in private should no longer be a criminal offence, the committee recommended that this silence of the law be applied to a new context and a different body: the male genital body in its genital relations with other male bodies.

In putting forward this proposal it had to define that place of silence. In the first instance it appeared to be reluctant to do so. In its report the committee suggested that the words 'in private' were not intended to have a legal definition. It continued:

> Many heterosexual acts are not criminal if committed in private but are punishable if committed in circumstances which outrage public decency, and we should expect the same criteria to apply to homosexual acts. It is our intention that the law should continue to regard as criminal any indecent act committed in a place where members of the public may be likely to see and be offended by it, but where there is no possibility of public offence of this nature it becomes a matter of private responsibility of the persons concerned and as such, in our opinion, is outside the proper purview of the criminal law. It will be for the courts to decide, in cases of doubt, whether or not public decency has been outraged, and we cannot see that there would be any greater difficulty about establishing this in the case of homosexual acts than there is at present in the case of heterosexual acts.
>
> (Wolfenden 1957: 25, para. 64)

Here the focus is upon a concern with the display of the genital body (Brown 1993). When translated into the law in the Sexual Offences Act 1967, 'in private' was defined in the following way:

> s1(2) An act which would otherwise be treated for the purpose of this Act as being done in private shall not be so treated if done –
> (a) when more than two persons take part or are present; or
> (b) in a lavatory to which the public have or are permitted to have access, whether on payment or otherwise.

In the first attempt at a definition in paragraph (a), display is widely construed; an act will be a display if a third party is present no matter where that display takes place. In paragraph (b), display is even more widely construed. The definition of 'in private' does not require the actual presence of a third party but the mere possibility of a third party.

This approach to 'in private' has been explained by way of case law. The one reported decision that has addressed the meaning of this statutory formula of privacy found in this act is *R. v. Reakes* (1974). Here the act that was the subject of the proceedings took place in an enclosed, unlit private yard at about 1 a.m. There was a gate separating the yard from the public road. In the yard was a 'water closet' (a toilet) used by patrons of two neighbouring restaurants and employees of a taxi business. Reakes had previously been to the yard and had used the toilet and had seen others using it. During the act of buggery no one came into the yard. The report tells us that someone came into the yard to use the toilet after the act that was the subject of the charge. The definition of privacy that was accepted by the Court of Appeal as clear and satisfactory defined 'in private' in the following terms:

> [Y]ou look at all the surrounding circumstances, the time of night, the nature of the place including such matters as lighting, and you consider further the likelihood of a third person coming upon the scene.

> (*Reakes* 1974: 615)

Here the emphasis is not merely upon display but upon the possibility of display. This approach to 'in private' suggests that the institution of silence enacted in the 1967 Act will be a particularly limited total silence. The mere possibility of display of the male genital body in juxtaposition with another male body will render those bodies capable of total visibility in law. 'In private' is to be haunted by the paranoid figure of an ever-present third party.

While these reform proposals and changes in the law seek to create a place where the law may not speak the name of buggery (or gross indecency), at the same time the reforms never intended to silence the law and thereby to erase the terror of the law or to erase the threat of blackmail. Subsequent to the 1967 reforms, the limited research conducted into the lives of gay men suggests that the creation of this formal silence has had little effect. The continued viability of the law–terror conjunction appears in the ongoing private appropriation of the terror of the law (West 1985: 126–8). Donald West, undertaking research on sexual victimization, found that the post-1967 practices of the police continued to mimic those of the blackmailer. He found that the male adults in his sample talked of verbal and physical intimidation while in the custody of the police, the police neglected complaints of criminal victimization, they threatened to make revelations to families or employers of the sexual orientation of men who co-operated with police enquiries; the price of silence was a confession of guilt (West 1985). The blackmailer's use of terror and the fear of double victimization by the agents of the law would appear to have currency still in the UK. More recently, the *Pink Paper* (27/8/93 and 3/9/93), a national newspaper for lesbians and gay men in the UK, reported a 'blackmail epidemic'. In the two weeks following the publication of a report on the work of a charity that specialized in providing support to the victims of blackmail, Glasgow City Liaison Group, over 600 blackmail victims from around the UK contacted the organization. More often than not, blackmail victims continue to be too afraid to report the matter to the police. The Glasgow City Liaison group found that the current practices of blackmail take forms similar to those practised before the Wolfenden review. They involve not only direct demands for money but also enforced payment through petty theft. They also continue to take the form of business operations, there being some evidence that organized gangs are involved in nation-wide extortion rackets. And as the Wolfenden Report recognized, while the law continues to offer the opportunity to terrorize by way of the offences of buggery, attempted buggery and gross indecency, to name but a few, the law will continue to promote blackmail.[33]

SILENCE AND THE REFORM OF LAW

The silence–buggery conjunction made a recent dramatic appearance in the UK during a parliamentary debate in the House of Commons on 21 February 1994. Members of Parliament were debating the proposals to reduce the 'age of consent' to genital relations between men from 21 to 16. The three-hour debate was dominated by speakers in support of the reform.[34] Two short contributions made by those who opposed reform are of particular interest. The first instance is to be found in an exchange made by two Scottish MPs, Sir Nicholas Fairbairn and Mr Bill Walker:[35]

SIR NICHOLAS FAIRBAIRN (Perth and Kinross)   I hope that the Committee [on this occasion the House of Commons as a whole was sitting as a committee] will not be misled by the fact that heterosexual activity is normal and homosexual activity, putting your penis into another man's arsehole, is a perverse – [at this point, shouting brought the debate to a halt]

THE FIRST DEPUTY CHAIRMAN   Order. We can well do without talk like that.

MR BLAIR   I do not think that I will answer that intervention.

MR BILL WALKER (Tayside, North)   On a point of order, Mr Lofthouse [the first Deputy Speaker]. For those of us who wish to speak in the debate, may I ask whether it would be in order to describe what it is that we are debating – the actual act? [HON MEMBERS: We all know?] We may all know, but would it be in order? Would it be in order to describe an unnatural act so that we can be absolutely certain that there is no doubt outside this Chamber about what we are debating?

THE FIRST DEPUTY CHAIRMAN   It is a matter of the words and language that are used.

(*Hansard*, House of Commons, Vol. 255, 21.2.94, col. 98)

The second instance appears in a speech made by Mr Tony Marlow. He interrupted the speech of Mrs Currie, who proposed the reform reducing the age of consent to 16, with the following observation:[36]

MR MARLOW   I am grateful to my hon. Friend [Mrs Currie]. She is seeking to persuade hon. Members to vote to legalize the buggery of adolescent males. Does she think that is what our constituents have sent us here to do?

MRS CURRIE   I merely repeat that I do not consider the private sexual practices of other people, including the hon. Gentleman, to be any business of the law. The debate in recent weeks has taught me that one person's sexual perversion is another person's preferred sexual practice. We should all be careful about pronouncing on what goes on next door.

(*Hansard*, House of Commons, Vol. 255, 21.3.94, col. 77)

In both incidents speakers refer, albeit in different ways, to buggery and silence. Both incidents demonstrate the continuing viability of a close proximity between buggery and an economy of silence. This is revealed in the way individuals respond to the naming of buggery. For example, it is manifest in the performance of a certain verbal decency. Here a trace of the injunction to silence remains in the self-conscious requirement that buggery may only be spoken of by way of a language that is sanitized. The first instance of the naming of buggery draws attention to another aspect of the contemporary significance of silence. The breaking of the silence, in this instance by way of a curious conjunction of a scientific term (penis) and a vernacular term (arsehole), has particularly dramatic effects. It unleashes a certain violence. In this instance it provoked an explosion of noise in the chamber of the House of Commons of such ferocity that it momentarily brought the unfolding narrative of the debate to a sharp (temporary) end with the call for 'Order'. It is followed by a plea to re-establish an economy of silence, then a dispute over the economy of speech – the lexicon – by which genital relations between men might be represented in the debate. In the second example, there is evidence of the deployment of another silence. Buggery is here to be confined to the silence of privacy. These examples draw attention to the way that buggery continues to operate as a powerful symbol that might have the power to disrupt and disturb. The speakers referred to above deploy that power with some effect. As the Honourable members demonstrate, far from producing ignorance the silence ensures that, 'We all know.' Silence is not about lack of knowledge; silence is consistent with knowledge and continues to produce very specific effects that are central to a particular knowledge of the body and a particular politics of representation.

SILENCE = DEATH: OUTING

The final example of the current importance and operation of an economy of silence in the representation of genital relations between persons of the same sex is to be found in the politics and practices of outing. Outing is a practice of naming. As such it seeks to appropriate the privileged position of speaking the name of genital relations between persons of the same sex. It is a politics of naming that recognizes the wide significance of the terms of representation. These have been explained in the following terms: 'gay is not about sex acts or about what we do in our bedrooms but is a much larger matter regarding identity and culture and community'

(Signorile 1993: 80). Outing is a practice of the politics of identity that has emerged at a particular moment, in the context of a post-liberation politics, Queer politics, and in a place and time where the trauma of HIV/AIDS has (again) made illness and death an overt matter of identity, community and culture. In this section, the analysis will focus upon the interface between an extant economy of silence and this new practice of naming. It will analyse the way in which the practices of outing both mimic that economy and at the same time seek to disrupt it.

Outing is a political practice that both situates itself and is situated within the context of a specific economy of silence. This is represented, for example, in the title of Johansson and Percy's study of outing: *Outing: Shattering the Conspiracy of Silence* (Johansson and Percy 1994), and in Michelangelo Signorile's observation that outing is a practice that has to be located in the context of the fact that: 'There exists in America what appears to be a brilliantly orchestrated, massive conspiracy to keep all homosexuals locked in the closet' (Signorile 1993: xiii). Outing is a practice that presents itself as a response to a silence that seeks to bring that silence to an end. However this tells us little about the nature of the particular economy of silence within which outing is located, the nature of the problem of silence it seeks to address or the techniques deployed through outing to respond to that silence. It is these matters I want to address.

In the USA, law has a particular place within the economy of silence that outing occupies and to which it responds. One aspect of this was demonstrated and given a high profile in the decision of the Supreme Court in *Bowers* v. *Hardwick*. This decision confirmed that the total criminalization of genital relations between men was not contrary to the US constitution. This demonstrates that, in the USA, outing is not a response to or an engagement with an economy of absolute silence. In *Bowers* v. *Hardwick*, in refusing to establish a right to privacy, the Supreme Court confirmed that the truth of genital relations between persons of the same sex might always be represented in terms of the limited economy of the lexicon of the law by way of the name of sodomy (homosexual) (Halley 1993 a, b, 1994), as articulated, without limit, by way of authorized speakers (Johansson and Percy 1994: 305–12). As such, the social order of representation that outing seeks to address does not produce a closet without limit. The closet is one that must remain outside and beyond the legal textual practices authorized by the Supreme Court. Outing might be said to respond, at least in part, to the impoverishment of representation that is institutionalized here.

There is a second dimension to the interface between outing, silence and the law. This second dimension is found in the context not of the criminal law but of the civil law. This is the law that seeks to deal with relations between individuals (in contrast to law, such as the criminal law, that is primarily a matter of relations between the state and the individual). In the USA, a formal silence (closet) in law might be constructed through this law between individuals. In the USA, two civil actions may be invoked by an individual to stop the deployment of the name by another individual: defamation and the invasion of privacy by public disclosure of a private fact (see Elwood 1992; Grant 1991; Wick 1991).[37] Both create a legally defined and enforced silence around the individual.

Outing sets itself up over against a silence formally constructed in the name of privacy (Mohr 1992: ch. 1). Michelangelo Signorile makes the point by way of an observation made by Benjamin Schatz, executive director of the lesbian and gay doctors' group, American Association of Physicians for Human Rights. The right to privacy 'plays right into our enemies' hands. Private is, after all, exactly what they want us to be. I believe we are in the long run fighting less for the rights to privacy than for the right not to have to be private' (quoted in Signorile 1993: 87).[38] Privacy is equated with silence and, within the parameters of an outing agenda, silence whatever its form is the object of concern: 'Outing may not be a vehicle to create living role models; it does however create visibility' (Signorile 1993: 81). Signorile argues that, through outing, lesbian and gay activists and journalists alike are challenging the very notion of 'privacy'. This, he argues, is inevitable where individuals come to understand their sexual identity as being similar to racial or ethnic identity, and where that identity is a matter of culture and community. In that context it is not appropriate to consider gay as merely a private matter (Signorile 1993: 80).

It would be wrong to conclude that the silence that the practices of outing address is exclusive to the law. The silence that outing addresses is both within and outside the law. The silence beyond the law, which lies in the shadow of the law, needs to be approached with some caution. Again outing is not a response to a total silence beyond the law. Signorile demonstrates this in posing the following question:

> DOES ONE HAVE TO TAKE THE C.I.A. CODE-BREAKING COURSE IN ORDER TO FIGURE OUT WHAT THE FUCK IS BEING SAID IN THE PAPERS THESE DAYS? IT'S UTTERLY HOMOPHOBIC OF US AND THE MEDIA TO CONSTANTLY BEAT AROUND THE BUSH, SPEAK IN CODES AND TREAT HOMO-SEXUALITY AS SOME SCANDALOUS SECRET, THE NAME OF WHICH WE CAN'T INVOKE.
>
> (Signorile 1993: 68, capitals in the original)

Outing's focus is not so much the operation of a total silence but the fact that identities founded on genital relations between persons of the same sex continue to be spoken by way of special (obscure) codes. Outing would appear to be a practice that demands genital relations be named in a very specific way, according to a specific code that grounds itself in a belief in sexual identity as authenticity.

Outing is a response to an economy of silence that has other important qualities. Signorile has drawn attention to this in the following observation: 'This conspiracy [of silence/speaking in marginal codes] forces many of us to live in shame and tremble with fear. Anyone who dares venture out of that closet is threatened with destruction. The vast majority heed the warning' (Signorile 1993: xiii). This draws attention to the fact that these codes are marginal vernaculars of identity and desire produced in response to an economy of silence that is also an economy of violence.

The effect of this economy of violence has been given a particularly high profile through the devastating effects of HIV/AIDS (Gross 1993: 33–5; Johansson and Percy 1994: ch. 5). HIV/AIDS has been used to rationalize prejudice, discrimination and violence against gay men and lesbians (Herek and Berrill 1992: 2; Gross 1993: 106). Awareness of the continuation and prevalence of this economy of violence has also gained a new visibility through work that seeks to catalogue the incidence of homophobic violence. Homophobic violence is a manifestation, and realization, of this economy of silence:

> Every such incident carries a message to the victim and the entire community of which he or she is a part. Each anti-gay attack is, in effect, a punishment for stepping outside culturally accepted norms and a warning to all gay and lesbian people to stay in the closet.
>
> (Herek and Berrill 1992: 3)[39]

Signorile argues that outing seeks to respond to a connection between the particular marginal vernaculars of identity and desire, the violence of HIV/AIDS and homophobic violence. His particular target is those who hide behind these codes:

> YOU SLIMY, SELF-LOATHING, HYPOCRITICAL MONSTERS. YOU GO TO YOUR PARTIES, YOU WHIRL WITH BIGOTS AND MURDERERS, YOU LIE AND ENGAGE IN COVER-UPS, YOU SELL YOUR SOULS – MEANWHILE WE'RE DYING.
>
> (Signorile 1993: 68, capitals in the original)

Those who practise and advocate outing seek to present it as a practice of naming that responds to the destructive effects of the existing practices of naming identity. Richard D. Mohr has addressed this point. He has suggested that:

> the sort of outing I have advocated does not invoke, mobilize or ritualistically confirm anti-gay values; rather it cuts against them, works to undo them. The point of outing, as I have defined it, is not to wreak vengeance, not to punish, and not to deflect attention from one's own debased state. It is to avoid degrading oneself.
>
> (Mohr 1992: 36)

Mohr's observations have another significance. They draw attention to the fact that while outing sets itself over against an existing economy of silence and violence it might also be interpreted as a politics and practice of violence, which mimics the violence that it seeks to disrupt. Fran Lebowitz characterized the practice of outing in the following terms: 'It's damaging, it's immoral, McCarthyism, it's terrorism, it's cannibalism, it's beneath contempt . . . to me this is a bunch of Jews lining up other Jews to go to a concentration camp' (Lewin 1990). It has been described as a form of 'fascism' (Signorile 1993: 75). A common feature of these criticisms is that they recognize the possible proximity between the violence of the status quo and the violence of contemporary practices of outing in order to condemn the practice of outing. Those who advocate outing have also recognized the possibility that outing may mimic the violence of the existing economy of silence. For example, Johansson and Percy explain that:

> we can say that inquisitors and police as well as spiteful gossips outed sodomites over the centuries. But now outing in the new sense means militant activists dragging the cowardly and disloyal out of the closet by trumpeting their proclivities to all and sundry, ostensibly in the political interest of the Queer Nation.
>
> (Johansson and Percy 1994: 4–5)

Here the proximity between the violence of the law and the violence of the practice of outing is recognized and celebrated. It recognizes that proximity advocating the use of violence for the fabrication of community; the Queer Nation. Gross gives another instance of this proximity in his observation that:

> Conventional notions of a community include the expectation that the community will protect its members, and may on occasion sacrifice some members to protect or further the interests of the group. Outing would appear to be an example of such a sacrifice. In traditional political liberalism, the members will, it is assumed, offer themselves voluntarily for possible sacrifice, but there are cases, such as the military draft, where the community compels members to sacrifice themselves.
>
> (Gross 1993: 127)

At the same time that the violence of naming is recognized and celebrated in the name of community, those who engage in outing recognize the need to regulate that violence or to use it strategically: 'The point of outing, as I have defined it, is not to wreak vengeance, not to punish, and not to deflect attention from one's own debased state. It is to avoid degrading oneself' (Mohr 1992: 36). In turn, those advocating outing have attempted to produce it as a science of social change, setting out an ethical framework through which outing may take place. (See Johansson and Percy 1994: ch. 8 'Tactical guide to outing'; Mohr 1992: 35–48.)

CONCLUSIONS

In the introduction to his study, *Gays/Justice: A Study of Ethics, Society, and Law*, Richard Mohr refers to 'the legally enforced invisibility of gay people' (Mohr 1988: 1). This chapter has attempted to explore the nature of that 'enforced invisibility'. At one level, Mohr's observation is an accurate one. This chapter has demonstrated the way in which genital relations between persons of the same sex have limited visibility, being represented in law by way of an impoverished lexical code. On the other hand, this study suggests that there is a need to proceed with some caution here, in that there is ample evidence that the representation of these relations within the law is far from a state of invisibility. There is a very long and verbose tradition of representation through which this body has been produced in the law.

This chapter has attempted to provide an insight into the nature of that system of representation, which produces both impoverishment and such a superabundance of meaning in the law. Through the injunction to silence it has been possible to learn much about the idiosyncratic nature of legal practice as a practice of representation. It is a practice that demands resort to a limited lexicon and the deployment of that lexicon by way of elaborate performances of verbal decency. It is a practice that both seeks to limit the generation of meaning and produce a wealth of meaning. This study has drawn attention also to the intimate relationship between the law as a practice of representation and law as a practice of terror and violence.

This chapter draws attention, finally, to the wider cultural significance of the injunction to silence that is made in the law. It draws attention to the way in which a politics of representation of the male genital body is always already situated within an economy of silence. It might be the object of political engagement and at the same time be structured by it, both making that engagement possible and limiting its parameters. The injunction to silence provides an actual limit to representation, but it is also implicated in the possibility of representation and the proliferation of meaning, both within the law and outside the strict impoverished lexical code of the law. It is to the proliferation of meanings that articulate and might be given a voice through buggery that the analysis now turns.

4

MAKING THE SENSE OF BUGGERY

INTRODUCTION

Buggery is not merely another term in the lexicon of the law, through which the male body in its genital relations with other male bodies is to be represented. Buggery has long been assigned an exalted position. This chapter is concerned with the way in which this nobility is generated at any one time, particularly the present, and repeated over time. The position of 'buggery' is intimately connected to the meanings that have been associated with and given voice through the use of 'buggery' to make sense and nonsense of this male genital body with particular reference to the English legal order. This chapter is an exploration of those meanings. In pursuing this line of analysis, the chapter seeks to achieve another objective: to explore the meanings that have been associated with and given voice through the term 'homosexual' in law. In the 1967 Sexual Offences Act, a connection is made between buggery and homosexual. It is made in the name of equivalence, between buggery and homosexual, and in the name of tradition. Tradition, as the bond that connects homosexual to buggery, is important in two ways. First, it suggests that the meanings that are henceforth to be associated with and given a voice through the use of 'homosexual' are those that have been produced by way of 'buggery'. Second, tradition suggests not only a sameness between homosexual and buggery but it also suggests a sameness in the repetition of 'buggery' over time. In pursuing an analysis of the meanings of 'buggery', this chapter seeks to challenge these claims of sameness and repetition.

The chapter seeks to draw attention to the multiplicity of meanings that inform and are given a voice by way of 'buggery' in the law. This multiplicity of meanings at any one time and over a period of time is not only offered as a challenge to the claims of sameness and repetition that is tradition but it also has another significance. It draws attention to the way in which, perhaps contrary to expectations, sameness and repetition might also be a vehicle for change. Having drawn attention to the changes that take place in the meanings that form and are given a voice through buggery, the analysis will then return to tradition as the production of sameness. Having attempted to challenge the claims of tradition as the production of sameness and repetition, at this point the purpose of the

66

analysis is to take these claims seriously. The objective here is to explore the nature of the legal practice that generates our experience of the truth of the text of law as tradition. This will involve an exploration of the legal practice that generates the experience of law as the endless repetition of the same: citation. The analysis will not only demonstrate the way in which the practice of citation works to generate the truth of the text of law as the present of the past but will also explore the way in which the practice of citation reveals and depends upon the gap that separates the present from the past. In pursuing this analysis, the general objective of this chapter is to problematize the meanings that articulate and are given a voice though the 'homosexual' of law, where that 'homosexual' is defined as buggery.

These objectives will be pursued by way of an analysis of a specific set of texts of English law: commentaries on the law and statutes that seek to codify and consolidate the criminal law.[1] Most of the commentaries referred to here were produced by judges, such as Sir Edward Coke and Sir Matthew Hale writing in the seventeenth century, William Hawkins and Sir Edward East writing in the late eighteenth century, and Sir James Fitzjames Stephen writing in the nineteenth century. In addition, attempts to codify and consolidate the law are of significance here. The first originates in the early nineteenth century. In the name of logic, rationality and ensuing enlightenment, the Offences Against the Person Acts of 1828 and 1861 bring together a large number of previously disparate offences, give them a certain commonality and hierarchy. Buggery is placed within this new distribution. The second code that consolidates the law that is of concern here is a more recent Act: the Sexual Offences Act 1956. In this reform, buggery shifts its position from being an offence against the person to being a sexual offence. This event is of particular significance in that for the first time English law was to be organized by way of a division between the sexual and the non-sexual. Both the commentaries and the codes, in different but interconnected ways, offer a rich source of data about the way in which the meanings of 'buggery' and 'homosexual' are made as sense and nonsense.

TAXONOMIES

Analysis of the commentaries and statutes utilizes a feature that is common to all these texts. Each is a work of classification. Each allocates offences within a hierarchical distribution (a taxonomy) of wrongs. A reading of these taxonomies in general and an analysis of the particular allocation of buggery within the hierarchy of these various texts provide an opportunity to consider the particular meanings and values that have been connected to the term 'buggery' and have come to be expressed through 'buggery' in law (Foucault 1970: preface). This study of the legal practices of classification facilitates an exploration of the sense (the intelligibility) and nonsense (unintelligibility) of the male genital body in its male genital relations that is made by resort to 'buggery' as an august wrong in law. It allows us to consider how the lofty values associated with and articulated through 'buggery' have been formed and reformed, gained an importance, been rendered more marginal and, in some instances, made obsolete.

The first taxonomy in this study is found in Sir Edward Coke's early seventeenth-century text, *The Institutes of the Laws of England* (Coke 1628). It is a text of particular importance and utility as it provides one of the earliest and most extensive scholarly meditations written after the first secular enactment of buggery in 1533 that contains a reference to buggery.[2]

Coke's work is made up of four volumes. The first deals with land tenure. The second is a compilation of Acts of Parliament,[3] which, with a few exceptions, deal with Common Pleas (actions between subject and subject brought before the king's courts as opposed to actions before the king's courts between the Crown and the subject). The third part of *The Institutes* is devoted to Pleas of the Crown, or what would now be called criminal offences. It brings together a mixture of statutory and Common Law (judge-made) offences. The fourth volume deals with the tribunals of adjudication and the procedures of the law. The third part of *The Institutes* is of particular interest, as it is in this volume that we find the chapter entitled, 'Buggery or Sodomy'.

The index of the chapters of the third volume of *The Institutes* places 'Buggery or Sodomy' in the following way:

1 High treason and of incidents thereto
2 Petit treason
3 Misprison of treason
4 Felony by the statute of 3 Henry 7 to conspire the death of the King, or Privy Counsellor
5 Heresie
6 Of Felony by Conjuration, Witchcraft, Sorcery and Inchantment
7 Murder
8 Homicide, and herein of Felo de se
9 Deodands
10 Buggery or Sodomy
11 Rape
12 Felony for carrying away a woman against her will
13 Felony for cutting out tongues etc
14 Burglary, and herein of Sacrilege
15 Burning of houses.

It then continues to catalogue a further ninety-one chapters dealing with other offences and matters connected to them.

In general the focus of concern here is the particular allocation of the chapter, 'Buggery or Sodomy' within this taxonomy of 106 chapters. In particular, our concern is with the factors that influence its specific allocation within this hierarchy of wrongs and thereby make its meaning.

The preface to Volume 3 entitled, 'A proeme to the third part . . .', is one source of information that can shed some light on the factors that inform, organize and are given a voice, not only throughout the general distribution of offences in this taxonomy, but also in the specific allocation of the chapter, 'Buggery or Sodomy'. Coke explains the themes that inform the selection and distribution of the offences in this volume in the following terms. First, he notes the connection that fuses all offences into a volume of work. They all:

> ... concerneth the safety of his Majesty, the quiet of the Commonwealth, and the life, honour, fame, liberty, blood, wife, and posteritie of the party accused, besides the forefeiture of his lands, goods, and all that he hath.
>
> (Coke 1628 [1979])

Thus to be included within this volume an offence must, in various ways, in full or in large part, be capable of being always already understood through these terms. Incorporation into this taxonomy in turn suggests that each term functions as an image through which these matters might be represented and thereby articulated again.

Coke notes other concerns that conjoin the named offences in this text and produce their specific distribution. He continues: 'We shall first treat the highest, and most hainous crime of High Treason, *Crimen laesae Majestatis*; and of the rest in order as they are greater and more odious than others' (Coke 1628 [1979]). Here he draws our attention to the fact that his distribution of the specific offences is informed by the requirements of hierarchy. The allocation of each wrong is the operation of an economy of gravity, and in turn the offence is made an image of that economy of gravity. Each offence articulates a particular gravity. The allocation of buggery to Chapter 10 within a taxonomy of 106 chapters suggests that it is always already taken as an extremely grave wrong and furthermore that it can be put to use as a representation of great danger.

Coke's preliminary observations announce a set of factors that generate the particular consistency and the specific comprehensibility of his text. These themes not only connect the separate offences but in bringing them together they also work to distribute the offences into a hierarchy. As such they speak through each offence in its particular distribution in the table of pleas of the Crown. They provide some of the key terms of the coherence or the intelligibility that fabricates and is given a voice through the distribution of offences into this particular hierarchy of wrongs.

This intelligibility, as Coke informs us, is to be understood in a very particular way. It is that which makes the text 'lightsome and easie to be understood'. As that which makes the light of the law these themes make law's sense and nonsense in general, and in particular they make sense and nonsense of the buggery or sodomy of law. This making of a sense of the buggery or sodomy of the law is offered in the name of banishing darkness. It is this intelligibility that staves off the buggery or sodomy of law as incomprehension and nonsense. These themes are the factors that offer to bring the absurdity of law in general and of buggery or sodomy in particular to an end. They work to produce the truth of law.

Being Chapter 10 in a text that is made up of 106 chapters, 'Buggery or Sodomy' is given gives a high priority within the taxonomy by Coke's expressive system. In general, its early appearance draws attention to its use as a vehicle through which an intense and noble odium might be articulated. Its general priority and its close proximity to various forms of treason suggests that at least by the date of this edition, 1628, buggery was an image that constituted a grave threat to majesty. At the same time it is more intimate with other offences. It appears most immediately below offences that name unlawful acts of violence that result in the death of the individual, murder and deodands (where death is caused by a moveable inanimate object or animate beast without the will offence or fault of the victim or of any other person[4]). It appears immediately above offences relating to the unlawful carnal knowledge and abuse of women. In connecting these offences, buggery or sodomy appears to be positioned as an extreme act, akin to death. As such it is made as a substantial threat to the life, honour, fame, liberty and blood of the accused: an act of civil death. Being between the extreme forms of unlawful killing and the most grave threat to the male/female carnal order, its appearance suggests that the sense of buggery or sodomy is to be made by way of extreme violence to the body that, on the one hand, is proximate to death and, on the other hand, is to be understood as an extreme violence to a carnal economy and a violation of a specific carnal order. The sense and nonsense of buggery or sodomy is made at the point of the intersection. By way of this expressive system, buggery or sodomy in law is to be a representation of extreme violence to the individual body, the carnal order and the wider order of the Sovereign and thereby the nation – the king's peace.

The detail of the chapter itself is also of some interest. As one of the most extensive meditations on buggery or sodomy within the legal practice of commentary in the Common Law, the chapter provides an opportunity to consider the way in which the expressive system works through the detail of the text itself.

The primary focus of the chapter, 'Buggery or Sodomy', is on the legal texts that introduce the term into the secular lexicon of English law, the first of these being an Henrician statute of 1533 and its Elizabethan re-enactment in 1562. Much of the chapter is taken up with a description of the wrong by way of reference to the language of the statutes. At times this takes the form of a summary of the statutory provisions. On other occasions it takes the form of a more detailed description of the meaning of certain words and phrases, such as 'carnal knowledge'. In addition, Coke proceeds to chronicle thirteenth-century secular legal references (Britton 1865; *Fleta* 1955; and the *Mirror of the Justices* 1893) that incorporate a reference to the proscription of sodomy and its severe punishment in England. He also notes an early parliamentary reference. A Parliament of Edward III condemned the practice. Finally, he glosses the language of the law by reference to a higher, atemporal authority, God, whose voice is located in a specific text, the Bible.

These aspects of the text draw our attention to a matter that is absent from the earlier analysis of the taxonomy of the text. One of Coke's major concerns is the novelty of the proscription created in the legislation. Much of the chapter seeks to erase the novelty of the proscription and to name the novel enactment as the mere repetition and redaction of an earlier practice of proscription (Moran 1993).

In addressing this matter he also draws our attention to some of the other factors that inform the legal writing of buggery or sodomy at this time. The date and terms of the Henrician statute are of particular significance. They highlight the fact that buggery was introduced into secular law in order to promote the use of 'buggery' in law. As such the inclusion of buggery and sodomy and its elevated status within this economy of gravity records the fact that buggery played an important part in the politics of the day, that is in the politics of the Protestant ascendancy, which was initiated and institutionalized during the reign of Henry VIII.[5] Bray, in his book, *Homosexuality in Renaissance England* (Bray 1982), provides a more general exposition of the place of sodomy (buggery) within this Protestant movement. He notes that a Catholic was:

> . . . the Papist, follower of Antichrist, servant of the terrible king of Spain and, as the propagandists of the reformation added sodomite. The Popish sodomite is a familiar figure . . . . Was not the papacy itself a 'second Sodom', 'new Sodom', 'Sodom fair', 'nothing but a cistern full of sodomy'.
>
> (Bray 1982: 19)

Thus the priority of buggery within Coke's scheme of Pleas of the Crown might be an expression of the significance of buggery within Protestant politics. Its particular position and its particular intelligibility is an expression of a certain theme of that politics. Here the sense of buggery or sodomy was to be made by way of the themes of majesty, religion, nation, body and danger. In particular, in buggery or sodomy they are worked together for an anti-Catholic politics. The Henrician enactment synthesizes a dynastic state and Protestant religion. It is in this context that the sense and nonsense of buggery as a grave threat not only to the individual but also to majesty and nation in the form of treason is made (Bellamy 1970, 1979).[6]

These themes are developed in this text in another context: in a conjunction between buggery and identity. Coke pursues this theme through the production of a conjunction between buggery and Englishness. He does this in various ways. He writes it in the production of an etymology of buggery. He notes that buggery is not only an ancient term but also one of alien origin. 'Buggery', he declares, is said to be Italian in origin, *bugeria*, with a Greek theme, *paederastes* or *paiderestes*. In addition, he writes of 'buggery' as a particular identity in reciting a history of its practice. His point of departure is that it was originally unknown to these lands. He proceeds to assert that its domestic presence is to be explained as the effect of a foreign (Lombardian) invasion in the reign of Edward III. Here Coke writes of buggery as potentially not only a threat to the king and thereby to majesty but also a grave threat to the sense of nation and the national identity of its people. For Coke, buggery or sodomy is of central importance to the meaning of Englishness. In the etymological analysis, buggery is that which is not English. In turn, he writes Englishness as nothing more than that which it is not buggery.[7]

Coke's commentary has another interesting aspect to it. He comments that a person comes to buggery by four means: by pride, excess of diet, idleness and contempt of the poor. This produces a list of the causes of the wrongful act (an aetiology). Here the focus is, in the first instance, not so much upon buggery or sodomy as an image of the aetiology of the decline of the nation, but rather as an image that might tell a story of the decline and fall of the individual. Here Coke suggests that the sense and nonsense of buggery or sodomy is to be made as the inevitable effect of a violation of several codes of civility (Elias 1978). Furthermore, Coke notes the effect of buggery or sodomy as a representation of total corruption; all parties to the act, both agent and consentient, are corrupted, guilty and must be condemned.

Finally, in analysing the detail of the statutory language Coke makes sense of buggery or sodomy by way of its place in a particular carnal economy. In the first instance, buggery or sodomy is to be understood as a form of carnal knowledge. This is represented in the conclusion that it shares with rape a requirement of penetration. The least penetration, Coke notes, is sufficient. Having made sense of it by way of its proximity to the carnal order, Coke also defines it as that which is against that carnal order, and so be understood as an extreme violence that is a threat to that order. Coke demonstrates how this is to be achieved by reference to the words that must appear in the indictment (the formal accusation). Buggery or sodomy is to be a carnal knowledge that is against the ordinance of the Creator, and against the order of nature.

This analysis of Coke's scheme of things is of importance in various ways. First, the distribution of 'Buggery or Sodomy' is not to be taken as the expression of a single factor but is the effect and expression of multiple meanings that join and conjoin at this particular location. Second, buggery may simultaneously be expressive of several different and disparate themes. Third, in its specific location we find the articulation of a particular sequence of these disparate themes producing an idiosyncratic coherence at a particular moment of interpretation.

Another insight into the allocation of buggery and the meaning that might be expressed though buggery or sodomy in the seventeenth century is to be found by way of a consideration of two texts by Sir Matthew Hale. The first is *Pleas of the Crown: or a Methodical Summary of the Principle Matters Relating to the Subject* (Hale 1678), and the second is *Historia Placitorum Coronae* (Hale 1736). Common to both texts is the distribution of buggery within the two taxonomies. Hale's work is of particular interest, as buggery is allotted to a very different place in his taxonomy. Here the sense of buggery is no longer made through its proximity to treason and no longer found at the conjunction of violent death and violation of the carnal economy.

In Hale's taxonomy, buggery is to be found in a different place: in chapters dealing with felonies enacted by Parliament. In the *Historia*, buggery appears in a chapter that collects together enactments from the times of Richard III, Henry VII, Henry VIII, Edward VI and Queen Mary, being one of seven chapters dealing with various statutory offences. Buggery now connects a felony of selling or delivering a horse to a Scotsman and a felony of being or disguising oneself as an Egyptian and remaining in Wales for one month at one or several times.

The chapter that contains buggery provides some evidence of the factors that inform this particular allocation. In writing buggery into the text, Hale's preoccupation appears to be with its legislative history: its enactment, repeal and re-enactment. He provides only a brief outline of the details of the offence. The sense of buggery and the particular allocation of buggery is made here by reference to its idiosyncratic source (statute law) and its particular chronology (it was enacted between the offence relating to the sale and delivery of horses and the offence of being or disguising oneself as an Egyptian in Wales).

While Hale's texts were being produced at a time similar to Coke's *Institutes* (Coke 1628), both the taxonomy in general and the particular allotment of buggery within Hale's texts differs considerably from that found in Coke's text. This might be explained in various ways. For example, the first book, *Pleas of the Crown*, which is thought to have been written about the time of the end of the reign of Charles I, was written for a purpose that differed from that of Coke. Hale's text was produced as a summary for personal use. Another explanation for the difference is found in the objective of the *Historia*, a much larger work. Hale explains the purpose in the preface to that text, 'the Proemium'. The book is organized so that it deals with 'what the law anciently was in these matters, what alterations have from time to time been made in it, and what it is today' (Hale 1736). This theme appears to have had considerable impact upon both texts. Thus while the gravity of buggery positions it in the volume dedicated to an exposition of the most serious, capital offences (both treasons and other grave felonies), it now appears to be remote from those specific offences that it was proximate to in Coke's work, such as various types of treason, heresy and apostasy, offences dealing with forms of killing, including homicide, deodands and manslaughter. In Hale, it finally appears after several chapters relating to property offences and eight chapters dealing with procedure, escapes and accessories, in a section of the work made up of six chapters that collect together felonies by Act of Parliament. How might this difference be explained and what is its significance not only for a specific understanding of the contemporary valorization of buggery but also for an understanding of the way that meaning is produced through the image of buggery?

The positioning of buggery within Hale's taxonomy is structured by reference to privileged terms in a series of binary oppositions that are referred to in the Proemium: the criminal as opposed to the civil, those to be punished by death in contrast to those to be punished by other means, the temporal in contrast to the spiritual, felonies in contradistinction to misdemeanours, the complicated rather than the simple, and statute law against the (judge-made) Common Law.[8] The title of Hale's work draws attention to the importance of another opposition between the diachronic (over a period of time) and the synchronic (at the same time). In giving priority to the former, Hale produces a text by reference to a temporality that emphasizes linearity and change against simultaneity and stability.[9] It is by way of Hale's particular focus on temporality that, in contrast to Coke's attempts to make

73

buggery or sodomy an image of continuity, Hale makes sense of buggery in law by way of novelty.

It is also useful to consider more closely Hale's taxonomies in the context of those produced by Coke. While both deal with similar and in many cases the same offences and while Hale is said to have frequently relied on Coke (Glazebrook 1971), the allocation of buggery differs for each author. While this suggests that different modes of making sense of buggery in law are at work here, it would be premature to conclude that this difference in the meaning and taxonomic allotment of buggery is produced through the operation of mutually exclusive expressive systems. The privileged terms of the system of binary oppositions so clearly displayed in Hale can also be found, at least in part, operating in the production of Coke's order of things. Thus while the two expressive systems deployed in the legal practices of Coke and Hale are similar and largely contemporary, it is important to recognize that, within these practices of making sense of law, buggery may take up two very different positions within coextensive schemes of distribution and may be used to express very different concerns. The difference would appear to be not so much the effect of the operation of two radically opposed expressive systems but the effect of two systems that have considerable similarity.

The difference in the position of buggery is more an effect of changes in the sequence or valorization of the various elements informing the expressive sequence producing different criteria of selection and addition, different require-ments of coherence and different patterns of intelligibility. Thus a greater emphasis upon common law and a stress upon the diachronic rather than the synchronic radically changes the position of buggery within the wider scheme of the text, giving it a very different significance. [10] The contrast between Coke's texts and those of Hale draws attention to the fact that, while buggery might continue to be positioned by both authors by way of extreme gravity, its particular allocation within a taxonomy might change. Thus, at the same point in time, buggery may express different priorities and be made sense of in different ways and made to express different values.

BUGGERY OVER TIME

A reading of later commentaries on the law draws attention to another important matter: the movement of buggery within taxonomies over a period of time. This enables us to consider the capacity of the sense and nonsense of buggery in law to shift over time. This matter will be considered first by way of a brief analysis of the taxonomies of three legal scholars whose writing spans over two hundred years. The first text to be considered is a commentary written by William Hawkins, *Pleas of the Crown* (Hawkins 1716–21). The second is a treatise by Edward East, published in the early nineteenth century, also entitled *Pleas of the Crown* (East 1803). The third text is *A Digest of the Criminal Law*, written by Sir James Fitzjames Stephen in the mid-nineteenth century (Stephen 1894).

Within Hawkins's *Pleas*, buggery appears early in the taxonomy. In this instance the sense of its (high) priority is made by reference to the persons against whom the offence is committed. It appears in the first group of offences. Their priority is due to the fact that they are to be made sense of as 'Offences more immediately against God'. The specific priority of buggery or sodomy is amplified, in that it is allocated to the first group of offences more immediately against God:

1 Heresy.
2 Witchcraft.
3 Sodomy.

Its prominence within Hawkins's general taxonomic scheme can be shown to be an effect of various factors. First the nobility of buggery or sodomy is a representation of the supreme nature of the one against whom the act is committed. Here it is made sense according to an economy of persons that places God before king or government or the individual. In turn, this sense of buggery or sodomy is made by way of a threat to the sacred order rather than a threat to the secular order. As a violence to a sacred order it is now remote from extreme violence to the natural body but is to be understood as an extreme threat to the sacred body of God. Its priority and sense are further made by way of a privilege of the Common Law over against statute law. Thus the proximity of heresy, witchcraft and sodomy is made, as they are said to be kindred offences of Common Law. Finally, it is also a proximity and a priority whose sense is made by way of them being capital offences in contrast to non-capital offences.[11]

In East's *Pleas of the Crown*, buggery has again been given a different location. This treatise consists of two published volumes. The taxonomic distribution in these volumes is organized by way of four general categories: offences against religion and the Church establishment, offences against the person and majesty of the king, offences immediately against the person, and finally offences immediately against property. Within this scheme of things, and by way of contrast with that found in Hawkins's text, while heresy and witchcraft continue to be prominent within East's taxonomy (they appear in Chapter 1) and continue to be made sense of as an 'Offence against Religion', buggery or sodomy is no longer proximate to them. Buggery or sodomy is now made remote from offences against religion. Furthermore it is also made remote from offences against majesty and the nation (treason).

In East's taxonomy, the sense and nonsense of buggery or sodomy is no longer to be a representation of an injury done to the supreme being. Now its sense is to be made in its connection with those offences that are to be understood as an injury done to the individual. Its sense and nonsense are now to be made in its proximity to homicide, mayhem or felonious maims, assaults, false imprisonment and kidnapping, rape and the unlawful carnal knowledge of female children, forcible or fraudulent abduction, marriage or defilement, polygamy or bigamy, and offences touching clandestine and illegal marriages. More specifically it is allotted to a place at the end of this list of kindred offences against the person and conjoins offences touching clandestine and illegal marriages to burglary.

Various factors might be at work in the production of this particular congeniality. One is violence to the body. A second is violence to the carnal order. More problematic is the connection between the carnal order and property. This can perhaps be best explained by way of a recognition of the fact that the exchange of women that takes place in and through marriage is also about the exchange and distribution of property. As a threat to the carnal order, buggery (sodomy) might also be made sense of as a violence to the system that circulates property between men.[12]

Finally, in Stephen's *A Digest of the Criminal Law* (Stephen 1894), buggery is given yet another position. In this instance it is no longer to be made sense of by way of a conjunction with other offences against the individual, but is to be found in Part IV, which deals with 'Acts Injurious to the Public in General'. Here it immediately follows offences gathered together in Part III: 'Abuses and Obstructions of Public Authority'. It comes immediately before those offences allocated to Part V, which gathers together 'Offences Against the Person, the Conjugal and Parental Rights, and the Reputation of Individuals'.

Sodomy and attempted sodomy are found in Part IV, Chapter 18. Here their sense is made as, 'Offences against morality'. This chapter immediately follows on from Chapter 16, entitled 'Undefined misdemeanours' ('Acts involving public mischief'), and Chapter 17, 'Offences against religion'. It is immediately followed by Chapter 19, 'Common nuisances – disorderly houses' and Chapter 20, which is entitled 'Vagrancy'.

The chapter containing the offence of sodomy proceeds in the following manner:

186   Sodomy
187   Attempt to commit Sodomy
188   Outrages on Decency
189   Ecclesiastical Censures for Immorality
190   Public Indecencies
191   Obscene Publications
191A Sending Indecent Letters
192   Procuring the Marriage of Parent of a Bastard
193   Unlawfully Defiling a Woman
194   Householders Permitting Defilement of Girls on their Premises
195   Conspiracy to Defile
196   Preventing the Burial of Dead Bodies and Disinterring them.

Here the sense of sodomy or buggery is to be made by way of a separate secular realm of morality. It is proximate to matters that relate to public order and public decorum. It is relatively remote from acts that are to be made sense of as a violence to the individual body. While it has a certain proximity to threats to the sacred order and thereby to the sacred body, here its particular sense is to be made by way of a violence done to the civility of the body politic (Elias 1978).

While in all three of these texts buggery or sodomy is given a particular prominence, its position within the legal order in these different places at different times draws attention to the fact that its position is subject to change. These changes demonstrate the different ways in which sense and nonsense is made of buggery or sodomy in law, and more specifically how it is made to represent many different ideas both at one time and over time. Thus for Hawkins the sense of buggery or sodomy is made by way of an emphasis on the binary opposition of the sacral and the secular. Here buggery is made as a grave threat to the sacral order. This is in contrast to the position of buggery within the taxonomies of Coke and Hale, where the distinction between the sacred and the profane has little significance. Nor for Hawkins, in contrast to Hale and Coke, is the sense of buggery to be made primarily by way of its chronology, though both chronology and idiosyncratic source are significant in Hawkins's allocation of buggery or sodomy. As an offence primarily against God, buggery or sodomy appears to be allotted within the classification by way of an understanding that it is expressive of a threat to the orthodoxy of the official Church. This is in contrast to later taxonomies, where its meaning and prominence are to be produced by reference to threats to individual life, or to the carnal economy, or to the patriarchal property rights over female members of the family, or to public decency and public tranquillity.

At the same time, when considering the mobility of buggery or sodomy within these various texts, it is also important to recognize that buggery or sodomy also has a certain stability within these different hierarchies. Thus it is always relatively intimate in various ways in these different texts to the secular concerns of the safety of the king and the state. There is also always some relative proximity to personal violence. At one point, its sense and nonsense is to be made by way of a conflation of authorized religion and government. At another time, a sense and nonsense of buggery or sodomy is to be made through a separation of the sacral and the secular, so that the act is now to be made sense of primarily as an offence against the person and to property and no longer primarily as an offence against God. Now distant from the need to preserve and protect the safety of his majesty, at another time it is now more intimately connected with the protection of the individual. Finally, in another place at another time, buggery's priority is specifically made to mean a threat to the realm of public order and public peace. Now buggery is no longer primarily expressive of a wrong done to the individual person, or as a type of violence to the private body. Here it is to be used to articulate a wrong done to the public weal. It is a grave act done to the body politic. Positioned within the domain of the public police, it is now the image through which secular as opposed to sacral concerns are given a prior voice. However, at the same time, while it is separate from and in contradistinction to the sacral it still retains a degree of propinquity with that other chain of meaning in that it appears as a category of public wrong that follows 'offences against religion'.

While the taxonomies in these various texts are different and evidence the ability to redistribute buggery within the legal order of things, from offences against majesty and offences against God and the religious order to offences against the individual and offences against public order, they are also similar and these different domains of meaning are connected. Thus the sacral order and the secular order might be conflated in the idea of majesty or nation. Buggery might thus be an offence against God and majesty. Proximity might also be found by way of the economy of gravity that gives buggery in both instances a particular priority. Both buggery and treason are capital offences.

Similarity and difference are produced through the shared multiplicity of elements. Thus in the production of difference there is not only the suggestion of new themes but also the repetition of old themes organized into new sequences expressive of new priorities that work to connect, separate and differentiate taxonomic orders. A common set of binary oppositions is at work in the fabrication of the sense and nonsense that is embodied in these various taxonomies. It includes the following: criminal/non-criminal, God/man, common law/statute, capital/non-capital, king/subject, person/property, private/public, synchronic/diachronic. The differences in the distribution of buggery within these different taxonomies are produced by way of this common stock of themes. Sameness and difference both at one time and over time lie in the combination of these common oppositions and in the assertion of their privileged terms. Thus, for example, while these oppositions are at work in the writings of both Coke and Hale, the distinctive position of buggery within Hale's writings is a product of and a testimony to the priority given to the opposition between the diachronic and the synchronic and the common law (judge-made) over against the statutory source, where the privilege of the diachronic in turn organizes the relations between judge-made law and statute.

MAKING THE TRUTH OF LAW

There is also another point of contact between these texts. Each is presented as the truth of the legal order. Like Coke and Hale before them, Hawkins and East offer formal expositions in support of their schemes of classification. Here the formal exposition is in good part produced as a recognition of the novelty of the taxonomies offered. For example, Hawkins explains the novelty of his taxonomy by reference to the design and method deployed. This, he tells us, is informed by the reasonableness of the law. As such the taxonomy is presented as a process of selection and display that is not so much the product of human artifice but is the expression of the nature of the thing in itself. As the presentation of an essential coherence, each new distribution is presented in contrast to the imperfect, incomplete and impoverished treatises that precede it. Edward East (1803) explains the novelty of his taxonomy by reference to modernization. His taxonomy is a response to a need to take account of the accumulation of new statute law and cases (East 1803 [1972]: v). It is informed by an economy of likeness as demonstrated by the need to bring together 'kindred offences'. A third theme is pragmatism. The novelty of his legal order is that it responds to the needs of convenience. He warns the reader that together these factors have led to the production of a taxonomy that departs from the more usual arrangement of offences (East 1803 [1972]: x).

These scholarly commentaries on the law draw attention to the fact that the history of the use of buggery as a way of making sense and nonsense of the male genital body in its male genital relations is a history that not only is complex but also reveals many idiosyncrasies. They also draw attention to the fact that the elevated position of buggery within the legal order has considerable durability and utility. They demonstrate that the positioning of buggery within the legal universe is an effect of a complex conjunction of values. Buggery or sodomy is a point of their concentration. As such it stands as an idea of this male genital body that articulates several associative chains of meaning. The particular position of buggery is both their point of intersection and their point of concentration. Its particular importance or unimportance as a way of imagining that male genital body should be understood as an effect of the sum of those energies that are concentrated upon it and articulated through it.

STATUTORY TAXONOMIES

Taxonomies are not a peculiarity of the legal practice of commentary. They are also to be found in Acts that seek to codify and consolidate the law. Through codification, Parliament offers to bring together, in a single statute, disparate matters, to name them as kindred and to organize them by reference to a common theme, a shared logic and a single unfolding reason. The incorporation of buggery into such a code gives a formal legality to a particular way of making sense and nonsense of the male genital body by way of specific genital acts as wrongful acts in the law. The taxonomies found in the statutes are often informed by the taxonomies generated through the practice of commentary that precedes them. At the same time, the production of statutory taxonomies differs from that found in the commentaries. In particular it is a relatively recent phenomenon within the common law that post-dates the taxonomic practices of many of the commentators. Perhaps the most important difference is that unlike commentary, which is merely an addendum that seeks to explain the law, the statutory taxonomies have the status of law itself.

The first enacted taxonomy that is relevant to this study is the Offences Against the Person Act 1828 (9 Geo. 4 c. 31). This is a statute of particular significance. It formally repealed the Elizabethan statute that originally made buggery a secular offence in perpetuity. It then re-enacted the offence of buggery in a new body of law. Through this codification, buggery was formally allotted to a new place within a statutory scheme of offences. No longer, within the general scheme of the law, was it to be allocated by way of a linear chronology.

The enacted taxonomy of the Offences Against the Person Act 1828 opens with offences relating to killing. It follows with attempts to kill and other lesser forms of violence to the body, which do not result in death but still attract capital punishment. It then turns to offences relating to procuring a miscarriage and the disposition of the body of a child in order to conceal a birth. This is followed by sections that deal with sodomy, rape and unlawful carnal knowledge of a girl under the age of twelve. A section dealing with the requirement of proof common to these offences against the carnal order follows. Subsequent to this are sections dealing with the abduction of women, child-stealing, bigamy and an offence of arresting a clergyman during divine service. They are followed by a collection of sections dealing with specific kinds of assault. The Act closes with several sections dealing with procedural matters.

The allocation of buggery or sodomy within the general order of offences against the person has a certain familiarity. Buggery or sodomy conjoins particular offences that relate to forms of unlawful killing with grave offences against the carnal order, of which rape is one. In its proximity to grave acts of violence to the body it is always already made sense and nonsense of as an acute form of violence. The conjunction with rape articulates their common concern with the carnal knowledge and violence to the carnal order. More specifically as offences against the person they are both to be understood as representations of grave violations of the carnal order of the individual. Another feature of this distribution is the priority given to buggery or sodomy within this taxonomy. One important factor at work here is the punishment it attracts – death.

Thirty years later this particular taxonomy was replaced with a new Act: the Offences Against the Person Act 1861 (24&25 Vict. c.100). Again, this Act is a codification. It enacts a taxonomy bringing together matters within a single statutory framework according to a particular logic, an idiosyncratic common reason, a truth. However, while the distribution of buggery or sodomy within these two Acts takes place in the context of common parameters – in both it is an offence against the person – the allocation of buggery or sodomy in the two Acts of Parliament differs.

The Act of 1862 opens in a familiar, if more verbose, way, with offences dealing with unlawful killing. This is followed by sections dealing with lesser offences of violence to the person, categorized according to various criteria: the severity of punishment (felony or misdemeanour), the degree of violence (grievous bodily harm, assault), the means by which the act was performed (by shooting, wounding, choking, chloroform, poison, starvation), and by reference to the object of violence (a servant, a clergyman, a magistrate, a peace officer, a seller of grain). There follows a collection of sections on rape, abduction and the defilement of women, child-stealing, bigamy, attempts to procure abortion, and concealing the birth of a child. Buggery follows. It now appears separated out under its own sub-heading: 'Unnatural Offences'. It is followed by two sections that deal with 'making gunpowder to commit offences' and 'searching for the same'. The Act closes with a collection of sections dealing with procedure and punishment.

In general, the scope of the enactment of 1861 is wider than that found in the Act of 1828. It incorporates a wider range of offences and it has a wider jurisdiction, being applicable not only to England and Wales but also to Ireland. It also puts a new taxonomy into circulation. Within this new taxonomy of offences against the person, buggery has lost something of its priority. More specifically, it is no longer immediately proximate to rape. It now appears towards the end of an enactment refashioned as an exceptional crime against the carnal order: 'Unnatural Offences'.

The resort to a formal division between natural offences against the carnal order and violations of that order that are to be named 'unnatural' is of some interest. On the one hand, the formal appearance of the category 'unnatural' works to bring together a series of offences previously formally unconnected: buggery, assault with intent to commit buggery and indecent assault upon a male person. In particular a new commonality has been forged, bringing together the offence of buggery with indecent assault on a man. Another novel characteristic of the use of 'unnatural' is that it is made to designate a commonality that makes light of the distinction between felony and misdemeanour. While the offences gathered at this point retain the distinction between felony and misdemeanour, their connection under a common title draws attention to the reduced significance of the opposition between felony and misdemeanour. The new proximity of these different categories of wrong draws attention not only to a new connectedness but also to the displacement of the other expressive forces that make that new connection possible. In particular it draws attention to recent reforms affecting punishment. In general, there had been a significant reduction in the availability of capital punishment and, more specifically, buggery had ceased to be a capital offence under the Act. This change produced various effects within the wider scheme of wrongs. Not only had the division between capital and non-capital offences become more significant but also the distinction between certain felonies and misdemeanours had become less significant. When refracted through these concerns, the allocation of buggery in this Act tends to place it by reference to its new remoteness from the capital offences of unlawful killing and by its affinity with other non-capital offences such as indecent assault. The new positioning of buggery under the rubric of the unnatural points to the deployment of these different considerations in making a new sense and nonsense of buggery in the law.

On the other hand, the natural–unnatural division separates buggery and the newly related offences from other offences with which they had in the past been closely connected. Thus buggery is now positioned as more remote from rape. Rape now takes priority at the head of a category of wrongs that might be named natural offences against the carnal order. However, at the same time, the category of unnatural offences carries with it the trace of the earlier order of things within which buggery was proximate to rape. The trace of a previous commonality in rape and buggery is retained in the requirement that both are defined as forms of prohibited carnal knowledge and to be evidenced by the same act: mere penetration.

THE SEXUALIZATION OF BUGGERY

This taxonomy continued until the middle of the twentieth century. At that time, the taxonomy of offences against the person was subject to a radical revision, which had particular significance for making sense and nonsense of buggery in the law.

This major revision of the law's taxonomies was achieved through the invention and use of a new category of wrongs in law: sexual offences.

In the name of a new commonality – the sexual – buggery was re-presented in the law. This was formalized in the Sexual Offences Act 1956 (4&5 Eliz. 2 c. 69). This Act takes certain offences out of the category of offences against the person and conjoins them with other offences and sets them up in a new and distinct division of the law. The long title of the new Act declares the theme that conjoins these disparate wrongs in the following terms:

> An Act to consolidate (with corrections and improvements made under the Consolidation of Enactments (Procedure) Act, 1949) the statute law of England and Wales relating to sexual crimes, to the abduction, procuration and prostitution of women and to kindred offences . . .

As such, the offences that appear within this new taxonomy are always already to be made sense of as the sexual and at the same time are declared henceforth to speak of the sexual. But as the long title of the Act declares, the taxonomy of the new sexual offences legislation is organized in a particular way. First are the 'sexual crimes'; then follow crimes relating to 'abduction, procuration and prostitution; and finally we have 'kindred offences'. Following the logic of this division and the headings that precede the various sections, 'sexual crimes' would seem to refer to those matters that are dealt with in the first sixteen sections of the Act. They are ordered in the following way:

Intercourse by force, intimidation, etc.

1 Rape.
2 Procurement of woman by threats.
3 Procurement of woman by false pretences.
4 Administering drugs to obtain or facilitate intercourse.

Intercourse with girls under sixteen

5 Intercourse with girl under thirteen.
6 Intercourse with a girl between thirteen and sixteen.

Intercourse with defectives

7 Intercourse with an idiot or imbecile.
8 Intercourse with a defective.
9 Procurement of defective.

Incest

10 Incest by a man.
11 Incest by a woman.

Unnatural Offences

12 Buggery.

13   Indecency between men.

Assaults

14   Indecent assault on a woman.
15   Indecent assault on a man.
16   Assault with intent to commit buggery.

As such, intercourse by force, intimidation, trick, with girls under 16, with defectives, incest, unnatural offences and assaults make up the corpus of sexual crimes. There follows a series of other offences relating to abduction, prostitution and procuration, solicitation, and the suppression of brothels. Various other matters then follow that relate to punishment, procedural questions, interpretation and a miscellany of points relating to amendments, adaptations and so on.

The commonality of the category of sexual crimes is set out in s. 44. The sexual refers to sexual intercourse, both natural and unnatural. The unity of this category is given in the common requirement that intercourse is penetration by a penis. While the assaults allocated to the category of sexual crimes do not involve intercourse (penetration) their proximity to crimes of intercourse can be explained as they are intimately connected to genital contact (Moran 1990).[13] The taxonomy of sexual crimes is then organized by the distinction between the natural and the unnatural. Again, in the actual presentation of the taxonomy within the act, the natural sexual offences are not overtly named as such but are to be named by way of the designation of those offences that are to be specifically named unnatural offences.

In naming the sexual, and in renaming specific offences against the person as now being within the sexual order of law, the statute demands that sense and nonsense of the male genital body in its male genital relations as wrongful acts should no longer be made by reference to a violence to the carnal order of the individual but by way of a wrong done to the sexual order. This is echoed in the fact that the legislation demands that the lexicon of the carnal must now be translated into a new lexicon: that of the sexual. Thus carnal knowledge is now to be 'sexual intercourse'. Penetration is henceforth to be known as 'intercourse'. However, it is important to note that at the same time the sense of this new taxonomy is still to be made by way of archaic terms, such as 'buggery' and the 'unnatural', which are taken from an earlier lexicon of the law.

While the new order of things repeats the natural–unnatural distinction, it is important to recognize that this new use of the distinction produces different effects. In the Offences Against the Person Act 1861, unnatural offences included not only buggery but also assault with intent to commit buggery and indecent assault on a man. In the act of 1956, indecent assaults on a man have been separated out from unnatural offences. While still within the parameters of sexual crimes and therefore associated with violations of the sexual order, they are separated out as they do not involve penetration. Here the sexual as intercourse

83

is mediated as a lesser form of touching. As such their commonality is not so much intercourse as a touching that is both remote from but connected to intercourse.

The separation between the natural and unnatural is a division that is made sensible by reference to the sex of the parties that engage in the forbidden acts. Thus the natural relates to wrongs that may only be performed in a cross-sex context. For example, at the time of the 1956 Act, rape could only be performed by a man against a woman and, more specifically, was an act of penetration that could only be performed by way of a penis being placed in the vagina. (By virtue of the 1994 Criminal Justice and Public Order Act, rape now includes the penetration of vagina or anus of any sex.) All the other offences that fall under the category of natural offences share this cross-sex requirement. The distinction between the natural offences and the others that are categorized as sexual crimes is that the other offences, with the exception of indecency between men, are indifferent to the sex of the parties taking part. Thus buggery is a wrongful act that might be performed by a man or woman with either another man or another woman (though it does not include an act of anal penetration performed between two women).[14] This indifference remains the case even where the sex of the offender is specified. In those cases the law is indifferent to the sex of the other party. The one exception that does not fit into this scheme of things is the offence to be found in s. 13, gross indecency between men. Its allocation as the offence that follows on from buggery perhaps testifies to the tendency to make sense of buggery merely by reference to forbidden relations between men.[15]

Thus the Sexual Offences Act 1956 introduces a completely new category into the law – the sexual. As such it fragments a prior taxonomy. It introduces new terms that point to the introduction of a new way of making sense and nonsense of the male genital body in the context of a wide range of specific wrongful acts. At the same time, however, this new taxonomy and this new way of making sense and nonsense of the male genital body (as the sexual) also preserves those terms that represent an earlier and now alien way of making sense and nonsense of this male genital body. Within that new taxonomy, the gravity of buggery is to be defined particularly by way of the sexual order rather than more generally as a threat to the person. However, while buggery might as a result be seen as a more specific threat, and thereby less dangerous to the individual, its great gravity is retained in that the sexual is understood as that which is the essential truth of the subject, and an act that does violence to the sexual is a crime that is to be celebrated as the most serious crime.

LEGAL PRACTICES OF CITATION: SAMENESS, DIFFERENCE AND REPETITION

The above analysis evidences the fact that the Common Law has demonstrated a considerable capacity to animate buggery over several hundred years. Furthermore, the constant repositioning of buggery within various taxonomies of Pleas of the Crown draws attention to the problematic nature of any claim that the repetition of buggery in these various texts achieves continuity or sameness, or that the many representations are all equal to the first use. The diffusion of buggery through the various distributions of the Pleas of the Crown suggests that its repetition cannot be reduced to the production of the same. They suggest that the meaning that might articulate and be articulated by way of buggery (or sodomy) is multiple and subject to change. At the same time, the analysis of these taxonomies, which span over three hundred years, draws attention to the persistence of buggery (or sodomy) over time. The repetition of buggery in these various texts brings us back to the claim that the constant invocation of the offence of buggery can be explained as the embodiment of a tradition of the Common Law.

Tradition and repetition are intimately connected. Both suggest sameness over time and place. They suggest that each appearance is equal to the previous one. Here all subsequent uses are homogenous with the first use. Tradition and repetition, as a practice of law, are techniques of transmission of meaning that suggest continuity. In naming not only the successive appearances of buggery but also the meanings of buggery as tradition and repetition there is the assertion that the appearance and meaning of buggery are the same over time. The Wolfenden Committee's proposal that buggery be retained and connected to 'homosexual' in the name of tradition is a recent assertion of sameness: that buggery and homosexual are the same. This particular declaration of sameness is important, as it marks the transmission of meaning from buggery to homosexual. It is a formal moment in the modernization of law. It is these claims of sameness and repetition in the face of multiplicity, difference and change that now need to be considered.

The commentaries provide a good vehicle through which to consider the nature of the practices of law that produce the law as tradition. Tradition appears by way of attempts to authenticate the new commentary. For example, in writing the entry on sodomy, East cites various authorities in the margins of the text: the Third part of Coke's *Institutes*, Hale's *Historia Placitorum Coronae*, Hawkins's *Pleas of the Crown* and Blackstone's *Commentaries*. Through the technique of citation, East suggests a certain relationship between his own new and idiosyncratic text and those texts detailed in the margin. Citation suggests a relationship of similitude between the earlier text and the current text rather then one of divergence. Through the practice of citation, East seeks to present his idiosyncratic concerns according to another temporality as the always already past. He seeks to present his own concerns as mere repetition, as continuity and an analogous statement of that which was written time out of mind.

The invocation of these earlier texts as signs of sameness has interesting characteristics. On the one hand, it is important to remember that each of the earlier texts cited in general, and the specific references to sodomy or buggery therein, were originally produced in a specific context (by specific authors, animated by and expressive of specific concerns, addressed to specific audiences). As such they are the antithesis of sameness. On the other hand, in being cited in another place at another time these texts appear to have the capacity to be legible at other times and in other places remote from the time, place and context of their original production (Derrida 1977). In order to work as a sameness over time, these texts have to be capable of breaking with the specifics of their production.

This might be illustrated by a consideration of the context of their citation in East's *Pleas of the Crown*. The taxonomy of each cited text differs from that found in East. The taxonomy of each text evidences the context of the original text, drawing attention to the idiosyncratic valorizations that inform and animate the expressive system and thereby produce the particular sense and distribution of buggery or sodomy within the general order of the text. Thereby each text draws attention to the particular use of 'buggery' and its significance at a particular time. The citation of these texts for another taxonomy expressive of different concerns draws attention to the fact that, in order to work, the citation depends upon a capacity of the previous text to break with the specificity of the past. Thus, for example, for the citation of Coke's taxonomy to work as mere repetition (an invocation of the same), the particular expressive regime that produced and animated Coke's text, which endows buggery (or sodomy) with such particular meaning, has to be forgotten. Thus citation, which is a practice used to produce sameness and continuity, the past as present, depends upon the opposite: the capacity to break with the past and to forget the past. Citation operates as a means whereby the past may be rewritten according to the needs of the present. Citation is a mechanism whereby sameness is produced through change. By means of the practice of citation, successive transformations of law as a discourse of truth are realized. Citation is a legal practice through which this truthful discourse continuously reshapes its own history (Foucault 1977: 151).

Citation draws attention to another important feature. It has already been suggested that the allocation of buggery within each order of things is the result of a plurality of determining factors. The citations evidence the operation of this multiplicity. While the various texts are structured by reference to similarity, and at times the same set of binary oppositions, they produce dramatically different taxonomies. Through the practice of citation this diversity is presented as an expression of sameness over time and at the time of citation. As such, citation evidences the elision and layering that is the plurality of significations that buggery expresses. Furthermore, it works to produce buggery's great instrumentality.

CONCLUSION

The distribution of buggery or sodomy within the various taxonomies over a span of time draws attention to the fact that the significance of buggery is capable of considerable change. In the allocation of buggery or sodomy within the total distribution of similarities and differences, each taxonomy demonstrates that a multiplicity of factors is at work in producing the sense and nonsense through which the hierarchy and distribution of wrongs is organized. At the same time, it is important to recognize that the particular filiation of the plurality of meanings, of the past and the potential, of the idiosyncratic position of buggery or sodomy within each taxonomy is the effect of a plurality of determining factors. The particular spacing through which it makes sense and nonsense is constituted by the elision and layering of meaning. In different temporal and spatial contexts, these elements fragment, join and conjoin, fabricating a new order of things, producing buggery through a new spacing productive of new propinquities and disparities.

This draws attention to an important point. Foucault has suggested that the buggery–homosexual division is a division between a concern with acts in contrast with a concern with identities. The analysis undertaken in this chapter suggests that this Foucaultian dichotomy is an impoverished one. It is wrong to reduce buggery to the representation of an act (no matter how wide the range of acts might be). The multiplicity of meanings connected to the term buggery draws attention to the fact that buggery operates as a metaphor. As metaphor it speaks of danger, violence, terror, love, lust, identity, nation and empire, to name but a few. As a metaphor, buggery is a dense transfer point of multiple shifting significations. It is through these multiple significations that the male genital body in its genital relations might be made in law in order to be destroyed by law. Furthermore it is through this multiplicity of significations that not only the immobility of making sense of this body of law is produced but also the mobility of making sense of this body of law is made possible. So, for example, this multiplicity is not only at work in the making of buggery as a grave offence punishable by death, but it is also implicated in the recent successful attempt of the Criminal Justice and Public Order Act 1994 to make certain acts of buggery rape (see McMullen 1990).

Its plurality is important in another way. It draws attention to the fact that, as a way of imagining this male body, buggery has considerable instrumentality. Thereby, it is always already in many different ways a prop or an anchor point; a point of support in a wide variety of ways of making sense (Foucault 1981a: 99). As such, the persistence of the importance attached to buggery cannot be reduced to a sign of the enormity of the danger to either the private individual or public order of buggery. Nor ought it to be reduced to a sign of society's continuing failure to control or eradicate buggery because of its intractability. Its persistence and profile within the Common Law is testament of its usefulness. The various taxonomies draw attention to the fact that it has been repeatedly invoked. As such it has been repeatedly recalled, revived, reused and recycled for many new and different projects that take the male genital body in its genital relations as their object.

In the context of this chapter, the importance of the Wolfenden Committee's deliberations and the Sexual Offences Act 1967 lies in the decision to retain the term 'buggery' and to propose that it be formally connected to the term 'homo-sexual' in the name of tradition. This chapter has been concerned with an attempt to understand the nature of that connection as a mechanism for the transmission of meaning. Metaphor is also of great significance here. Again contrary to Foucault, who proceeds on the basis of homosexual as identity, my analysis draws attention to the need to understand 'homosexual' as a metaphor with the capacity to voice all the concerns articulated by way of buggery, but also to inflect them in a different way and to articulate different concerns. In making buggery homosexual in the name of tradition, the multiplicity of meanings that gives form to and can be given a voice through buggery might be articulated in a different form, as homosexual.

At the same time, the analysis problematizes that connection. That connection is particularly difficult in that the Wolfenden review straddles the moment when Parliament transformed buggery or sodomy from a crime against the person into a new wrong: a sexual crime. It is to that transformation of buggery into a (homo)sexual crime that the analysis must now turn.

Part II

THE HOMOSEXUAL(ITY) OF LAW

5

THE ENIGMA OF 'HOMOSEXUAL OFFENCES'

The meaning of 'homosexuality'[1] was an immediate and enduring problem for the Wolfenden Committee. The committee addressed the matter by way of a consideration of the meaning of the phrase 'homosexual offences', which was to be found in the terms of reference given to the committee by the government of the day. The committee was directed to consider 'the law and practice relating to homosexual offences and the treatment of persons convicted of such offences by the courts'.[2] The problem of the meaning of the phrase 'homosexual offences' plays an important role in the Wolfenden review. Throughout the deliberations, the phrase appears to stand as the enigma in need of resolution at the heart of the review. As such it is important to recognize that this enigmatic phrase worked as an engine that promoted a great proliferation of speech about homosexuality in general and 'homosexual offences' in particular (Barthes 1990; Moran 1991a). These discussions not only dominated much of the proceeding before the committee, but also dominated its own deliberations and the discussions that circulated around the final report (see Grey 1992; Hall 1980; Jeffrey-Poulter 1991; Newburn 1992; Evans 1993). The Wolfenden review has particular importance as it provides a snapshot of the process whereby homosexuality comes to be imagined as the 'homosexual' of law.

The objective of this chapter is to undertake an analysis of the emergence of this 'homosexual' in the law. First, consideration will be given to the Wolfenden Committee's attempts both to formulate and to resolve the enigma of 'homosexual offence'. While the committee offers a solution to the enigma in its definition of 'homosexual offences', the analysis will demonstrate the way in which this solution merely reformulates the enigma and sustains it. Thereafter, taking the material presented to the committee, the second half of the chapter, drawing upon Foucault's insights into the historicity and materiality of sexuality (Foucault 1981a), will seek to provide an alternative view of the meaning of the 'homosexual' that makes sense and nonsense of the phrase 'homosexual offences'.

The enigma of the meaning of the phrase 'homosexual offences' appeared to the Wolfenden Committee in the following way. The committee found that the phrase 'homosexual offences' did not refer either to a particular named offence or to a discrete category of criminal offences known to English or Scots law.[3] Nor, at the start of the deliberations, was the task of unravelling the meaning of 'homosexual offences' assisted by the existence of a wider general legal category of 'sexual offences'. The enactment of the Sexual Offences Act in 1956 post-dates the start of the Wolfenden review. Furthermore, while this Act attempted to bring together sexual offences, it had nothing to say about the meaning of the category 'homosexual offences', as it did not organize the existing offences in England and Wales relating to the sexual by way of a division between heterosexual and homosexual offences. Finally, the committee was given no guidance on the meaning of 'homosexual offences' from those (the government) who had originally set the agenda.

On the other hand, the committee's experience was that the phrase 'homosexual offences' was readily deployed as an organizing category by all those who both were connected with and participated in the review.[4] This drew the committee's attention to the fact that the phrase 'homosexual offences' already had a certain legibility and currency, at least within popular discourse and certain specialist official discourses connected to the law, if not formally within the law itself.

However, the repeated citation of the phrase did not appear to resolve the difficulties over its meaning. In an early draft of the final report the committee commented that:

> At every stage we have been driven to face the question of terminology. From the literature of the subject, from the memoranda submitted to us, from our conversations with witnesses, and from our own discussions, it has become clear that an accepted terminology is an essential precondition to any useful discussion of this tangled and complicated matter.
>
> (PRO HO 345/11, CHP/DR/3)

Here the committee drew attention to the fact that the problem of the meaning of 'homosexual offences' appeared to be not so much that it was a phrase that had no meaning but more a phrase that had many different and problematic meanings. As such the repeated use of 'homosexual offences' might not so much resolve the enigma of meaning as sustain it and compound it.

An important formulation of the enigma of the meaning of 'homosexual offences' is to be found in the committee's consideration of the conjunction of 'homosexual' and 'offence'. It noted that the conjunction of these two words was particularly problematic:

> It is important to make a clear distinction between 'homosexual offences' and 'homosexuality' . . . homosexuality is a sexual propensity for persons of one's own sex. Homosexuality, then, is a state or condition, and as such does not, and cannot, come within the purview of the criminal law.
>
> (Wolfenden 1957: 11, para. 18)

While the word 'offences' referred to acts designated as criminal and thereby within the general agenda of the review, the addition of 'homosexual' rendered that problematic. 'Homosexual' appeared to define the wrongful acts by way of 'homosexuality', a term that refers to a 'state or condition'. 'Homosexuality' was not and never had been illegal. As such, the committee concluded, 'homosexuality' was not an object of concern of either the law in general or the criminal law in particular. Thus the conjunction of 'homosexual' and 'offences' brought together in one phrase a term that appeared to be primarily a reference to matters outside the law and thereby outside the legal interests of the committee, with another term that referred to an object firmly within the purview of their investigations. The enigma was that their combination in the key phrase, 'homosexual offences', threatened to name an object that was unintelligible within the law and thereby beyond the committee's agenda.

THE HOMOSEXUALITY OF 'HOMOSEXUAL OFFENCES'

The committee followed two strategies in its attempts to understand and resolve the relationship between 'homosexual' and 'offence'. The first pursued the meaning of 'homosexual offences' by analysing its association with 'homosexual acts' and 'homosexuality'. The second strategy was to name 'homosexual offences' through the production of a list of those offences. Each approach to the discovery of the meaning of homosexual will be considered.

The attempt to discover the meaning of 'homosexual offences' through a consideration of the relation between 'homosexual offences', 'homosexual acts' and 'homosexuality' led the committee to address the causes and nature of homosexuality. This brought it up against the limit of its agenda: how could the committee consider homosexuality when the law had no interest in that state or condition?

It found the solution to this problem in the terms of reference that dictated the parameters of the review; these terms directed the committee to consider not only the law and practice relating to homosexual offences but also the treatment of persons convicted of such offences. It was in the context of the treatment of offenders that it found that questions of the nature and origins of homosexuality already had a currency within the legal system. Therefore it was legitimate for the committee to engage with that general domain of knowledge through which such questions might be asked and answered, and in particular it enabled the committee to engage with the numerous submissions that addressed the question of the nature and causes of homosexuality.[5]

The management of this material and its application to the task at hand was, for much of the review, delegated to the two psychiatrists sitting on the committee, Drs Curran and Whitby. On behalf of the committee they formulated an analysis of the homosexual(ity) of acts and offences by way of an exegesis that flowed from two propositions. The first was that not all homosexuals indulge in homosexual acts. The second was that not all those who engage in homosexual acts are homosexuals. Their analysis produced interesting results.

The analysis of the first proposition proceeded in the first instance by way of the category of overt homosexual behaviour. While Dr Curran accepted that the level of participation in homosexual acts by homosexuals might vary, in the final instance he concluded that total abstinence from such acts would be extremely rare.[6] He reached this conclusion on the basis that few would abstain from the most common homosexual act: homosexually motivated masturbation.[7] Thus the review rejected the first proposition as it applied to overt homosexual behaviour. It was to proceed on the basis that all homosexuals indulged in overt homosexual acts.

However, this did not exhaust the consideration of the first proposition. The matter was complicated by the introduction of a new dimension, the concept of latent homosexuality. This threatened to problematize the conclusion that all homosexuals indulged in homosexual behaviour in two respects. First, homosexuality now could be something absent or invisible, a mere potential for presence and visibility. Likewise, the homosexual act was rendered problematic, since an act might now be an act of homosexuality even though it did not appear to be an overtly sexual act. Thereby homosexual acts might take many forms. For example, the experts suggested that homosexuality might be latent in poor relations with a wife or in a completely unsuccessful heterosexual love affair, or in neurosis of various kinds, or inferable in psychopathic manifestations (PRO HO 345/9, CHP/107: 12).[8] In the first instance the invisibility of both homosexuality and homosexual acts associated with latent homosexuality threatened to make it more difficult to support the conclusion that all homosexuals engaged in homosexual acts. However, in the final instance, latent homosexuality did not so much disturb Dr Curran's conclusion that all homosexuals indulged in homosexual acts but rather reinforced and elevated the importance of that conclusion by creating the possibility of discovering homosexuality in acts that had heretofore been thought to be outside the boundaries of the sexual. Thus the homosexuality of individuals who had fallen outside that category of identity might be produced.

The introduction of the distinction between overt homosexual acts and latent homosexual acts draws attention to some important features of homosexuality. Here homosexuality is shown to be not just a self-evident quality of certain acts or individuals but an effect of interpretation. While it may be a practice of self-definition it is also shown to be a practice of reading, by which 'homosexuality' is ascribed by others to an individual by way of a reading of that individual's actions. Through these practices of naming, others may give the name of homosexual to that behaviour even though the one who is the subject of that act, and/or the object of attention of those who seek to give that act a name, has neither defined himself or his acts as homosexual nor had any awareness of the possibility of his or their homosexuality. Finally, through the concept of a latent homosexuality, homosexuality is liberated from any discrete notion of sexual (genital) acts.

The addition of latent homosexuality and its effects generated some concern. Roberts, the Secretary to the committee, expressed his concern at the notion of latent homosexuality in a handwritten marginal note to his redraft of the general chapter on homosexuality in the following terms:

The difficulty about 'a homosexual' is that according to some psychos [*sic*] we're all homosexuals on this definition.

(PRO HO 345/17)

The problem appeared to be that the idea of latent homosexuality in general and the sexuality of non-sexual acts in particular offered to transform homosexuality and homosexual acts. From being an ontological essence peculiar to a distinctive, exceptional and aberrational class of persons, whose identity was made manifest in a strictly limited range of gestures or acts, it threatened to change 'homosexuality' into a reference to an ontological category that was universal and the norm. 'Homosexual acts' might now be not so much a category of acts limited to particular gestures and acts but the expression of an identity capable of being discovered in an endless variety of gestures remote from the overtly sexual. This threatened to increase the importance of Dr Curran's original conclusion that all homosexuals engage in homosexual acts. However, at the same time it also threatened to render this conclusion less important as it appeared to explain less about the distinctive and peculiar nature of homosexuality and homosexual acts.

While in the final report the Wolfenden Committee accepted the idea of latent homosexuality, the members also demonstrated a determination to limit the great homosexualizing potential that was found to be associated with the concept of latent homosexuality. While they concluded that the existence of latent homosexuality was an inference validly drawn, they also commented that it was to be limited in two ways. First, latent homosexuality was an inference that could in general only be drawn in specific circumstances by certain individuals – for example, after a formal examination made by a specialist such as a doctor, who had been trained to discover the symptoms that evidenced a homosexual component. Second, while certain signs might be read by lay persons as self-evident proof of latent homosexuality, the committee wished to limit the number of signs through which (homo)sexuality might be read. Several examples were given from which homosexuality might be inferred: an individual's outlook or judgment; a persistent and indignant preoccupation with the subject of homosexuality; participation in certain occupations, particularly those that called for service to others or services that were of great value to society such as teachers, clergy, nurses, and those interested in youth movements and the care of the aged. By these mechanisms the committee could recuperate and reinstall the idea that homosexuality was an ontological state peculiar to a distinctive, exceptional and aberrational class of persons, whose identity was made manifest in a strictly limited range of gestures or acts. In turn this might help to recover the importance of the conclusion that all homosexuals engage in homosexual acts, which suggests that the act is a manifestation of a specific identity: homosexuality.

Having thus suggested that homosexual acts, either overt or latent, were necessarily a manifestation of homosexuality, Drs Curran and Whitby proceeded to explore the second proposition: that not all those who indulge in homosexual acts are homosexuals. They concluded that on many occasions homosexual offences

95

(and thereby homosexual acts) were committed by individuals who were not predominantly homosexual. They offered various examples of same-sex acts that were not the acts of homosexuals: situational homosexuality, acts performed in adolescence, and also the acts of 'certain primitive types who wanted sex and were indifferent as to whether the partner was male or female' (PRO HO 345/9, CHP/107: 4). The committee's final report added other examples.

> [S]ome of those whose main sexual propensity is for persons of the opposite sex indulge, for a variety of reasons, in homosexual acts. It is known, for example that some men who are placed in special circumstances that prohibit contact with the opposite sex (for instance in prisoner of war camps or prisons) indulge in homosexual acts, though they revert to heterosexual behaviour when opportunity affords; and it is clear from our evidence that some men who are not predominantly homosexual lend themselves to homosexual practices for financial or other gain.
>
> (Wolfenden 1957: 11, para. 19)

While Drs Curran and Whitby had concluded that all homosexual acts, both overt and covert, were the acts of homosexuals, this evidence appeared to suggest something different. Homosexual acts might be the manifestation of neither overt nor latent homosexuality. Drs Curran and Whitby attempted to capture this emerging paradox in their conclusion that neither social reputation nor even legal conviction was a sound criterion for what might be called the percentage of homosexuality in a given case or the Kinsey rating of that case (PRO HO 345/9, CHP/107: 6).[9] Their analysis appeared to suggest that a homosexual act, and thereby a homosexual offence, might be not only the overt or latent manifestation of homosexuality but also the manifestation of bisexuality or heterosexuality.

Various attempts were made to express this complex state of affairs in different drafts of the final report. One example is to be found in a draft of Chapter III of the Report:

> Where we refer in this report to 'a homosexual', we mean a person in whom this propensity exists and not a person who indulges in homosexual acts . . . a person who indulges in homosexual acts is not necessarily 'a homosexual'.
>
> (PRO HO 345/17)

While the definition of homosexuality as 'a propensity' expresses the idea that the homosexuality of 'homosexual acts' may be both overt and latent, this connection is rendered problematic in the further observation that a person who performs a 'homosexual act' is not necessarily a homosexual. In a later draft of the same chapter we find another formulation:

> [I]n this enquiry with [sic] the law relating to homosexual acts, the adjective 'homosexual' as applied to such acts will be used indifferently whether or not

those who engage in them are by nature or disposition of the exclusively homosexual type.

(PRO HO 345/18, CHP/DR/11, replacing CHP/DR/3)

While this definition attempts to preserve the nexus between sexual identity and sexual act, if only in the suggestion that temporary or transient homosexuality will result in transient or aberrational homosexual acts, at the same time it also suggests that there is no necessary connection between the sexual identity that is used to name a category of unlawful act and the sexual identity of the person that performs the act. These attempts to explain the homosexual of 'homosexual acts', and thereby the homosexual of 'homosexual offences', seem to suggest that it cannot be understood as a reference to the sexual identity of the one who performs the act or offence. As the analysis proceeds towards its object that object threatens to disappear; the homosexuality of homosexual offences appears to refer to no sexual identity at all (Zizek 1991: 3–12). Rather than offering a solution to the enigma of the homosexual of 'homosexual offences', the conclusions offered here appear to reformulate and sustain the enigma.

LISTING 'HOMOSEXUAL OFFENCES'

A second major attempt to explore the meaning of 'homosexual offences' occurred in the context of attempts to list those offences. Several different lists are to be found in the papers submitted to the committee.[10] In the final report of the Wolfenden Committee, 'homosexual offences' was used to name two lists of offences; one referred to offences in England and the other applied the rubric to offences in the law of Scotland. In England, the phrase 'homosexual offences' was to incorporate the following: buggery; attempted buggery; assault with intent to commit buggery; indecent assault on a male by a male; indecent assault on a female by a female; acts of gross indecency between men; procuring and attempting to procure acts of gross indecency between males; persistent soliciting or importuning of males by males for immoral purposes (where the 'immoral purposes' involve homosexual behaviour); and offences involving indecency contained in by-laws (where the offences involve acts of indecency between persons of the same sex). The list for Scotland differed from the list for England in that it made no reference to buggery but included references to sodomy. It also included offences that were absent from the list of 'homosexual offences' in England, in particular the Scottish common-law offence of lewd and libidinous practices and behaviour (between male persons), which has no equivalent in England.[11]

These two lists have interesting characteristics. They differ in various ways from other lists of 'homosexual offences' found in memoranda submitted to the committee. In general, the lists contained in the final report of the Wolfenden Committee are more expansive. They include, for example, an offence that is notably absent from most other lists of 'homosexual offences' presented to the committee: a criminal offence applicable to genital acts between women.[12] This is in sharp contrast to the lists of offences produced by central government; both the Home Office and Scottish Office had commented that homosexual acts between women were not criminal offences. Second, the Wolfenden lists are more expansive in that they include a potentially extensive range of offences (by-laws) created by town, city and regional government. Third, they show a sensitivity to jurisdictional differences between Scotland and England that are notably absent from the memoranda submitted by the Home Office and the Scottish Home Department. In particular they take note of the distinction between buggery (a term of English law) and sodomy (a legal term in Scots law) and of the existence of offences in Scotland that have no equivalent in England.

The Committee provides no overt explanation of the common denominator that joined these offences together under the title of 'homosexual offences'. However, the papers of the committee's deliberations provide some evidence of the factors that informed the production of this affiliation. The issue was addressed by Drs Curran and Whitby, who noted that the phrase 'homosexual offence' already had a currency as a rubric for a list of offences: 'Taylor, a prison medical officer... stated that in his experience [homosexual offences] can be divided into four main groups namely (1) indecent assaults on boys under the age of 16, (2) importunity [*sic*], (3) buggery, and (4) gross indecency' (PRO HO 345/9, CHP/107). Drs Curran and Whitby concluded that this classification had certain virtues. First, it was simple. Second, if the majority of cases appearing in the criminal statistics could be brought under this scheme, it would also have the virtue of intelligibility.

While the catalogue of wrongs found under the heading 'homosexual offences' in the Wolfenden Committee's final report might be explained by reference to the criteria used by the prison medical officer, it also differs in various ways. For example it incorporates a wider range of offences. As such it might be said to have a greater intelligibility. In particular the list includes all indecent assaults between men, indecent assaults by women against women, and a wider range of lesser offences. However, this still tells us little about the factors that bring the offences together under this common rubric.

An attempt to formulate a statement of the common denominator is to be found in a letter by Dr Curran attached to a draft of the chapter on general considerations relating to homosexual offences. He suggested that:

at least the majority of offences would I think fall into the general statement 'a meeting between two or more male persons during which the genital organs of one party are deliberately brought into contact with or pressure against any part of the body of another or wilfully exhibited or inspected with intent (admitted or reasonably presumed) to obtain sexual excitement'.[13]

This definition of 'homosexual offences' has interesting characteristics. Of particular note is the absence of any reference to the sexual identity of the participants and the absence of any reference to women. Furthermore, while this definition might explain the presence of some of the offences that fall under the title 'homosexual offences', it is problematic with regard to most of them. At best it would appear to be directly relevant to only two of the offences named: gross indecency and importuning. Gross indecency was first introduced into the law in s. 11 of the Criminal Law Amendment Act 1885, which provides that:

> Any male person who, in public or private, commits, or is a party to the commission of, or procures or attempts to procure the commission by any male person of, any act of gross indecency with another male person, shall be guilty of a misdemeanour, and being convicted thereof shall be liable at the discretion of the court to be imprisoned for any term not exceeding two years, with or without hard labour.[14]

This section would appear to fall within Dr Curran's definition of 'homosexual offence' as it is an offence exclusive to men. Further, the use of the term indecency, while undefined in the Act, is a term in law that might include genital contact or display.[15] However, it is important to note that when s. 11 was introduced into the law it was not defined as an offence that related to homosexual acts. The legislation describes it as a wrongful act that is an outrage on decency.[16] Nor in its original manifestation is the offence to be found in a statute whose main purpose is sexual relations in general or sexual relations between men in particular. The purpose of the Act of 1885 is described in the preamble as an Act 'to make further provision for the Protection of Women and Girls, the suppression of brothels, and other purposes'. The legislation is primarily concerned with cross-sex relations in general and cross-sex prostitution in particular. The naming of the offence as a 'homosexual offence' would appear to be at best a *post hoc* classification.

The incorporation of the offence of importuning is more problematic still. Importuning is now defined in s. 32 of the Sexual Offences Act 1956:

> It is an offence for a man persistently to solicit or importune in a public place for immoral purposes.

The section itself does not specify the sex of the object of the accused's soliciting or importuning. The reduction of the offence to behaviour between men is of particular interest. While soliciting or importuning is also an offence in Scotland,[17] its interpretation differs from that in England and Wales. The limitation of the offence to men who seek genital relations with other men is unique to English law. It is largely an effect of English police practice and judicial interpretation which the history of the statutory provision suggests is far from either the necessary or inevitable meaning of the terms of the prohibition (Cohen 1982).

The incorporation of other offences into a list of 'homosexual offences' presents greater difficulties. Both buggery and sodomy are problematic. Contrary to expectations generated by the rubric of 'homosexual offence', neither buggery nor sodomy is exclusive to male-to-male intercourse. In England and Wales, buggery is now made an offence by virtue of s. 12(1) of the Sexual Offences Act 1956: 'It is felony for a person to commit buggery with another person or with an animal.'[18] By virtue of the paragraph heading, buggery is an unnatural offence. Section 44 of the Act further defines buggery in giving a meaning to the phrase 'sexual intercourse':

> Where, on the trial of any offence under this Act, it is necessary to prove sexual intercourse (whether natural or unnatural), it shall not be necessary to prove the completion of the intercourse by the emission of seed, but the intercourse shall be deemed complete upon proof of penetration only.

As such it is a wrongful act that may be performed by one man with another, by a man with a woman and by a human with an animal.[19] In Scots law the definition of the criminal act of sodomy differs from this. It does not include acts of unnatural intercourse between a man and a woman. These acts are not an offence in Scotland (Gordon 1978: 894). The common incorporation of bestiality in the definition of these two offences also draws attention to the fact that neither offence is sex/gender- (or species-) specific.[20] Similarly, the laws that define acts of indecent assault on a man or a woman do not proceed to limit these wrongful acts to situations where the wrongdoer is the same sex as the object of the assault. Section 14(1) of the Sexual Offences Act 1956 merely declares that: 'It is an offence . . . for a person to make an indecent assault on a woman.'[21] Section 15(1) states that: 'It is an offence for a person to make an indecent assault on a man.' Furthermore, while the committee did not give details of the by-laws that might fall under the rubric of 'homosexual offences', it did note that these laws, made by town, city and regional government for the 'good rule and government' of their areas, provide penalties for indecent behaviour that are not specific to sex, sexuality or gender (Wolfenden 1957: 45, para. 125).

These factors have a particular significance. They draw attention to the fact that, in order for Dr Curran's definition to work as a statement of the factors that connect the offences listed, much has to be ignored and forgotten. In particular it is necessary to forget that the most common overt homosexual act, solitary masturbation with homosexual fantasies, has never been criminalized.[22] It is necessary to forget that most of the offences that are to be found under the rubric 'homosexual offence' are equally applicable to heterosexual relations and might equally be described as 'heterosexual offences'. It is also necessary to pass over the jurisdictional idiosyncrasies of England and Wales on the one hand and Scotland on the other, thereby erasing the cultural and historical idiosyncrasies of the different practices of criminalization. It is necessary to ignore the fact that Dr Curran's definition cannot explain the absence of any reference to sexuality in a definition that purports to name a category of offences by way of a particular sexuality. It is necessary to ignore the fact of the general absence of women from both the definition of homosexuality and the particular definition of 'homosexual offence'. Nor can his definition explain the one reference to wrongful acts between women in the final Wolfenden list of 'homosexual offences'. It is necessary to forget that when viewed through sexuality in general, or more specifically the binary of hetero/homosexuality, as a reference to genital acts performed with the opposite sex in opposition to genital acts performed with the same sex, the criminal calendar appears to be absurd and incoherent.

The production of a list of wrongful acts under the rubric 'homosexual offences' is an attempt to install a new configuration within the law. This citation of 'homosexual' appears to be a reference to a complex process of selection and reorganization that works to create a new coherence and incoherence in the law by filling in gaps between wrongs that otherwise have little or no connection and separating out offences that had previously been proximate to each other. It partially reorganizes elements of the law by means of selection and addition, producing dramatic rearrangements, making drastic new connections, and censoring knowledge of previous practices, histories and cultural differences. It is by this process that 'homosexual offences' is made to appear as a category that makes sense in law. It is also by this process that the traces of other earlier ways of making sense of prohibitions are now to become part of a new nonsense or a new unintelligibility. In order to be a success, 'homosexual offences' depends upon and seeks to install a certain amnesia in the law and demands a certain forgetfulness by those that cite the phrase 'homosexual offences'.[23]

Forgetfulness is also a theme to be found in the earlier analysis of homosexuality, homosexual acts, and 'homosexual offences' conducted by way of the proposition that not all those who indulge in homosexual acts are homosexuals. As the analysis demonstrates, in citing the phrase 'homosexual offences' it is necessary to forget that the 'homosexual' in that phrase is not necessarily a reference to the sexual identity of the actor made manifest in the wrongful act. At best it might be said to be a mere reference to the fact that both parties who perform an act that attracts a penalty are of the same (male) sex. Furthermore, the analysis of the proposition that not all homosexuals indulge in homosexual acts draws attention to the importance of recognizing that the use of the term 'homosexual' is not so much the use of a term that describes the essential nature of an act or the truth of the identity of the actor, but is a reference to a practice of naming, performed by authorized speakers, according to a limited set of signs that, when deployed, attribute a particular truth that purports to refer to the essence of the object(s) so named. More specifically, the Wolfenden analysis draws our attention to the fact that the citation of 'homosexual' is a reference to 'a whole machinery for speechifying, analysing and investigating' (Foucault 1981a: 32). It is a reference to a set of practices performed and a particular knowledge of the (male) body and its desires that is produced and enforced not so much by the one who is placed in the position of the object of consideration,[24] but, as the Wolfenden Committee noted, by authorized and duly qualified speakers such as psychiatrists and prison doctors. The Wolfenden analysis suggests that as the machinery works towards the discovery of the essential truth of the thing that is the object of knowledge – homosexuality – it is faced with the prospect of discovering that, rather than being a reference to a specific identity, homosexual(ity) refers to no specific thing. That is not to suggest that the 'homosexuality' of 'homosexual offences' has no meaning, but it does draw attention to the way nothing can give rise to something. It is as a signifier without a signified. 'Homosexuality' is a fantasy space or a kind of screen onto which are projected and articulated multiple desires, memories and anxieties (Zizek 1991: 3–12).

'HOMOSEXUAL' AS A TECHNOLOGY OF PRODUCTION

The analysis draws our attention to the fact that the 'homosexual' of 'homosexual offences' is a reference not only to a machinery of naming that has a great capacity to incite, extract, distribute and institutionalize the discourse of (homo)sexuality but also to a machinery for putting sex into discourse that has unruly tendencies, produces unexpected meaning, and is in need of control. The final report of the committee draws attention to two mechanisms through which that control might be produced: through the distribution of those authorized to speak the name 'homosexual' and those who cannot speak its name, and through the designation of a specific lexicon or code that may be spoken and read as the signs and symptoms of that identity. The Wolfenden review suggests that the 'homosexual' of 'homosexual offences' is nothing more than a reference to the machinery through which the very legibility of homosexuality and 'homosexual offences' is produced.

The use of 'homosexual' in the phrase 'homosexual offence', in the original terms of reference, is a reference to the fact that by the time of the Wolfenden review a machinery for speechifying, analysing and investigating homosexual(ity) in law was already a possibility. The references to treatment, the prison medical service in general, and the prison medical officer's use of the category 'homosexual offence' in particular draw attention to the fact that these naming practices implanted within the legal system had already produced a possibility of the legibility of 'homosexual' and 'homosexual offences' within the substantive law.[25] The reference to 'homosexual offences' as a central category in the Wolfenden reform proposals seeks to formally deploy these practices and knowledges developed elsewhere for a different purpose: for the invention of a new category of wrong in law. Using the materials presented to the Wolfenden Committee, the remainder of this chapter will focus upon the technology of homosexual(ity) and the knowledges that were produced and deployed at the time of the Wolfenden review.

THE TECHNOLOGY OF HOMOSEXUAL(ITY)

One mechanism is of particular importance, the examination. It is a complex apparatus that has various dimensions. First, it is a conjunction of various technologies: observation, questioning, listening, formulation and recording. Second, these surveillance and recording mechanisms are intimately connected with other technologies that generate the agents who articulate them. Finally, it is a technology through which schemes of knowledge of the male genital body in its genital relations with other male bodies are produced and deployed in making this body for the law. The analysis will proceed first by way of a consideration of the memorandum submitted to the Wolfenden Committee by the British Medical

Association (BMA) (PRO HO 345/9, CHP/95). The memorandum is particularly useful here as it draws attention to the importance of the examination as a naming practice through which a particular schema of knowledge (a medical knowledge) of the male genital body and its desires was deployed and produced. It also provides a valuable snapshot of the uses of the technologies of examination within the processes of the law at the time of the Wolfenden review.

The report notes that in general the examination might operate in two contexts: first, in the context of the offence itself, and second, in what is described by the BMA as a medico-psychiatric context. In the former, an examination might be undertaken in order to facilitate the process of detection and/or to assist the court in its decision as to whether there was sufficient evidence to justify conviction. In the latter case, the examination might occur at various points in the legal process – pending trial, after conviction but before sentence, or after sentence – and might be commissioned by the prosecution, the defence, the court itself or the penal authorities. The BMA suggests that this second type of examination might have various uses. Pending the trial it might be used to assess the quality of the case. Post-conviction it might be used to determine the causes or reasons underlying the conduct or to inform the court's disposal of the offender. This attempted categorization of examinations draws attention to three important points. First, the two functions need not necessarily be carried out in separate examinations; there is evidence of overlap between, for example, the fact-finding function and the pre-trial medico-psychiatric function. Second, during the processing of an in-dividual within the law, that individual might be subject to many examinations; he might be examined upon arrest, before trial, before sentence, after sentence, and in the course of entrance and placement in prison or in other institutions of punishment or treatment. This does not exhaust the matter as he might also be subject to examinations during the period of punishment or treatment, especially before release on parole. Finally, examination may take place after release as a condition of that release (Ellis 1954: 41–7). These points evidence the fact that by the time of the Wolfenden review the technologies through which the male genital body and its desires might be put into discourse were well implanted within the processes of the law.

While the BMA document draws attention to the many uses of examination, it tells us little about either the range of techniques deployed within the examination itself or the detail of each of the techniques. A document submitted to the Wolfenden Committee by the Admiralty provides an example of an official examination handbook. It is particularly useful as it details some of the practices associated with the 'fact-finding' examination (PRO HO 345/7, CHP/21).

Having stressed the importance of the examination, the Admiralty orders proceed to explain the purpose behind the examination. The general objective of the examination is said to be to produce a written record that contains a clear and definite opinion. The written record should always incorporate certain informa-tion. It must record the detail of the act[26] and establish whether it has occurred on one occasion or on several occasions. It must record all signs and symptoms, whether direct or indirect, and all findings, both positive and negative. It must record both active and passive participation. It must contain a record of any physical signs and symptoms of venereal disease and include the venereal history of the man. The orders state that it shall contain the appropriate conclusions, and gives explicit instruction as to what that evidence shall be; the only certain medical evidence of the commission of the offence of buggery 'is the presence of semen in the anal canal'.[27]

The orders then proceed to document the detail of the examination procedure. In this instance we find not one but three examination procedures. The first is applicable to the passive 'partner'. A second procedure is designed for the active 'agent'. A third procedure is specific to the examination of the self-confessed homosexual. In general, each individual is to be subject to at least two examinations: both the passive and the active.

The orders instruct that, as a prerequisite, where two persons are suspected of a 'guilty relationship', they are to be kept apart from each other during the course of the examination and given no opportunity to communicate. Then, in the case of the passive, the orders direct that the examination should be conducted in the following manner:

1 Note the general appearances. Look for feminine gestures, nature of the clothing and the use of cosmetics, etc.
2 Visual external examination of the anus for:
   ● Appearance of bruising or inflammation.
   ● Whether redundancy or thickening of the skin is present.
   ● Evidence of irritation, inflammation or presence of thread worms.
   ● Recent tears, lacerations, fissures and piles, old scars due to previous ulceration, or any physical sign that might be present and might cause dilation or relaxation of the anal sphincter.
3 Examine the anus for size and elasticity (it is useful to measure the size of the opening by some standard measure such as the number of fingers) and note any discomfort or otherwise during the examination. A speculum may be used.
4 A swab must be taken from inside the anus with the aid of a proctoscope or speculum for demonstration of spermatozoa, and another from surrounding parts for identification of lubricant and spermatozoa.
5 The anus should be examined most carefully for the presence of V.D. The presence of any discharge from either the anus or urethra should be noted and slides and swabs taken for the identification of gonococci.... When possible all cases in whom V.D. is suspected should be sent to the venereologist for examination at the earliest opportunity.
6 If it is alleged that the practice has been carried out recently, the underpants and shirt should be examined for the presence of stains which may still be damp. Any suspected stained articles should be wrapped in cellophane or brown paper and sealed for transmission to a laboratory. If it is possible to

collect a specimen of liquid semen from an article of clothing, it is desirable to send this in a suitable container. In some cases the blood group of the donor can be detected.

7   Other suspicious objects such as tins of lubricants, should be sent to a laboratory for examination for the presence of spermatozoa or pubic hair.

In the case of the active agent, the examining officer is instructed that the examination is to have a particular focus: the penis. The purpose of the examination is to establish whether the penis has in fact been subjected to friction and is contaminated with faeces, lubricant and spermatozoa, which are strong evidence of an offence. The orders direct the attention of the examiner to search for the strongest evidence of an offence: the mixture of faeces, lubricant and spermatozoa. Thereafter the eye and hand of the examining officer are instructed to proceed as follows:

1   Examination of the penis for evidence of friction, for the tearing of phrenum and presence of faeces especially beneath the prepuce if uncircumcised. Also for the presence of lubricant which should be collected on a swab as well as any suspicious material. Examination of the base of the penis should be made for contamination with faeces and spermatozoa.
2   Examination of clothing, in this case the front of the pants, trousers and shirt, for fresh stains and again for a mixture of semen and faeces, the clothing being treated as mentioned previously.
3   Examination of objects in the possession of the suspected person such as handkerchiefs, rags, etc., and also of tins of lubricant, in a similar manner to that already described.

At the end of the examination, the report must be written. The directions that guide the eye and the hand of the examiner are to be the organizing themes that produce the record of the examination. The report should be framed following the line of the examination. But it must also go beyond the examination. It should contain appropriate conclusions, bearing in mind the fact that the only certain medical evidence of the commission of the offence of buggery 'is the presence of semen in the anal canal'.

The third interrogation procedure is specific to the examination of the self-confessed homosexual. Here the orders direct that the examination should be conducted by particular specialists: a venereologist and a psychiatrist. While the orders direct that this examination must be carried out on the general lines already indicated, this examination is also very different. The procedures are modified to shift the focus away from a recent act. The objective here is not to be limited to producing and documenting a particular act or series of acts. Here the objective is the documentation of a life history and an identity.

Again the examiner is directed to document negative as well as positive findings, with supporting reasons for any conclusions reached at any stage in the examination. The examiner is specifically required to state in his report that he considers that the man is telling the truth, or that the man is lying, or that he cannot give an opinion on this point.

The orders also contain certain cautions applicable to all the different examinations. For example, in the examination of the anus the examiner is warned that the 'classical' appearance of the anal sphincter described in many books is most uncommon. The orders go on to advise that the 'conical' anus occurs only in the confirmed practitioner. The orders note that the anus, which is the object of so much attention, is problematic in other respects. The 'dilation of the anus by itself is not a specific sign of the homosexual and that this sign can be due to other causes, e.g. old standing piles, or it may follow operations on the rectum, or it may be due to some disease of the nervous system, etc.' Further difficulties are noted in the context of the examination of the self-confessed homosexual. The examiner is warned that: 'Medical evidence may be completely negative even in a well-established case; and as the rating who voluntarily confesses may not be a confirmed addict, abnormal physical signs are unlikely to be met.'

While the examination procedures appear to be of general significance, applicable to the fact-finding process for a wide range of listed 'offences of immorality',[28] the examination procedures appear to have a very particular focus. This is demonstrated by the emphasis given to the distinction between active and passive, which returns in the prominence given in the interrogation procedures to the anus and the penis respectively. As a technology that is designed to produce the truth of the anus and the penis in their conjunction, this technology appears to be oriented to the production of 'the fact' of one particular offence – buggery (the only offence in the list that directly involves the penetration of the anus by the penis) – rather than upon the full range of offences. A second feature is also of note. In general the orders purport to be concerned with setting out an examination procedure dedicated to the detection of an unlawful act. It is, however, apparent from directions contained in those orders that this is not the only intended product of the interrogation. For example, the direction to examine appearances in general and to examine the presence (or absence) of feminine gestures, the nature of clothing and the use of cosmetics in particular suggests that the object of the technology of examination is not merely the act itself but also the signs or symptoms of an identity that is to be produced through the act and installed behind the act in order to be named as its cause and essence. Nor is identity only to be read from signs remote from the wrongful act. Act and identity are presented in close proximity by an assumption that the 'unnatural offence' (buggery), and more specifically particular uses of the anus, is a manifestation of homosexuality (Bersani 1987: 197). Here the fact-finding and the medico-psychiatric functions are not necessarily separate functions of separate examination procedures but one and the same. These orders suggest that if the fact-finding examination is concerned only with establishing the fact of the offence then the sexual desire and thereby the sexual identity of the accused has become one of the facts of the offence to be established (Ellis 1954: 41).[29] Thereby they suggest that the nature and cause of homosexuality are not matters confined to post-conviction deliberations.

The technology's concern with identity is also confirmed by the presence of a psychiatrist as an officer in the fact-finding examination of the self-confessed homosexual. Here the interrogation is concerned primarily with the production of a sexual biography rather than the detail of a particular act. The examination procedure applicable to the self-confessed homosexual is of interest in other ways. In particular, Admiralty orders draw attention to the fact that the authenticity of identity is not so much an effect of self-identification but an effect of the machinery of examination, produced through the scrutiny of specialists and subject to their endorsement. Thus while the technology of examination is organized by way of a demand that the self-confessed homosexual speak of his homosexuality, the technology questions the authenticity of that speech. Where the homosexual names himself, that naming of homosexuality appears to become more rather than less problematic. The orders warn the examiner of the dangers of self-definition. Here the homosexuality of the self-confessed homosexual has to disappear in order that it reappear as the product and effect of the process of examination. Perhaps contrary to expectations, the presence of the self-confessed homosexual doesn't so much undermine the need for the technology of examination as reinforce the importance of that technology. Here self-confession is only ever an ambiguous sign of homosexuality. The examiner is warned that the self-confessed homosexual may become more difficult to detect as he may carry none of the signs of homosexuality.

Thus, the self-confessed homosexual presents a threat; in part this threat lies in the fact that he is not an authorized speaker. The threat of the self-confessed homosexual also lies in the possibility that he may present his homosexuality in ways that do not comply with the canonical code by which homosexuality is represented and as such may threaten to disturb and disrupt that code. The Admiralty orders show that, in the final instance, the homosexuality is to be produced or authorized by a designated speaker and through a particular code of representation dedicated to the production of 'the truth' of homosexuality. As a particular specialist, a psychiatrist is required to determine the truth or falsity of the self-confession, and by means of the examination document the self-confession of the accused according to the requirements of the canonical discourse.

Before leaving the Admiralty orders it is useful to note that they draw attention to the importance of another aspect of these techniques of knowledge. This is to be found in the requirement that practices of interrogation and documentation are in general to be carried out by particular personnel, medical officers, or in specific situations by particular specialists – psychiatrists and venereologists. Each in turn requires complex training: the completion of a course of medical training, with supervised clinical experience, contact with the psychological disciplines, the creation of particular attitudes, the installation of particular personality characteristics. All have their place in the production of the art of observing, questioning and listening.

The Admiralty papers only provide us with evidence of a fragment of those aspects of the technologies of examination that focus upon the art of observing, questioning and listening. Evidence of the detail of these art forms (both of their content and complexity) can be seen in material that is largely contemporary with the Wolfenden deliberations.

In 'Interrogation of Sex Offenders', Albert Ellis[30] documents some of the requirements that produce these arts (Ellis 1954). In general the requirements that must be satisfied in order to produce these arts are concerned with:

> making it easy for the questioner to face his informant, to win his confidence, to show him that he has non-judgmental attitudes toward his desires and acts, and to handle any difficult situations that may arise in the course of the interview.

> (Ellis 1954: 42)

They take many forms. For example, interrogators should be drawn from persons that have had a reasonably active sex life, preferably including some nonconformist sex behaviour. They should come to the object of surveillance with a distinct scheme of knowledge already in place. Thus he directs that they should have distinctly liberal attitudes toward sex and should believe that there is nothing inherently wicked, nasty or evil about acts like exhibitionism, homosexuality, or disseminating literature, and should have no exaggerated horror of such antisocial sex acts as rape or relations with a minor. Furthermore they should operate not through a single schema of knowledge but a multiplicity of different schemata of knowledge. Thus, in addition to their knowledge of the science of human behaviour, they should also have a specialized knowledge of the historical, socio-logical and anthropological aspects of sex, love and marriage. They should have a general knowledge of criminology and a special knowledge of sex crime. As subjects of these technologies of production they must also be subjected to very specific requirements. They should be sufficiently stable and non-hostile individuals who are able to gain and maintain rapport with even the most truculent and uncommunicative kinds of offenders. They are to be trained to be fully capable of easily and unembarrassedly employing the most down-to-earth language and of showing their informants, in every possible way, that they are not in the least afraid of any sex topic. They must be trained in the ways of clinical 'intuition' and judgment. The art of questioning must make them capable of sensing when some of their questions have struck home, and aware of which questions are to be directly or subtly followed up while others are, temporarily or permanently, dropped. The satisfaction of these requirements will not only maximize the successful deployment of clinical interrogation techniques but they will overcome other inadequacies in technique.

Ellis documents another aspect of these technologies of production: questioning techniques. He proceeds in the following terms. The first technique of questioning demands that the interrogator develops a rapport with the one who is the object of the interrogation. Ellis notes that this may effectively be done by convincing him that, even though you are interviewing him in some official capacity, you are essentially on his side. It might be achieved in various ways: by demonstrating that you want to help him to get at the root of his sex and other problems; that your function is not a punitive one; that you would much rather see him treated than be jailed; that you do not in any way loathe him because of the act he has committed, but understand instead how he could have done so; that you generally sympathize with him and are much more interested in his physical and emotional well-being than in his 'immortal soul'.

A second dimension of the art of questioning focuses upon the phrasing of the questions. This theme is of particular importance as it may make considerable difference between getting maximum and minimum information. It is to be achieved, Ellis informs us, in various ways:

> You should normally assume that the respondent has participated in almost every sex act, 'normal' and 'abnormal', known to man, and you should express surprise and incredulity when he claims *not* to have indulged in them. . . . The underlying tone of your questioning should imply that virtually every normal person does this or that, and that therefore the informant probably has done it too.
>
> (Ellis 1954: 43)

The order of the questions is also of major importance, particularly, Ellis notes, if the respondent is shy or guilt-ridden. So, for example, questions about the offender's love life should precede direct questions about his sex life as the former (because they are generally considered to be less embarrassing than the latter) serve as a good introduction to the latter. Innocuous questions about schooling, physical health, and relations with parents may give invaluable psychological background to the respondent's sex activities.

Questioning techniques must also respond to the specifics of the case. With regard to sexual matters the problem of privacy is particularly important. Ellis comments that: 'there is little that is not private about the whole procedure, and the offender generally realizes that anything that he says may be held against him' (Ellis 1954: 43). Ellis notes that this disadvantage may be minimized through the techniques of questioning. The interviewer must convince the 'informant' that his main purpose is to help rather than to punish him. By means of the questions the interviewer must demonstrate that the main object of the interview is to get at the 'true facts' in order to understand *why* the offender committed his offence and not merely to discover *what* he did. In other words, the questioner must let the informant feel that he understands that:

> a sex offense was committed, and he knows that such offenses are often committed, but he wants to discover why this particular offender committed this particular offense, in order to minimize the element of blame and to maximize that of treating the offender so that the offense will not be

committed again and so that the offender will keep out of trouble in the future.

(Ellis 1954: 43)

Again the particular questions draw attention to the importance of sexual desire as the object of the examination, even where that examination is concerned with the fact of the offence. The interrogation is designed to promote the expression of desire. The repeated reference to treatment in the formulation and documentation of these techniques of interrogation is also of importance. It draws attention to the schemes of knowledge that are produced, invested and deployed through these technologies of production. Furthermore it also draws attention to the need to be sensitive to the 'incessant back and forth movement of forms of subjugation and schemas of knowledge' (Foucault 1981a: 98). It is to schemes of knowledge that the analysis will now turn.

Many papers presented to the Wolfenden Committee provide us with evidence of the knowledges of homosexuality according to which the outpourings incited by the examination machinery might be organized, presented and absorbed. These diverse and different knowledges tend to take a particular form. In general they are produced as a system of classification. Each tends to be organized by a series of concerns. Each seeks to name homosexuality by way of its causes and origins, its particular manifestation and its treatment. Beyond that, they exhibit a rich diversity. A small number of examples will be considered.

The first is to be found in a paper presented to the Wolfenden Committee by Dr H.K. Snell, then Director of Prison Medical Services (PRO HO 345/9, CHP/86: Appendix 1). He begins with a threefold differentiation of homosexuality: congenital, acquired, and pseudo-homosexuality.[31] (This, he notes is a much simplified classificatory scheme.) This is a classification that is primarily organized by way of a concern with causes (aetiology) though, in the reference to 'pseudo-homosexuality', it is also informed by a concern with the form of the practice. He proceeds to draw attention to a more elaborate classificatory differentiation: a distinction between paedophilia and homosexuality between adults, between active and passive forms, between the various forms of physical acts, between homosexual behaviour and sexual perversions both homosexual and heterosexual. His colleague, Dr W.F. Roper, Senior Medical Officer at H.M. Prison Wakefield, provides a different classificatory scheme, though one that is organized by way of many of the same themes that articulate the classification of his immediate superior (PRO HO 345/9, CHP/86: Appendix 4). Again this scheme of knowledge is organized by reference to the patterns of homosexuality and types of homosexuality. The patterns of homosexuality, he notes, are very diverse. However, he then proceeds to write them by way of a series of oppositions, which he explains in the following way:

a. Obligate and Facultative

Obligate homosexuals are those who have no other possible shared sexual outlet because of a total lack of desire for the opposite sex.... At the other extreme are men who prefer women but will take on men when it is convenient to do so, as may be the case when no women are available. In between lie all gradations of bisexuality.

b. Paederasts and Adult seekers

At the one extreme are those who have no interest except in pre-pubertal boys; at the other are those who desire their partners to be fully mature. There tends to be an overlap in the middle since many paederasts are prepared to encroach into early adolescence and many adult seekers like youth, provided they are past puberty.

c. Active and Passive

Some have no use for homosexuality unless they can take the dominant male role and others will always take the female role. But in the majority of these cases there is a good deal of interchangeability depending on the age and the mutual relationship of the partners.

d. Cultists and Non-cultists

A few derive their greatest thrill from coupling in company; others require the normal conditions of privacy. Some couple in private but like to belong to a homosexual circle in which some interchange of partners occurs and which serves to recruit new members.

e. Promiscuous and Non-promiscuous

Some men are entirely promiscuous and never seek the same partner twice; they are often forced to take great risks by frequenting urinals and the like in the course of their search for new partners. Others remain with the same partner as long as they can and are rarely seen in prison unless they favour juveniles or adolescents.

f. Profit seeking and Non-profit seeking

Some are interested in homosexuality purely for gain and may have a lively heterosexual life as well. Others are accustomed to paying their partners or, if this is not necessary, are very generous to them. Many others are somewhere in between. A person disposed to blackmail is easily led on to the exploitation of the position and some paederasts report that even little boys may engage in petty blackmail.

g. Religious and Anti-religious

In some homosexuals interest in religion is strongly developed and this interest appears to be reinforced by their guilty activities. . . . At the other extreme are those who profess a hearty contempt for religion and conventional morality. Most fall somewhere in between.

h. Feminised and Virile

Some homosexuals are feminised and in their mannerisms and attitudes, others take a very hearty and aggressive line. Most of them lie in between.

i. Sodomists and Masturbators

Some men are not much interested in anything less than anal intercourse; others think this loathsome and concern themselves solely with mutual masturbation but most try both. Oddities such as oral intercourse, fetishism and transvestitism are not infrequent and there are cases of pansexualism in which homosexuality is merely one aspect of the determination to explore all means of sexual stimulations.

This scheme is offered as the basis for a 'truly scientific study of homosexuality, which would entail plotting a man's position so as to get a quantitative formula for his condition'. However he went on to conclude that this procedure was not yet a reality. In order to meet this inadequacy he concluded that investigation and the production of understanding should proceed by means of another schema of classification in the following terms:

There are three main types, which may then be further subdivided.

A. Paederasts, which may be further classified as 1. Maternalistic, 2. Inadequate or 3. Psychopathic.
B. Adult seekers who may be subdivided into 1. Aggressive, 2. Pansies, 3. Inadequate.
C. Finally the third general category is Pseudo-Homosexual which in turn may be divided into 1. Adolescent, 2. Deprived and 3. Mercenary.

Beyond the prison medical service the classificatory schemes took many forms. Two further examples will be given to demonstrate their rich diversity and recurring obsessions. The first is to be found in the memorandum of evidence submitted by the Institute of Psychiatry (PRO HO 345/8, CHP/57).[32] This classificatory scheme operated with five main categories and a number of sub-categories. The schema is of additional interest in that it draws attention to the proximity of the theme of aetiology and the theme of treatments. This takes place in the context of an analysis of the causes and nature of homosexuality together with an evaluation of the effectiveness of different available treatment regimes. These regimes of treatment are described as follows: analytical therapies [ANALYT], psychiatric teamwork, [PSYCH], sexual sedative medicine [SED], social work supportive measures [PROB] and penal [PEN]. Their suitability is marked within this schema by way of a crude scale: + = useful, ++ = very useful and +++ = essential. In their conjunction they formed the following classification;

a) Adolescent and mentally immature adults disliking their perversion.
    – those experiencing home and other influences which make for sexual maladjustment.

Treatment.
PSYCH +++

ANALYT ++

SED+	for brief period to give confidence and to reduce anxiety.
PROB	not very useful.
PEN	usually contra-indicated, though appearance in court is often helpful.

b) Severely damaged personalities.

i) very effeminate, self-advertising, female-impersonating, ... affected manner, mincing gait ... wears frilly underclothes, make up etc. A much misunderstood group. Not socially dangerous.

PROB++

PSYCH ++	doubtfully more effective than probation.
ANALYT	not tolerated.
SED	makes little difference.
PEN+	they are afraid of penal action and it helps them to modify their activity; approved schools and Borstals contra-indicated. Sometimes small hostels are effective.

ii) inadequate, down trodden, dull, very passive, who are unable to make affectionate relationships.

Not socially dangerous.

PROB+)	very difficult to help; usually no family with which to
PSYCH+)	work.
ANALYT	incapable of co-operation.
SED	they accept it for a while and then lapse.
PEN	only temporarily effective.

iii) deeply resentful, anti-social ... coming from a neglectful home and hostile home. May not be homosexual and may often have a hetero-sexual life and exploit homosexuals.

PROB+

PSYCH	can't co-operate and are estranged from their families.
ANALYT	inapplicable.
SED	inapplicable unless they recognise in themselves strong desires and are frightened of punishment.
PEN+	probably not very effective, hardens them.

c) Homosexuals in relatively intact personalities, otherwise well socialised.

either young and comely who have digested any scruples and are having a good time often at the expense of the wealthy homosexuals or old homosexuals, experiences, knows dangers, rarely approach anyone before they are sure it is safe.

– happy, hold useful jobs.

– subject to depression, don't want to change.

PEN+	healthy respect for law which keeps their behaviour within bounds.
PROB+	may help a little with the young.
PSYCH+	may help a little with the young.
ANALYT	not accepted.
SED	not accepted.

d) Latent and well compensated homosexuals.

– strength of personality who may not appear in courts until middle life. They either genuinely do not know what their real difficulty is or else have struggles against it. Very often intelligent, perhaps married with healthy children and may be professional.... offence at the time of some additional stress.... children are often objects of their choice.

PSYCH++	(+++ if they have been in prison when rehabilitation is usually essential.)
SED++	
PROB+	
ANALYT	usually too late.
PEN	no more effective than a court appearance.

e) Definite homosexual predisposition co-existing with other serious mental disability, e.g. intellectual defect, brain damage, psychosis, gross personality defects, sadistic tendencies.

PEN+++	need to be segregated until rendered harmless. Actual punishment... is probably less effective here than in any of the groups – mental hospital may be indicated.
PSYCH ++	
SED+++	but co-operation cannot be counted upon.
ANALYT	unsuitable.
PROB	unsuitable.

In common with all the classificatory schemes presented to the Wolfenden review, this grid has both an individualizing and a totalizing dynamic.[33] It seeks to name homosexuality in general by way of its causes and origins and particular manifestation and seeks to name the nature and causes of the homosexuality of the particular individual. The grid is of particular interest as it demonstrates the interface between the classificatory schemes and treatment regimes. This draws attention to the way in which these knowledges of homosexuality are closely linked to projects of control and eradication. When deployed through the process of interrogation, the naming process seeks not only to incite and extract but also to distribute and institutionalize the (male) body and its desires, attributing it with a particular nature and connecting it to a particular project of treatment that might further encode it in particular practices or work towards its total eradication.

CONCLUSIONS

The citation of 'homosexual' in the phrase 'homosexual offences' is a reference to a complex of interconnected matters: to technologies of examination; to the arts of questioning, interrogation and observation; to schemes of classification and projects of management and eradication. The reference to 'homosexual offences' in the original terms of reference of the Wolfenden review points to the always already existing implantation of these devices through which homosexuality might be spoken about and through which homosexuality might be induced to speak for itself within various practices of the law. In particular it points to the existing installation of these technologies in the specific context of regimes of containment, treatment and punishment.[34]

The Wolfenden review worked as a nexus connecting disparate sites of production both outside the law and within it, facilitating their further extension and insitutionalization within the law. More specifically the Wolfenden proposals, and the later enactment of the phrase 'homosexual offences' in the Sexual Offences Act 1967, proposed the formal installation of these technologies and knowledges in a different context, within the practices through which substantive law is imagined and more specifically through which the (male) body and its desires are both criminalized and decriminalized.

There is evidence to suggest that the Wolfenden Committee hoped to install a technology of the homosexual within English law that would both limit the meaning of homosexuality in law, further enhance its installation and promote its eradication. Two strategies of eradication are proposed by the Wolfenden reforms. The first is one of juridical eradication. By arguing that certain homosexual offences be decriminalized when they occurred in private the committee hoped that homosexual acts might disappear into a space beyond the law. The second and related project of eradication is also connected to the proposal to decriminalize certain offences. The committee hoped that the proposal to decriminalize would enable homosexuals to come forward without fear to seek treatment for their condition. In turn that treatment would then lead to heterosexuality, abstinence or the performance of homosexual acts in private. Finally, the project of eradication is connected with the committee's proposal to embark upon a major investigation to discover more about homosexuality.

However, there is ample evidence in the Wolfenden papers that demonstrates that any project to install these technologies of production would be doomed to failure. Thus it is important to note that the descriptions already given of the technologies of examination describe the optimum conditions for success. These descriptions ought to be placed in the context of their actual operation. Day-to-day practice might not mirror these formal requirements. Evidence before the Wolfenden Committee draws attention to the fact that the use of the examination was a partially realized and idiosyncratic practice rather than a systematic one. For example, a survey of homosexual offenders remanded to Brixton prison in 1946 showed that, out of sixty-six prisoners, the magistrates had called for a report in only thirty-nine cases (Taylor 1947: 525–9). The Cambridge survey (Radzinowicz 1957), conducted immediately prior to the Wolfenden review, found that the courts called for medical reports in only 20 per cent of cases. Evidence pointed to the fact that the use of medical examinations by the courts depended upon the offence charged. Thus the Cambridge survey suggested that the use of medical examinations was higher (31.7 per cent) where the accused was charged with indecent assault. Dr Snell, the Director of the Prison Commission Medical Services, also noted that courts asked for reports much more frequently on cases of indecent assault but he also added that the same pattern emerged with regard to persons charged with importuning (PRO HO 345/9, CHP/95). This draws attention to the fact that the courts had a discretionary power to order medical examinations rather than a duty to request such interrogations. Finally, medical officers did not undertake examinations uniformly (PRO HO 345/9, CHP/86: Appendix 1).

Other instances of the failure of these technologies abound. For example, the classificatory grid referred to above demonstrates, in its references to the treatments available, that the success of the treatments was problematic. Furthermore, memoranda submitted to the committee demonstrate that while many classificatory schemes might have features in common they also differed in many respects. It should not be forgotten that in part the difficulties facing the Wolfenden Committee arose out of the need to make sense of the multiplicity of classificatory schemes that produced a proliferation of categories of homosexual. This proliferation of categories points to the effects of the tension between the totalizing tendency and the individualizing tendency, which promotes the proliferation of new categories and sub-categories, which in turn threatens to undermine the technology and invalidate the knowledges it seeks to produce and disseminate. As Dr Landers, the prison medical officer for Wormwood Scrubbs, noted: 'over classification of the different types of homosexual adds nothing to our knowledge and, if anything, leads to confusion' (PRO HO 345/9, CHP/95). So in some respects the multiplicity of classificatory schemes, fragmenting ontologies and multiplying aetiologies that were designed to clarify the nature and the origins of homosexuality had the opposite effect; they made it more difficult to talk about the nature and origin of homosexuality. This draws attention to the fact that these knowledges are not monologic (Foucault 1979: 26–9). These technologies are capable of producing knowledges that are not only partial but also problematic, multiple and unstable. These technologies may produce knowledge as sites of contestation rather than knowledge as an exhaustible and stable exposition of the truth.

In addition, it is important to note that those knowledges that are produced in order to eradicate the homosexual have other effects. Of particular importance is the fact that they are also implicated in the production of the homosexual as a subject that makes claims upon the law for recognition and respect. Also in this reversal (Foucault 1981a: 100–1) or inversion lies the birth as well as the limit of the homosexual as a sexual minority (Sedgwick 1991), and so also of the agenda of gay rights. The post-Wolfenden era, which has seen an escalation of talk about homosexual(ity) and law, attests to this fact. Rather than being a successful project to limit speech in law on homosexuality, to confine it by way of authorized speakers and the imposition of a code of representation, to relegate it to the silence of a private space or the silence of total eradication, the Wolfenden review ought to be seen as the inauguration of a new era that formally installed an incitement to put homosexuality into the discourse of English law and in other legal systems within the UK.

Before leaving the homosexualizing moment in English law it is also important to return to buggery. The proposal to make buggery homosexual in the name of tradition sought to install the technology of homosexuality in conjunction with different and remote knowledges that articulated and might be given a voice through buggery. While the project of tradition was one of making buggery homosexual, the realization of such a project was at worst doomed to failure or at best likely to produce a multiplicity of unforeseen and unexpected possibilities.

In undertaking this analysis of the technologies of homosexuality, particular attention has been paid to one site of their introduction and operation: the prison medical service. It would be wrong to conclude that this was the only site of their installation in law at the time of the Wolfenden review. Another site of their installation and operation is police practice. It is to these practices of production that we shall turn in the following chapter.

6

POLICING AND THE PRODUCTION OF THE HOMOSEXUAL(ITY) OF LAW

INTRODUCTION

Any attempt to study policing as a complex technology of production that incites, extracts, distributes and institutionalizes the homosexuality of law has to address a general problem. Until recently the police (like other agents of law) have been in a privileged position with respect to the production of the male genital body in its genital relations with other male bodies in law. This privileged position can be explained in various ways. First, it is a position that reflects the fact that, as agents of the law, the police have not only been duly authorized to deploy the limited lexicon of the law through which this body of the law might be imagined, but have also developed the practices whereby this lexicon might be deployed on a day-to-day basis. Second, the privileged position of policing reflects the fact that access to the lexicon of the law was also access to the silence of the law. This has produced particular effects. Policing has played a central role on the more general production of the male genital body in its genital relations with other male bodies, creating and enforcing silences at the same time as producing an immense verbosity by way of the official lexicon of the law. This has particular consequences for a study of policing. For example, until recently, public access to information about practices of policing was very limited. It was largely confined to the official reports of cases contained in the law reports and more generally in media reports of police operations or court proceedings. In addition it must also be recognized that these records of police practices produced this male body of law in a particular way. Here it is a body produced by way of a specific lexicon and a body that is made sense and nonsense of by way of particular schemata of knowledge that produce that body as a criminal body, a pathological body and a marginal body.

Only in the relatively recent past has this state of affairs changed. To a large extent this change has come about as a result of the creation of homophile organizations. In the UK these homophile organizations have collected and documented the experiences of those who have become the object of these police techniques of production and subjection. These organizations include the Homosexual Law Reform Society (later the Sexual Law Reform Society) (Grey 1992); the

118

Campaign for Homosexual Equality (CHE); the Gay London Police Monitoring Group (GALOP, established in 1984); Stonewall (a gay and lesbian law reform pressure group based in London); Outright (a lesbian and gay reform organization concerned with lesbian and gay rights in Scotland); and more general civil liberties organizations such as the National Council for Civil Liberties (now known as 'Liberty'). A second development has also had some significance here: the slow emergence of academic – in particular sociological and historical – research into the social practices of policing the male genital body in its genital relations with other male bodies (for example, Truman 1994; Cant and Hemmings 1988). Finally, the writings of lesbian and gay police officers provide another new source of data relating to police practice (Burke 1993, and in the USA Leinen 1993). Together these other sources of information are particularly important, as in many instances they are produced in opposition to the criminalizing, pathologizing and marginalizing frames of reference that have dictated the terms of understanding for so long (Foucault 1980: 81–4). In order to develop an analysis of the connection between the technologies of policing and the production of the homosexuality of law, this analysis will utilize all these knowledges.

This chapter is concerned with an exploration of the general place of policing in the production of the 'homosexual' of the law. This matter was first considered by the Wolfenden Committee. It pursued the point by way of an analysis of the factors at work in the production of the official statistics that purported to document the prevalence of homosexual behaviour. The analysis then proceeds to use material presented to the Wolfenden Committee and subsequent material gathered by homophile organizations to describe the range of strategic opportunities that are available to deploy the machinery of policing. This will provide a context within which a more detailed analysis of particular police technologies of production will be undertaken in Chapter 7.

HOMOSEXUALITY AND POLICING

The Wolfenden Committee found that the official statistics suggested that there was a substantial increase in the prevalence of homosexuality. In general, they concluded that the statistics could not be interpreted merely as an accurate representation of levels of homosexuality or homosexual behaviour. Many factors were at play in the production of this statistical representation of homosexuality.[1] Of particular significance was the relationship between this image of homosexuality and various police practices reflecting a specific intensity and efficiency (Wolfenden 1957: 19, para. 43).[2] So they concluded that the particular increases in the statistics for England and Wales, which immediately preceded the Wolfenden review, were not a picture of an increase in homosexuality in general or of homosexual behaviour in particular, but a reflection of more intensive training given to police officers in recent years and of changes in the methods of detection. They were also the effect of efforts to improve the methods by which offences known to the police were recorded. However, in seeking to draw conclusions, the

119

committee also noted that there was a need to proceed with caution. The final statistics only gave a very crude picture of police practices. In particular they did not reflect either differences between police forces or differences over time within the same police force.

Variations between and within forces could be explained in various ways. In some parts of the country the laws appeared to be administered with 'discretion'; in some police districts no proceedings were initiated unless there had been a complaint or the offence had otherwise obtruded itself upon the police – for instance, by a breach of public order and decency. In other parts of the country it appeared that a firm effort was made to apply the full rigour of the law as it stood (Wolfenden 1957: 46, para. 129). Sometimes these differences would be a reflection of the intensity of the ups and downs of public indignation or public annoyance caused by the behaviour of the offenders. They were also a reflection of the outlook of the senior police officers.

The conclusion that the statistical representation of homosexuality and homosexual behaviour was a picture of the police production of a homosexuality is not peculiar to the period prior to, or contemporary with, the Wolfenden review. Research conducted after the 1967 reforms, undertaken by the Government Home Office Research Unit, draws similar conclusions. Again the analysis focused upon a statistical increase, this time a 100 per cent increase in the number of offences of indecency between men recorded as known to the police between 1967 and 1973, and a 150 per cent increase in the number of persons prosecuted in England and Wales (Walmsley 1978).[3] This production of homosexuality is of special interest for various reasons. First, it occurred subsequent to reforms designed in general to decriminalize sexual relations between men in certain limited circumstances in England and Wales. Second, it occurred in response to a reform that had specifically attempted to bring to an end some of the police practices that had been shown to have a significant role in the earlier statistical growth of homosexuality and homosexual behaviour. In particular, s.7 of the Sexual Offences Act 1967 prohibited the prosecution of an offence committed more than twelve months prior to the start of proceedings.

Walmsley, who conducted the Home Office research, suggested that the statistical increase in both offences known to the police and in the number of prosecutions was closely related to the Act of decriminalization (cf. Hall 1980). The limited scope of decriminalization (to acts performed with consent by not more than two individuals in private over the age of 21) had reinforced the criminality of all other sexual acts between men.[4] The Act had not only been taken by the police as a clarification and modernization of the unreformed laws criminalizing certain genital acts between men, but it had also been interpreted as a reinforcement of those laws. This had been translated into a reinforcement and reinvigoration of the technologies of policing through which the homosexuality of law might be produced. The statistical increase also represented the fact that the 1967 Act made prosecutions for the offence of gross indecency in England and Wales much easier. The reformed law provided for the greater use of summary trial procedure as an alternative to jury trial. Walmsley found that the greatest statistical growth of homosexuality and homosexual behaviour occurred in the context of these simpler and speedier trial procedures. Thus reform in general and decriminalization in particular had not reduced the police need to invest the male genital body as homosexual(ity). Nor had it frustrated the impetus to detect its presence. On the contrary, it appeared to have created new policing needs to invest the male genital body as homosexuality and to subject that body to the new homosexuality of law.

Subsequent to Walmsley's study there has been little systematic research into the connection between the statistical picture of homosexual acts and policing practices. The statistics continue to document substantial periodical increases in the prevalence of criminalized homosexual behaviour. There is no evidence to suggest that the factors that influence these more recent changes are significantly different from the factors outlined above.

STRATEGIES OF PRODUCTION

So far the analysis has focused upon the general importance of the machinery of policing in the production of the homosexuality of law. In this section, the objective is to look at the technologies of policing in more detail, and in particular to consider the context in which these technologies of production might be brought into play and thereby to consider the policing context in which a homosexuality might begin to be produced for the law.

The Wolfenden review again provides a useful point of departure. The committee produced one of the first systematic inventories of these policing opportunities. The inventory arose out of the committee's consideration of a set of police reports relating to the 480 men who, during the three years ending March 1956, were convicted in England and Wales of 'homosexual offences' committed in private with consenting adult partners. This general category of offences (now decriminalized by virtue of the 1967 Sexual Offences Act) is a particularly useful vehicle for a consideration of police practices, because the homosexuality and homosexual behaviour produced through these police operations as 'homosexual offences' represented, at the time of the survey, the acts most difficult to investigate and detect owing to their private nature.[5] As such they catalogue the opportunities of production that are most difficult to achieve.

Within this sample of police investigations, the committee found that the great majority of the incidents, 64 per cent[6] (304 of the men), came into the legal process as the result of police investigations into other offences committed by one or other of the partners.[7] The following is an example of this type of production moment. It is an account of particular interest. While it is not an account taken from the sample considered by the Wolfenden Committee (the report contains many examples), it is an account that is contemporary with the Wolfenden review. It is an account of policing that has special interest, as it is not an account produced by the police but one taken from a letter sent to the Homosexual Law Reform Society.[8] As such it is

121

an account produced by an individual who became the object of police attention and was subjected to the homosexualizing technology of policing.

> I was until the beginning of this year living in a flat with my partner whom I love dearly. All our furniture, our personal effects and our money were shared equally; but most of all our two lives existed as one . . .
>
> However, although we kept ourselves to ourselves, and never had dealings with our neighbours, the police discovered what we had, although unwillingly, to keep a secret to the outside world.
>
> On January 2nd this year I was involved in a larceny offence which resulted in police action. Although at the time of the offence we were together, my partner was not involved but nevertheless was instructed to accompany me to police headquarters. On arrival there I admitted the offence of larceny and explained that my friend was not involved. (The larceny offence has since been dealt with by the Court.)
>
> However, after being asked various questions relating to this offence, the police officer in charge of the case informed us that the police intended to search our flat for traces of stolen property.
>
> In the meantime the police had dropped hints as to there being in existence a homosexual relationship, but did not ask this outright. Naturally neither of us said anything relating to this matter.
>
> We were then informed that I would accompany the police to the flat. . . . The Police never requested permission to search, but informed us outright that this was their intention.
>
> In the car, during the journey back to the flat, the police again hinted to me that they suspected homosexuality. I did not admit to any knowledge of this. On arrival at the flat the police made an extremely brief search of the premises, in fact not questioning anything that might have been stolen.
>
> However they were extremely curious to search the bedroom. They still persisted in questions pertaining to homosexuality and still nothing was admitted. On searching the bedroom, they found and removed the following articles:
>
> Tin of talc powder,
> jar of Nivea cream,
> piece of towelling,
> several commercial physique magazines,
> two pairs of briefs.
>
> After a direct accusation by the police I had no alternative but to admit that I was homosexual. (The admission was made under stress, the police not using violence but using threatening terms.) I denied that my friend was also homosexual, but naturally the police disbelieved this. After a prolonged battery of questions intermingled with threats I admitted to his homosexuality.

On return to police headquarters we were not permitted to see each other. I was taken to another office and made a statement, whilst my friend waited elsewhere in the building, in total ignorance of what had taken place at the flat or what in fact was happening to me.

In my statement it clearly pointed out that no relationship other than that between ourselves was taking place. After some hours I was informed that the police now intended to obtain a statement from my friend. We were still not permitted to see each other.

When my friend was called to make his statement he was informed that the police had removed the above listed items from the flat and asked what he had to say about them. . . . He was then informed that I had made a statement admitting to homosexuality and that it would save a lot of trouble all round if he would do the same. They also informed him that as far as he was concerned, second and third parties were involved. Naturally he thought that I had informed the police of the two relationships – one casual, the other semi-permanent – which he had before we met, and so he admitted to these in his statement, which also bore out my statement of our independence from other parties during our relationship.

He was then asked if he would consent to a medical examination. In the meantime I was informed that he had admitted these two previous affairs and was requested to give details of my previous relationships. These I informed them were merely 'casual', giving the name of one party, which the police seemed to want to ignore. Even to this day they have ignored this, but followed up on the names given by my friend.

I was then asked to consent to a medical, and we were permitted to wait together. After some time we were called to an inspector's office and informed that we would be allowed out on bail on the following verbal conditions:

1 That I would remain at my parent's address until bail expired at 2 p.m.
2 That my friend would remain at the flat.

We reluctantly agreed to these conditions.

On Monday, 4th January we both appeared at the police station and underwent a brief medical, afterwards being told that the police were again returning to the flat to remove the sheets from our bed, for forensic testing. We were then told that our 'bail' was extended indefinitely on the same terms as before.

On return to the flat the sheets were taken without permission; I was allowed to gather together some clothing. We were then informed that we were not to see each other under any circumstances. I was then taken back to my parents'. The police informed my parents that we were not to see each other at all, otherwise it would mean being remanded in police custody.

We heard nothing more until Friday January 15th, when the police called on both of us requesting samples of hair. We had by this point . . . sought legal advice. . . . Up to this point we have heard nothing further; we have not been charged; we don't know what is likely to happen.[9]

A further letter written to the Homosexual Law Reform Society four months after these events explained that the writer had returned to his flat on 24 March in consequence of an argument with his mother, who then informed the police, as a result of which the police called at the flat the same night, gained admittance through a neighbour instead of ringing the flat door bell, and told the two men that they had received orders from their inspector that they wanted to see them that night at the station, and that they could go peacefully or by force. The letter continued:

> When we asked if we were arrested they replied with a hesitant 'yes'. We dressed and prepared to go whereupon the officer in charge informed us that they had received a complaint from my mother to the effect that she had been assaulted.
>
> They *later* informed us that this complaint had been unjustified – but not until we were on the way back home. On arrival at the station we were separated and had individual interviews with the duty inspector, who to us appeared to have no knowledge of our case or the fact that we were being brought before him. Naturally on both your and our solicitors' advice we said nothing, but the police tried to say that we had in fact broken our 'bail'. We informed them that according to authoritative sources their 'bail' was non-existent. Upon hearing this they immediately refrained from mentioning 'bail' again.
>
> They eventually decided that we could leave and they brought us home.
>
> After that we heard nothing further from the police or our solicitors until last evening (i.e. for a further 4 weeks, making a period of in all 16 weeks between interrogation and a charge being brought). At 9.15 p.m. the police again obtained entry to the premises by the same method as before, and presented us with warrants for our arrest and duly cautioned us. We were handcuffed together and taken by car to the station where we were jointly charged with Buggery and Gross Indecency. We were then remanded in custody overnight and appeared before the Magistrates this morning.
>
> A final point we would like to make is that with regard to the previous relationships with other parties which we mentioned in my case no attempt to trace the person concerned has been made. As far as my friend is concerned, his two previous relationships have been followed up, but it does not appear that charges are being brought against the parties concerned; although a charge of buggery with one of the parties is being brought against my friend. [This is untrue, and has since been denied to the police by the person concerned.]

(Hall Carpenter Archives)

Here, the writer and his partner start from the point of being invisible: unknown to neighbours and the law. What follows is a description of the process of homo-sexualization in law and for the law. The process of homosexualization arises out of an act that is subject to police investigation, remote from the genital male body: larceny. But that other event provides the context for a series of examinations, insistent observations, and repeated interrogations that are designed to extort admissions and confidences. This letter describes policing as an institutional incitement to speak about homosexuality. Here policing is shown to be a determination on the part of the agents of law to hear homosexuality spoken about. From a point of silence, the machinery of policing brings into play a demand to speak of homosexuality and homosexual behaviour through explicit articulation and through the accumulation of detail (Foucault 1981a: 18). Here policing might best be understood as an apparatus for producing an ever-greater quantity of discourse about (homo)sexuality. Together, the technologies on display in this example – the arts of observation, questioning, listening, formulating and record-ing – work to produce a specific object for the law: homosexuality and homosexual behaviour.

Not only did these investigations produce homosexual behaviour for the purpose of an immediate offence, they also evidence the way in which the machinery of policing is concerned with a different and more diffuse focus: the production of homosexuality in general. The following illustration taken from the Wolfenden Report provides an example of this focus of policing practice.

Case IV

E., aged 53, was convicted of buggery with F., aged 31. To quote from the police report,

'The offence was discovered when it was observed by police that E., a man known to spend a great deal of his leisure time in company with men considerably younger than himself, was during the evening, returning to the shop at — where he was employed. He was joined by F., and the two men frequently did not leave the shop until after midnight. Observation could not satisfactorily be carried out on the premises and F. was interviewed by the police. He made a statement admitting that over a period of two years he had at regular intervals committed buggery with E. E. was interviewed and made a statement admitting buggery with F.'

(Wolfenden 1957: 47)

Of particular interest here are the references to the character of individuals and patterns of behaviour. Far from being confined to the investigation and detection of specific offences, strategies of initiation are practices that might be dedicated to a more general surveillance devoted to producing information about homosexuality as character and identity.[10]

The example of police practices taken from the archives of the Homosexual Law Reform Society is of interest in another way. It draws attention to the potential of the police technologies to produce homosexuality not only in the original incident (or in this instance an incident proximate to it) but also in other contexts remote from the original incident and investigation.[11] The Wolfenden Committee suggested that this aspect of the practices of policing was of particular importance. It was a practice of policing that had given rise to widely held beliefs that the police were involved in a nation-wide 'witch-hunt' against homosexuals (Wolfenden 1957: 48, para. 130).[12] This pattern of production had common characteristics, which the Wolfenden Committee described in the following general terms:

> A man is questioned by the police about an offence under enquiry, and in the course of the interrogation admits having indulged in homosexual behaviour with men whom he names. These men are then confronted with the statement made by the first man, and, in turn, make statements, inculpating further men. The process repeats itself until eventually a large number of men may be involved.
>
> (Wolfenden 1957: 48, para. 133)

While the committee found no evidence of any police 'drive' to produce homosexuality and homosexual behaviour on a national scale, they did conclude that there was evidence that, from time to time, there were local police campaigns to produce homosexuality and homosexual behaviour on a large scale. These events arose either as a result of a deliberate drive by the police alone or in response to local public indignation. Police forces differed in their practices of production deployed in the context of these events. While some confined interrogation and documentation to the particular offence under investigation, in others, interrogation techniques were used much more widely (Wolfenden 1957: 48, para 133). In particular the committee found that these techniques of production were used to bring to light offences committed many years earlier. Examples of this practice reproduced in the Wolfenden Report show that these practices of investigation had produced 'homosexual offences' committed up to thirteen years before the police investigation began (Wolfenden 1957: 49, Case VIII).

These strategies of production are not peculiar to the pre-1967 state of affairs. There is also much evidence, documented by homophile organizations, of their importance and use after the 1967 reform. For example, a report produced by the Campaign for Homosexual Equality, submitted in 1979 to the Royal Commission on Criminal Procedure, provides a more recent instance of a large-scale police production of homosexuality and homosexual behaviour. The investigation took place in the county of Cornwall in 1977. During the course of this particular investigation, some sixty-eight men were charged with various homosexual offences. Most were charged with ten or more offences (CHE 1979).[13] The investigation took the following form.

In early January 1977, Z, aged 19, was questioned by his step-father about the way he spent his evenings. Z confessed that he used to pick up men in public lavatories for sex. His step-father took him to the local police station where, under interrogation, he admitted that he had had sexual relations with nearly a hundred men. He supplied the names and addresses of several of these, together with details of his sexual activity with them. The police arrested these men and under questioning further suspected offences came to light and more people were arrested or taken in for questioning. All this took place within a few days of the police questioning Z.

As a result of the interrogation of Z, the police called on T, a clerk with the Inland Revenue aged 50, at about 9.00 p.m. on the evening of 3 January, and asked to speak privately with him. They told him that Z had made a statement that T had had sex with Z some months previously in a cemetery. T admitted this, was arrested and taken to the local police station where he was told he would be kept in the cells for the night and interviewed in the morning. At about 11.00 a.m. the next day, T was taken to his home by two arresting officers who asked if they could look around his bedroom. He was asked to provide the police with a photograph of two friends, who, the police had learned, had stayed with T nine months previously. During the search they seized some 'girlie magazines' and took T back to the station and put him in the cells. About an hour later he was told that he had to make a statement about his sexual relations with Z and with his two friends, which he did. After a further hour he was photographed and finger-printed and then given police bail.

At about 5.15 p.m. on Sunday, 9 January 1977, two policemen called at the home of Q, a labourer aged 25, and asked to speak to him privately (he lived with his parents). They asked him to accompany them to the police station, but because he had been suffering from bronchitis for a week he refused. The police insisted so he agreed to go with them. His father appeared at the door and on asking why his son was being taken away was told that he was being arrested and charged with buggery. He was kept in the cells overnight and the following morning was interviewed by two policemen. He was told that X, a postman aged 41, had made a statement that he and Q had had sex some twelve times, twice in a car. Q agreed that this was so. He was given the names of eight other men and agreed that he had had sex with them. He mentioned during this interview that he was the local agent selling *Gay News*. All this information was taken down in the form of a statement. He was then fingerprinted and returned to the cells where he remained until the following day, Tuesday, 11 January. On the Tuesday morning he was taken with two other men to the police station in a neighbouring town and was medically examined by the County Police Doctor. Q was then returned to his local police station, charged with gross indecency, and given police bail. At 4.00 p.m. on Tuesday he was taken back to his home by two policemen who then searched his bedroom, without asking his father's permission to enter the house or his permission to search his room. The police seized all his copies of *Gay News*, some personal gay magazines as well as his card index of customers.

At about 2.00 p.m. on Monday, 10 January 1977, two policemen called at the home of Y, a chef at the local police station aged 21. He was asked to accompany the officers to the local police station but was given no reason for this. On the way he was officially cautioned. He was interviewed at the station and told that his fiancee would be involved if he did not co-operate. After the interview he was returned to his cell. He was kept in his cell overnight and the following morning was photographed, fingerprinted and charged. Later that morning he was taken with Q and another man to be medically examined by the County Police Doctor. He complained about having his anus examined and was told that everyone else enjoyed it and asked for more. He was returned to his local police station and given bail and taken home, where he was told to tell his parents to permit the officers to search his bedroom or he would not be permitted bail (according to the bail form Y was to be released on bail some 15 minutes after he arrived home). He agreed to this and the officers searched his room and seized some gay magazines. Y was charged with two offences of gross indecency with R.[14]

At approximately 7.30 p.m. on Monday, 10 January 1977, two policemen called at the home of R, a social worker aged 29, and told him that he was being arrested on suspicion of having committed gross indecency and buggery. He was taken to the local police station where he was interviewed. He was told that Y had alleged that Y and R had had sex on the night of Y's 21st birthday party, which took place two days before his actual birthday, and on one other occasion. R denied this and was told that a night in the cells might make him change his mind. The following morning he was photographed and fingerprinted and again interviewed. He repeatedly denied the allegations and was then released on police bail.

This was not a policing practice unique to the policing of one remote part of England. Galloway has suggested that between 1967 and 1983 over twenty major 'police trawls' were conducted in England and Wales (Galloway 1983b: 114). Paul Crane noted that between 1976 and 1982 there were major police inquiries in Belfast, Bradford, Leicester, Rotherham, Leamington Spa, Glasgow, Northampton, Hull and Huddersfield (Crane 1982: 53). As a result, thousands of men were interviewed in what, in each instance, effectively turned into a far-reaching investigation.

While some of these investigations (such as that in Cornwall) had followed on from the discovery of a particular incident relating to specific 'homosexual offences', Galloway and Crane noted that other large-scale investigations had different origins and formats. Some arose out of police raids on clubs and pubs, producing names and photographs from membership records. For example, in December 1980 police launched a major investigation of men in and around the northern town of Huddersfield. It was instigated through a raid on a local gay club called the Gemini Club. The police initially arrested twenty men for alleged activities in an open yard. Investigations followed into the backgrounds of more than a hundred members of the club and a major police trawl began involving repeated visits to the club (Galloway 1983: 113).[15] Raids on newly emerging gay pubs and clubs were being developed by the police as a new opportunity to demand that homosexual(ity) speak its name.[16] Such raids were exploited as opportunities to gather names, to undertake lengthy interrogations, to document by means of reports and photographs, and to threaten prosecution sometimes under licensing laws, sometimes under laws specific to the sexual.[17]

Other trawls have been based upon data gathered by the infiltration of meetings and recording the numbers of the cars of individuals attending meetings (Galloway 1983: 114–16). For example, in 1978 in Rotherham the police made a practice of noting the number plates of the vehicles of people attending meetings and caused a great deal of anxiety to members of a group enjoying their lawful right to peaceful assembly (CHE 1979: 2). This type of surveillance and documentation operation has been given a further momentum and legitimacy by way of the development of the idea that the 'gay movement' is to be understood as a pressure group seeking to destabilize society, and receives its share of surveillance. Harold Salisbury, former Chief Constable of West Yorkshire, explained that gay activists were regularly monitored as 'a danger to the family' (Galloway 1983: 116). Surveillance work has included photographing Gay Pride rallies, monitoring meetings, tapping telephones and opening the mail of gay activists. Various high-profile proceedings in the 1970s appeared to be informed by this sensibility: for example, *Knuller* v. *DPP* (*Knuller* 1971, 1972), and the *Gay News* trial, *R.* v. *Lemon* (1978, 1979). In the 1990s, the legal proceedings in *R.* v. *Brown* (1992a, 1992b, 1994) dealing with 'homosexual sado-masochism' have been a major focus of attention.

A more recent example of the collection of car registration numbers of individuals whom the police believed to be homosexual was reported in *Gay Times* in 1994. In this instance the initial data production exercise was not part of a surveillance operation focusing upon a formal gay organization. In this instance it was a practice that focused upon a more informal meeting of men: cruising in open spaces. Here the police collected car registration numbers of men using an open space to meet each other (*Gay Times*, July 1994; see also *Pink Paper*, 8 July 1994).

Crane and Galloway noted that several large-scale investigations had taken a particular form: murder inquiries. They noted that, while some of the murders that had inspired these investigations had a 'homosexual' (or gay) element to them, sometimes the 'homosexual' (gay) connection had been extremely tenuous.[18] The most recent example of a large-scale investigation that had this dimension was code-named 'Operation Spanner' (see Chapter 8). While many stories have been told about the origins of this investigation, one told by the police is that it arose out of the activities of the Obscene Publications Squad of the Metropolitan Police, who believed they had come into possession of a 'snuff movie' (a film that records the killing of an individual). The investigation began in 1987.[19] Court proceedings arising out of that investigation were completed in the UK in 1994.[20] Over a hundred gay men were interviewed over a wide geographical area. Over forty men were arrested. Sixteen men were finally charged and found guilty (Thompson 1994, 1995; Farshae 1993; Kershaw 1992). While murder has been repeatedly invoked as an explanation and justification for the lengthy and extensive investigation, there appears to have been little to suggest that murder was an enduring central preoccupation of the police.

What is of special interest in this particular type of large-scale production of homosexuality is the way in which the framing of the investigation, as a murder, has been put to work to promote the prospect of producing admissions of homosexuality and extracting confidences relating to homosexual behaviour from interviewees. Crane and Galloway noted that these investigations have tended to proceed according to a common pattern. The police interview a couple of gay men and take from them the names and addresses of friends and acquaintances and any other information they can obtain about them. When the police say they are investigating a murder and the information will be useful in finding the killer, people questioned are invariably anxious to help and will talk freely and indiscreetly about their own and their friends' private lives. Even people wary of the police say that in these circumstances they have been seized by the irrational fear that the police seriously suspect them of murder and they have co-operated with the full knowledge of the other charges they may lay themselves open to. In the course of these investigations, interviewees have been encouraged or pressured to reveal the names and addresses of gay friends and acquaintances, required to sign statements acknowledging their homosexuality and giving extensive details of their personal history. According to one man interviewed in the course of a murder inquiry in Northampton, where more than two hundred gays were interrogated in a case where homosexuality was irrelevant:

> I was visited by two detectives who said they had got my name from a gay in Northampton who gave them a total of seventy names. In addition to the usual questions – where was I at the time of the murder and could I prove that I was at home – they asked me about other gays in the area. I refused to give them any names. They also asked me about paedophilia, people attracted to children. But what concerned me was the number of detailed questions they asked me about myself. I could not see that they were in any way relevant particularly as there was no evidence that this was a homosexual murder. They said they had so far interviewed 200 gays in the area.

> (Crane 1982: 53–4)

While such inquiries would not get off the ground if the gay men interviewed by the police did not freely and indiscriminately provide irrelevant information about their friends and acquaintances, those who have participated in police enquiries have found that this may have negative consequences. There is a long tradition of men who 'help the police with their enquiries' later being charged with sexual offences, despite police assurances to the contrary given beforehand. Often information gathered is not returned or destroyed, remaining on police computers. Such operations are particularly dangerous for gays in the closet, or in vulnerable occupations. Relations between the police and the community after such trawls are often so bad that the gay community advises against direct co-operation even in murder inquiries.

While murder might provide the context for mass examination, mass observation, and mass recording, these examples suggest that the technology of policing focuses upon the mass production of the male genital body not so much in order to produce signs of the guilty murderer (for example, a recent survey conducted in *Gay Times* (1994, July, p. 24) concluded that the clear-up rate for murders of gay men is substantially lower than that for murder in general) but in order to mass-produce homosexuality in general and homosexual acts (not necessarily connected to the original criminal act) in particular. The repeated examinations and insistent observations that have extracted confessions and confidences evidence a determination to produce an immense verbosity about this homosexuality.[21] Police practices produce homosexuality in general by means of constructing files that map social networks and hierarchies, catalogue sexual habits, document names and physiognomies (photographs).

The Wolfenden inventory of the moments that both create and are created as opportunities for the police to bring the whole machinery of 'speechifying, analysing and investigating' (Foucault 1981a: 32) into play, in a demand that homosexual(ity) speak its name, is of interest in another respect. It draws attention to a certain correlation between particular police practices and particular types of prohibited 'homosexual acts'.

A report submitted to the Wolfenden Committee by the then Commissioner of Police of the Metropolis, Sir John Nott-Bower, noted that, in general, acts of buggery or indecency came to the attention of the police not by means of direct discovery during the performance of the act but by indirect means. At best they become a vehicle for the production of homosexuality by way of other investigations into other wrongs. When they came before the police through a formal complaint, the acts tended to involve 'youths or boys'. This draws attention to way in which the particular opportunities to invoke the production of homosexuality through the machinery of policing may be framed by way of specific offences.

Sir John Nott-Bower's report also drew attention to the way in which particular offences might be closely associated with very specific techniques of production. One offence, persistent soliciting or importuning, is singled out in this respect. Nott-Bower's memorandum to the Wolfenden Committee explained the particular significance of this offence in the following way. Between 1946 and 1953 the offence of importuning accounted for over 30 per cent (and sometimes as much as 50 per cent) of the total of all 'homosexual offences' within the London area.[22] Between those dates, arrests for importuning had increased over 200 per cent: from 188 in 1946 to 374 in 1953 (PRO HO 345/7, CHP/10: Appendix C). These police practices also had a wider importance. Proceedings initiated by the London police on the basis of importuning accounted for the vast majority of all charges of importuning brought in England and Wales; in 1954, of the 425 convictions in Courts of Summary jurisdiction (the Magistrates Courts) 323 related to offences committed in London. Outside London the highest figures were forty-nine at Birmingham and twenty at Portsmouth (Wolfenden 1957: 43, paras. 119–20).

The Chief Constable then went on to give some considerable detail about the particular policing operations that were connected to this offence and the dramatic increase in the number of arrests. The rise in the number of arrests between 1946 and 1953 within the London (Metropolitan) Police district was closely related to the number of officers exclusively engaged in police practices connected to the investigation of this type of offence. The number of officers dedicated to this offence had risen over 200 per cent from 1946 to 1953; from three men per week in

1946 to over seven in 1953.[23] These officers were deployed in a particular way. They were not spread across the London area as a whole but were concentrated in particular 'divisions' within the police area, 'B' and 'C' division,[24] and upon particular lavatories: Victoria Station, South Kensington Underground Station, Dudmaston Mews, Clareville Street and Dove Mews in 'B' Division, and Piccadilly Underground Station, Leicester Square, Babmaes Street, Providence Court, Dansby Place, Falconberg Mews, Three Kings Yard and Grosvenor Hill in 'C' Division.

The only other publicly available information given to the Wolfenden Committee about these specific practices related to some of the detail of these operations. These were explained in the following terms:

> To obtain a conviction for importuning... necessitates a long observation most of which must usually take place in a urinal. Patrols of two men in plain clothes are specially authorized by a senior officer at New Scotland Yard to observe and detect these offences.... Because of the unpleasant nature of the work this duty is most unpopular and the officers posted to these patrols are not normally employed for more than 4 weeks at a time and substantial intervals elapse before they are again so employed.
>
> (PRO HO 354/7, CHP/10: para. 25)

This information of the particular police practices used to produce homosexuality through the vehicle of the offence of soliciting or importuning is of interest in various ways. First, the offence of importuning appears to be one instance where there is a very close relationship between the machinery of policing and the production of the homosexuality of the law. However, in sharp contrast to the emphasis on the close correlation between policing and the active production of homosexuality by way of this offence, Sir John Nott-Bower seeks to emphasize the passivity of the policing in this context: the great majority of these offences were said to be detected *in flagrante delicto*. These particular policing practices are also of interest, as they appear to be an example of an instance of a means of production of homosexuality that, at one and the same time, is both intensely localized and also highly productive at a wider (national) level. This offence is also of special interest in that it appears to produce a homosexuality of law in a very specific context (public urinals) by way of a very specific type of police practice (the use of plain-clothes officers).[25] Finally, it is a vehicle for the production of homosexuality that not only was popular prior to and during the era of the Wolfenden review, but that also has retained its popularity subsequent to the 1967 reforms. Walmsley's Home Office research provides evidence that the use and importance of the lesser offences in general and offences such as importuning in particular have continued to grow as an important vehicle of police practices of homosexualization. Subsequent to the 1967 reforms, the annual rate of prosecutions for offences of indecency doubled. Convictions more than tripled (Walmsley 1978). The offence of soliciting and importuning[26] had an important place in this increase. Walmsley commented that, particularly in those areas with high prosecution rates, most of the increase related to offences investigated and detected in public conveniences. More recently the lesbian and gay press in the UK has begun to document the continuing importance and regularity of these police practices with 'Cottage Alert' warnings. In September 1995, the national lesbian and gay magazine, *Gay Times*, noted that, within one month (July 1995), sixty men had been arrested by way of such practices in various parts of the country. It is to the techniques of production developed in the context of the offence of importuning that I shall turn in Chapter 7.

7

THE SOMATIC TECHNIQUES OF POLICING

INTRODUCTION

The aim of this chapter is to undertake a detailed analysis of a particular technology that incites, extracts, distributes and institutionalizes a legal discourse of the male body in its genital relations with other male bodies. This machinery takes the form of a particular collection of techniques of investigation and detection that are deployed in a particular way: plain-clothes police operations in public conveniences.[1] Plain-clothes police operations are of importance for many reasons. They form a collection of techniques of policing that is said to have particular strengths. First, their strength lies in the fact that they are perhaps one of the most effective means of investigation and detection of certain criminal genital acts[2] between men. They give full and immediate access to the men who perform these acts (Humphreys 1970: 25). Second, it is a technique of policing that is particularly efficient. Unlike low technological surveillance in public conveniences (which involves watching and invisibility by means of physical absence: spy holes, two-way mirrors, etc.), which might require extended periods of surveillance,[3] the use of the plain-clothes officer as *agent provocateur* need not necessitate long hours of duty (sometimes in cramped conditions) by men who may be needed elsewhere. In formal terms its success lies in the fact that it produces a high arrest rate over short periods of time, elicits ready confessions and guilty pleas, and meets with little resistance.[4]

For the purpose of this study their importance is in the way in which these technologies work to produce a representation of the male genital body in its genital relations with other male bodies in the law. The chapter will explore how these technologies produce a homosexual of the law in a very specific way. This chapter will also explore the shape and form of these technologies of production. This objective will be pursued by way of a consideration of some of the problems encountered in the deployment of these technologies of production. The first problem that faces the police is that this particular kind of police observation is difficult to carry out successfully. Surveillance demands a certain invisibility. This chapter will explore the technology of policing that has been developed to meet the demands of invisibility in the 'public space' of a public toilet. The analysis will

134

explore the problematic 'public' nature of these places and acts. It will explore the way the private nature of these 'public' encounters informs the technology of surveillance.

Sources of information that document the detailed operation of these technologies of production are still rare. Until recently they have largely been confined to the decisions of a few reported cases published in the law reports and in media reports of arrests and prosecutions. In the relatively recent past this state of affairs has begun to change. Official records, such as Sir John Nott-Bower's memorandum, have entered the public domain, providing another, albeit rare, example of the documentation of these police practices. The growth of homophile organizations has also been significant as a source of additional data on policing practice from new perspectives. Finally, there is a small but important body of academic writing that has some significance here. *Tearoom Trade* by Laud Humphreys (1970) is an exceptional study of genital encounters between men in public toilets ('tearooms') in the USA. Through metaphors of the game and economics he attempts to develop a science of these encounters. While Humphreys's work is not an attempt to write a science of the practices of male genital encounters as a technology of policing in these places, it has particular significance for an analysis of the techniques of policing that are deployed in these places. In this study, Humphreys's work will be used as a resource through which the complexity of the machinery of sexuality in the practices of policing might be explained and understood.

TECHNIQUES OF PRODUCTION

The published law reports provide some detail of the techniques of production used in plain-clothes police operations in public toilets. *Horton v. Mead*, a case reported in 1913, provides one of the earliest examples.[5] The report records that Horton was watched by two police officers over a period of time: from 11.10 p.m. to 11.50 p.m. on 31 May and from 12.05 a.m. to 1.00 a.m. on 1 June 1912. During that period the police conducted a surveillance exercise and documented his behaviour in the following terms:

> At 11.10 he entered the public lavatory at Piccadilly Circus and remained there four or five minutes; he then walked to Leicester Square, where he entered the public lavatory and remained for seven minutes; he then walked to Dansey Yard lavatory and remained there three or four minutes; he then walked back to Piccadilly Circus and entered the same public lavatory as before, remaining there five minutes. He then walked in the direction of Leicester Square, but the officers lost sight of him at the corner of Wardour Street at 11.50. At 12.05 a.m. he was again seen to enter the lavatory at Piccadilly Circus, where he remained for a few minutes; he then walked to Leicester Square, where he entered the lavatory and remained a few minutes; he then walked to Dansey Yard, entered the lavatory and remained for five

minutes. He then walked to Leicester Square tube station, where he was arrested.

(Horton 1913: 154–5)

The law report records some of the features of the techniques of surveillance and examination that work to produce the male genital body in law. Here it is shown to be a technology of observation and searching examination that is repeated[6] and insistent. In this instance the techniques of production occupy a place of specific significance. They work to produce this body in law, not as a result of a complaint but despite the absence of any complaint. There was no evidence before the court that anyone other than the agents of the law had noticed Horton's perambulations in general. Nor was there any evidence, apart from that produced by the agents of the law, that any person had been solicited by Horton. The law report records that, beyond the machinery that incites, extracts, distributes and institutionalizes a discourse of the male body in its genital relations with other male bodies for the law, Horton's body in general, and his body as a male genital body and its desires, had a certain social invisibility and a certain transience, without a fixed or limited reality. Through a technology of surveillance, examination and practices of documentation, his desires and his body as a genital body are given not only a visibility but also a particular and permanent meaning.

As a machinery of surveillance, policing is organized by way of an incitement to speak of this body. The duration of the surveillance draws attention to the installation of an institutional determination on the part of the agents of the law to hear the male genital body in its genital relations with other men spoken about, and to cause it to speak (Foucault 1981a: 18). The law report draws attention to the way in which surveillance operates as a machine that proliferates a discourse of a body by way of the accumulation of detail about that body: about its perambulations; about its gestures: 'While in the lavatories and also while in the street he smiled in the faces of gentlemen, pursed his lips, and wriggled his body.' Here what is not done and not said is as important a detail as what is said and done. 'He did not at any time during this period speak to anybody or touch anybody, nor did he attempt to speak to or touch anybody.' It intensifies the surfaces of the body and imprints its difference in the record of the event: 'At the police station the face and lips of the appellant appeared to be artificially reddened, and in the pocket of the appellant was found a powder puff with pink powder on it.' It isolates certain utterances: 'Upon being arrested and told of the charge, persistently soliciting or importuning for immoral purposes, he answered, "Oh dear this is very annoying" ' (all quotes from *Horton* 1913: 155). In all, the insistent observation and examination is concerned with the valorization and intensification of the surfaces of the body to produce that body as a set of decipherable signs. Through a method of interpretation a body is shaped in law according to schemes of knowledge that normalize and pathologize the surfaces of the body, its gestures and its movements, its utterances, its interactions, its social space.

The importance of these various practices of documentation and the signs of the body it produces is explained by Chief Justice Lord Alverstone in the following terms:

> It is found as a fact that while in the lavatories and also while in the street he smiled in the faces of gentlemen, pursed his lips, and wriggled his body. His face and lips appeared to have been artificially reddened, and his pocket a powder puff with pink powder upon it was found, not unimportant in connection with an offence of this kind.
>
> (*Horton* 1913: 157)

Its constitution and its truth is completed in the recording of it. As Chief Justice Lord Alverstone concluded:

> A magistrate no doubt always carefully scrutinizes the evidence of those who are watching this class of men; but to say that, because on the particular occasion he does not succeed in attracting the notice of anyone, there is no evidence upon which he can be convicted of solicitation is an argument which we cannot adopt.
>
> (*Horton* 1913: 157)

Here the truth originally verified in the police documentation is then subject to assimilation and further documentation in the text of the judgment of the magistrate. Thereby it becomes installed as the truth of law. Where that which precedes the law and lies outside the law cannot be brought into the service of the law (the absence of complaint and the absence of any evidence that Horton had been noticed by a specific individual), the law will satisfy its own needs:

> It seems to me on the facts stated in the case that we must of necessity draw the inference that what the appellant did was apprehended by the senses of the persons intended to be solicited.
>
> (*Horton* 1913: 158)

Here the truth of the body and the truth of the law lies in the fantasy of the body generated through the practices of surveillance and examination within the law.

Horton v. *Mead* is of significance in a more general way. It draws attention to the importance of surveillance. Here surveillance works to produce the intensification of the surfaces of the body and it is through these practices of the agents of the law that the body as (homo)sexuality might be constituted in the law. What is absent from this report is further information of the detail of the police practice of surveillance. Some information about the nature of this surveillance is found in Horton's response to the police when arrested: 'Oh dear this is very annoying' (*Horton* 1913: 155). This suggests that he meandered through the streets of London in ignorance of the surveillance operation. We learn nothing from the report about the nature of the policing techniques that generated this invisibility. This is of particular interest as the surveillance operation appears to have taken place in close proximity to Horton and in various public places, on the street and more intimately inside the public conveniences.

TECHNIQUES OF INVISIBILITY[7]

Other reported cases suggest that a wide range of techniques is utilized by the police to make surveillance possible. For example, in the more recent reported case of *R.* v. *Howells* (1976), the surveillance operation by two police officers began outside a public lavatory. After a period of some ten minutes their surveillance practice then changed its form and location. They entered the public toilet and found the only two cubicles in the lavatory engaged. Surveillance then continued by means of the police officers looking under the door of one of the cubicles. While in this position outside the cubicle and thereby in a state of relative invisibility they conducted their surveillance. There they proceeded to observe and document: they watched him masturbating; they noted his trousers were up; they observed a hole in the wall between the two cubicles. They later recorded that it was possible to see the occupant of the other cubicle and to be seen by that person through that hole. Here the invisibility of surveillance does not appear to require either special facilities, sophisticated technology or the expenditure of large amounts of time. Little more is revealed in this instance about the techniques of observation.[8]

R. v. *Redgrave* (1981) provides evidence of other techniques by which surveillance becomes possible. In common with the practice demonstrated in *Howells*, the surveillance began outside a public convenience. In this instance it was undertaken not by two but by five police officers of the local police Vice Squad. It was a surveillance operation undertaken according to the requirements of a very particular technique: the use of plain-clothes officers.

They undertook observation on the public convenience between 4.45 and 5.00 p.m. on 13 November 1979. During that time, they observed and documented the movements of the accused: he went in and out of the convenience on four separate occasions. The report also records a slightly different technique of surveillance. On at least two occasions the surveillance operation was undertaken inside the public convenience. While this might be similar to the practices of surveillance found in *Howells*, in this instance it is a practice that differs from those found in that case. In this instance the surveillance in the public convenience took place in the presence of Redgrave and with his knowledge. The law report records that, in the presence of and before two plain-clothes officers, who had gone into the public convenience separately and before Redgrave, the accused masturbated for about a minute near the urinal. In that exposed and visible position the officers observed the accused and documented his activities; the accused masturbated openly, noisily and violently and stared at the officers while doing so. Little further information about the police behaviour in the convenience is contained in the case report. All we learn is that the police officers asked the appellant to leave the convenience and then formally arrested him.

In this instance the police practice of observation takes place in a very different context from that revealed in *R.* v. *Howells*. In the *Howells* case, while surveillance takes place in the public convenience it is a practice of surveillance of which those being observed are ignorant. Here the practice of surveillance appears to be relatively remote from the performance of the unlawful genital act. In *Redgrave*, the act of observation takes place in a different context. The police practice of surveillance deploys a series of techniques that enable it to be undertaken in the full presence of, and with the knowledge of, the accused. This particular type of surveillance operation has interesting features. In particular it is a technique of surveillance that is more closely implicated in the illegal act. This policing technique requires that the agent of the law take up the position of the object of the desire of the one that will subsequently be arrested and charged. This particular technique of policing is generally indicated by reference to the phrase 'plain clothes'. *Redgrave* suggests that this particular technique of policing involves a simulation of the male genital body in its genital relations with other male bodies.

This particular aspect of policing practice is not unique to one case. It appears again in the more recent case of *R. v. Kirkup* (1993). Here the agent of the law was installed in plain clothes and positioned in a urinal prior to Kirkup's entry. Kirkup was made the object of the law and, as the law report records, subject to the law, by means of this surveillance technology. This enabled the police officer to map the body of Kirkup in the following way:

> ... he stood at a urinal for about four minutes;
> ... he was not urinating;
> ... he was ... looking around at other men using the urinals;
> ... going to the wash basin to wash his hands and to the dryer to dry them;
> ... to another set of urinals, again not urinating but looking and smiling at other men;
> ... he went to a urinal which was one space away from where a police officer was standing;
> ... he looked and smiled at [the police officer] while masturbating his own erect penis.

The officer recorded that throughout the defendant engaged in conduct that showed, tacitly, that he was inviting the other men to engage in homosexual activity with him.[9]

While these tactics and practices of surveillance are similar to those found in *Redgrave*, *Kirkup* is of particular interest as the law report records the simultaneous presence of not one but two surveillance techniques. First, surveillance was undertaken by means of the physical presence of the police. Second, the public convenience was surveyed by electronic means: a video camera. Here the multiplicity of technologies of surveillance draws attention to the extraordinary effort that might be put into the task of producing an immense verbosity around the male body as a genital body in its genital relations with other men. Here that constant and attentive technology contacts male bodies and intensifies particular surfaces: the hands, the penis, the mouth, the look. It is attentive to every move be it great or small. Its goal is to record each gesture (either instantaneously on the videotape or first in the mind of the officer and later in his note book) and simultaneously, by means of particular schemes of knowledge, to produce those gestures as a set of decipherable signs with a very specific meaning. Finally, it is important to recognize the difference between the two types of surveillance technology used in this example. In this instance the video surveillance technology was visible; the police officer standing at the urinal while physically present was invisible for much of the time.

The presence and absence of the police in the technique of surveillance in the context of a plain-clothes operation is of particular interest. It is both a fundamental requirement and one that is particularly problematic. The requirements of invisibility that operate here are influenced by specific factors. For example, many problems associated with this particular type of policing arise from the fact that while the genital acts that are the object of interest are performed in public places, the 'public' nature of these acts is problematic. These 'public' places and encounters also have an important private dimension. This may be demonstrated in various ways. For instance, while these genital encounters are performed in places that are potentially accessible and thereby potentially visible to all (hence 'public'), their use as a place where men meet other men for such encounters is not 'public' knowledge. They are both hidden from most people and easily recognized by one who already has prior knowledge.

INVISIBILITY, AND THE PRIVACY OF PUBLIC PLACES

In his study, *Tearoom Trade*, Laud Humphreys noted that this relative invisibility is the manifestation of a demand by the participants for privacy. The privacy of these 'public' encounters is demanded by participants for various reasons. First, it is demanded because the behaviour is potentially the object of criminalization and the object of much social derision. Participants are keen to ensure that the acts are performed in private in order to avoid an encounter with people in general and the officers of the law in particular. Second, while these activities are carried on 'in public', because the men are participating in acts associated with the intimate and thereby with the private, there is a strong wish to avoid the scrutiny of others. Privacy is also demanded as many of these men are married and wish to retain the appearance that they are dedicated to cross-sex relations.

Humphreys's work is of interest at this point in another respect. He demonstrates the way in which the men who use these 'public' places might exploit the always already private dimension of 'public space' and further privatize it in order to ensure that their activities remain private. For example, they exploit the privacy of 'public places' in the selection of the sites for these encounters; not all public conveniences or open spaces become places for such encounters. In part the selection exploits, for example, the privacy designed into the public convenience in the form of urinals (stalls), cubicles, doors and frosted glass. The erotic performance itself is organized according to the requirements of privacy; nothing is spoken. Silence not only secures the anonymity that preserves the private life of the participants, it also works to ensure that those outside the encounter know nothing of it. Humphreys also found that users would adapt such buildings or spaces in

140

order to promote further privacy: by breaking windows in order to provide a lookout to ensure that encounters only take place in private or by removing light bulbs to deter the casual user and to ensure that there is no sign of activity from the outside (Humphreys 1970: ch.1). To reduce a building or a space to its 'public' aspect and thereby to record the acts that take place within them as necessarily 'public' ignores these factors. More specifically, it ignores the way in which a building or space might be the site of two or more different sets of practices, in this instance one public (urination) and one private (a sexual encounter). It is important to recognize that the 'public' and the 'private' of the same space or building are socially constructed patterns of use (Humphreys 1982: xi). Humphreys's work draws attention to the way in which, in a public convenience, these two different functions may alternate in quick succession (from one person to the next), depending upon various factors: time, space, technology, information, and inter-personal contacts. Thus the building may in quick succession (or simultaneously in its various parts) function in various social and sometimes morally contradictory ways for varying clienteles without conflict.

Foucault's work draws attention to another aspect of this multiple use of space. His work suggests that there is a need for caution in characterizing these different uses as either separate and successive uses or as knowledges and performances that relate to separate communities. In particular, Foucault warns that a silence with regard to the sexual, either in an official designation of the use of public conveniences or in their 'public' character, might be problematic. Take the design of the public toilet; one might have the impression that the silence with regard to sexuality that informs references to the proper use of 'public' conveniences suggests that sexuality was irrelevant to the design of that institution. But one only has to consider the architectural layout to discover that the question of an erotic encounter is a constant preoccupation. Several examples suggest that, at least since the police appeared in public toilets, those designing and building public toilets have considered the sexual explicitly, taken it permanently into account to maintain a state of perpetual alert, which the overall design, the size, number, and spacing of the various facilities, the materials used, the attention to the detail of the fixtures and fittings, never cease to reiterate.[10] Foucault describes this as the internal discourse of the institution – the one it employs to address itself, and which circulated among those who made it function. It was largely based not only on the assumption that this sexuality existed but also that it was precocious, active and ever present.

Foucault's insight draws attention to the fact that the public, non-sexualized, convenience is always already imagined as a sexualized space of private encounters; its very existence speaks not only of a taboo around urination/defecation and the fact that it now has to be undertaken in private but that the removal of these functions into a private space generates other private dangers. The private and sexualized nature of that space is written in the division between male and female space; in the use of frosted glass that might provide natural light but prevent a public display; in the design of the stalls; in the erection of barriers between the stalls to secure individuality during the private act of urination; in the separation of space into individual private cubicles; in the provision of lockable doors to secure that individual space; the installation of ceiling to floor partitions to ensure the division of one from another; in the use of brick and stone to guarantee the separation of bodies; etc. (Foucault 1981a: 28–9). As Foucault reminds us, the silence with regard to these private and sexualized aspects of 'public' places is perhaps less the absolute limit of discourse than an element that functions alongside the things said, with them, and in relation to them within overall strategies. That silence not only marks the place of requirements relating to the different ways of not saying such things, but also marks the place of those requirements that designate who can and who cannot speak of such things and provides for their distribution. Silence also relates to the type of discourse by which one might be authorized to speak of such things and the form of discretion that is required (Foucault 1981a: 27). The silence with regard to the private sexualized aspects of 'public places' is of particular importance. It draws attention to the type of discourse by which one might be authorized to speak of such things – namely law. The law plays a particularly important role in transforming what might otherwise be a private encounter between men into a public one. For example, it is institutionalized in s. 1(2) of the Sexual Offences Act 1967, which declares that:

> An act which would otherwise be treated for the purposes of this Act as being done in private shall not be so treated if done
>
> (a) when more than two persons take part or are present; or
> (b) in a lavatory to which the public have or are permitted to have access, whether on payment or otherwise.

This section not only authorizes but also, in the narrowness of the definition of privacy, positively promotes references to the private and the sexualized nature of 'public places'. The section installs a demand that these things be spoken in the law. It also designates who can and who cannot speak of such things and provides for their documentation and distribution. The designated speakers, authorized to speak of the sexuality of these private spaces and thereby to render them public, are those who are or who purport to be agents of the law, such as the police or the park attendant. This is echoed in Laud Humphreys observation that, up to now, the police and other law enforcement agents have been the only systematic producers of knowledge about these encounters between men, and he adds: 'In some locals, these agents have been very busy' (Humphreys 1970: 17).[11]

It is the privacy of these 'public' places and encounters that makes the possibility of a police presence particularly problematic. To appear, particularly as a policeman in uniform (as a public official), would instantly eliminate the privacy and thereby the acts that are the object of surveillance, frustrating all possibility of investigating and detecting performances of unlawful action. Many have pointed out that this ought to be recognized for what it is, the ultimate success of policing, especially where policing is dedicated to crime prevention rather than to detection after the act. In turn, many have repeatedly asserted that this is, other than in exceptional circumstances, police practice (PRO MEPO 3/990). Many more have asserted that this ought to be the primary mode of police surveillance (Royal Commission 1928, 1929). However, innumerable examples, including most recently evidence from lesbian and gay police officers (Burke 1993: 44–61) have repeatedly demonstrated that police technologies are rarely deployed in this instance to produce the visibility of the public agent of law in order to prevent the male-to-male genital encounter. Policing technologies are more concerned with securing the production of the male-to-male genital encounters and more specifically with the production of this male genital body as a (homo)sexualized body.

In that event, the technologies of policing, dedicated as they are to the production of male-to-male genital acts and the male genital body as homosexuality are unavoidably at variance with the demands for privacy of the men who are to be subject to these technologies as the objects of attention (Humphreys 1970: 26). In these private places the agents of the law are strangers (the public) and thereby likely to generate suspicion in this world where privacy is paramount.

The technology of investigation and detection that the police have developed in order to investigate these situations is to a large extent a recognition of this demand for privacy, a response to it and reproduction of it. As the evidence of police practice already presented has suggested, to be successful these technologies of investigation and detection must be concerned with invisibility, or more specifically with dissimulation, making the police presence appear to be something other than it is: a wall, a door, a cupboard.[12] All these produce the presence of the police at the point of surveillance, at the same time that they produce the immediate physical absence of the police. Other techniques of dissimulation respond to and reproduce the privacy of these places in a different way. These techniques are concerned with securing the absence of the police at the same time as they seek to secure the immediate physical presence of the police. 'Plain clothes' is such a technique. It seeks to produce this state of affairs through the technique of making the policeman appear as a mere man. It is to the detail of these techniques that we shall now turn.

INVISIBILITY AND SOMATIC TECHNIQUES

An example of a case that illustrates these techniques of policing is the case of *R. v. Ford* (1978). The case report of the police operation is brief. A police officer in plain clothes stood outside a public lavatory in the seaside town of Bournemouth. He was approached by Ford who persistently suggested to the officer that he should go back with Ford to his flat for homosexual purposes.[13] An interesting feature of this case, one that sets it apart from those considered so far, is that the Campaign for Homosexual Equality (CHE) obtained information about this encounter and published details of it in their report to the Royal Commission on Criminal Procedure. It is of particular interest in that it provides more information about the nature of the techniques of policing that generate surveillance in this instance.

It would appear from the CHE report that the particular incident that is described in the law report is but one instance of a much longer and complex police operation. The CHE report describes the encounter between the man and the plain-clothes officer in the following terms:

> In October 1976 in Bournemouth, a plain-clothes officer entered a public lavatory and was followed by X, a civil servant, who stood at the other end of the room from the officer, watching him but making no attempt to speak to him. The officer left the lavatory and sat on a bench outside, eyeing X who had followed him from the lavatory and stood nearby. The officer got up, strolled slowly away and then stopped to let X catch up with him when he realized that X was behind him. X said to him 'I wouldn't leave your car here for very long if I were you, the fuzz come here a lot.' He then asked the officer if he would like to come back to his flat. The officer asked if he meant for sex, and when X replied yes he was arrested for persistently soliciting. At his trial, the prosecution admitted that the officer had been lying in wait for homosexuals. X was found guilty and fined £50.
>
> (CHE 1979)

When installed in plain clothes the police officer appears as a mere man. Here we learn a little more about the nature of the techniques whereby that mere man is performed: about some of its movements, its gestures, its perambulations, and its utterances.[14]

Humphreys's work on the demands of the privacy of these public places, however, suggests that this is a partial and insufficient explanation of the nature of this technique of policing. It is not sufficient that the policeman appear either as a mere man or as 'an ordinary member of the public'. In the context of a public convenience for men, a man is not always an insider. He may be a stranger, an outsider, who will generate suspicion. In order to disappear as an agent of the law the policeman must become an insider.[15] As Laud Humphreys noted, in order to observe without being exposed as a stranger and thereby as hostile, it is necessary 'to enter the subculture as would any newcomer and to make contact with respondents under the guise of being a gay guy' (Humphreys 1970: 24). While the initial entry of the police into this world of private acts in public places is not difficult to accomplish, the real problem is one of making the contact with the subculture 'stick'. It is in this light that we should read the documented encounter between Ford and the plain-clothes officer. Here the officer appears not so much as a mere man but by way of a performance of a man who seeks genital encounters with other men. Thus policing techniques, if they are to create the possibility of surveillance, must involve the deployment of that set of codes and conventions of the male genital body in its genital relations with other male bodies that they seek to make the object of the law: dress, gestures (he wriggled his body and smiled into the faces of men), the use of the eyes for communication, the adoption of silence, an intimate knowledge of certain places. Securing absence at the same time as securing immediate physical presence, as Laud Humphreys noted, does not come easy (Humphreys 1970: 24).

THE SOMATIC TECHNIQUES OF THE MALE GENITAL BODY

Some evidence of the detail of these policing techniques is documented in the case of *R. v. Gray* (1982). Here the surveillance didn't relate to a public toilet but was undertaken on the street near a well-known gay pub in the Earls Court district of London. The case report records that a police officer in plain clothes was standing in a doorway at about 11.30 p.m., when many male homosexuals were congregating outside a public house on the other side of the road, as was frequently so at that place and time of day. The police officer observed Gray, who was said to be sauntering around and smiling at people outside the public house. The case report tells us that Gray crossed the road, spoke first to a man with fair hair and then to a black man. He then moved towards the police officer and smiled at him, believing the police officer was a homosexual. After a short conversation, the police officer told the court, he was invited back to Gray's nearby flat to partake of a glass of whisky and to spend the night. Shortly after this the officer revealed his identity as a police officer. At that point the appellant was arrested.[16]

Again, this law report is of special interest as it deals with a police investigation and detection practice that not only takes an interesting form but also appears to have had considerable durability and generated information about police practices outside the context of law reports. Numerous examples of this type of operation were reported to the newly formed Gay London Police Monitoring Group (GALOP), and were recorded in their annual reports (GALOP 1984, 1985). Many of the recorded reports evidence a common police practice. One example will be taken from the first annual report to illustrate these police practices.

> Douglas left the Coleherne at closing time and was walking to his car, in Wharfedale Street. A young man wearing a tight T-shirt and tight jeans with a rip across one buttock smiles at Douglas. They begin a conversation, the young man questions Douglas very directly, does Douglas want to fuck or does he just want a blow job? Douglas is hesitant to talk about sex immediately and suggests they go back to Douglas's place south of the river. The young man says that is too far to go – he has a place around the corner. They walk up Warwick Road and when they reach Nevern Square, Douglas has his arm put behind his back and the young man and a third man identify themselves as police officers and Douglas is arrested. At Earls Court police station he is charged with persistently importuning. Whilst he is at the police station pressure is put on him to tell the police how he intends to plead and when he tells them 'not guilty' further pressure is put on him to plead guilty because it was only a minor charge and it would be unfortunate if his

employers were to discover that he was gay, his parents or next door neighbours for that matter. The police go on to assure that if he pleads guilty at the Magistrates Court he won't receive any bad publicity.

(GALOP 1984)[17]

The examples of Gray and 'Douglas' are important in various ways. They draw attention not only to the fact that police techniques of investigation and detection might be intimately connected with the illegal acts that are the object of the police practice but also to the nature and complexity of these techniques. To describe these police practices as 'plain-clothes' operations fails to take note of the particular nature of the techniques that produce this invisibility in order to facilitate surveillance, examination, interpretation and recording. Both examples provide evidence of a particular set of policing techniques. These techniques are dedicated to the production of the disappearance of the policeman and his reappearance in a very specific form: as 'a homosexual'. The policing techniques that produce this homosexual of the law have particular features. They might require the development and deployment of particular corporeal qualities: a 'pretty policeman' or 'a young man'. They might involve resort to a particular sartorial code: 'wearing a tight T-shirt and tight jeans with a rip across one buttock'. They include the use of a set of very specific interpersonal conventions: 'at closing time . . . he smil[ed] at Douglas', and a specific stock of key words and phrases: 'does Douglas want to fuck or does he just want a blow job?'. Here all are shown to be important techniques of the law.

While these examples provide some important evidence of the nature of the police practices they don't document the detail of the deployment of these technologies within those private 'public' places. A rare example of evidence of this type of police practice (within the Metropolitan Police district) is found in a report, now preserved in the Public Records Office, London, prepared for the Metropolitan Police in 1933.

'M' Division
Tower Bridge Station.
25th August 1933.

STATEMENT of —— , Police Constable,
528 'M' Division, who saith:

At 11.15pm. on the 24th August 1933, I was on duty in plain clothes, accompanied by P.C. 565 'M' Division —— , keeping observation on the public lavatory situated at the junction of Fair Street and Tooley Street, Bermondsey, in consequence of complaints having been received of indecent behaviour by male persons, when I saw two men enter the lavatory, they remained there until 11.35pm. I entered the lavatory and the two men then walked out. A short time later the prisoner, —— , entered the lavatory and went to the stall immediately opposite the one in which I was standing. In

146

about a minute later P.C. 565 'M' —— entered and stood in the stall nearest the entrance which was between the prisoner and myself. After a short time the prisoner left the stall in which he was standing and came round towards me stopping near the stall on my left hand side. I then saw P.C. 565 —— move round towards the stall which the prisoner had left. Two other men then entered the lavatory, one of them behind P.C. 565 —— and came around to the vacant stall directly on my left, the other men remaining near P.C. 565 —— The prisoner then said to me 'Will you give me a light please?' He then walked behind me and took up a position in the stall immediately on my right, which P.C. 565 —— had previously occupied. After a few minutes the prisoner made a half-turn towards me, stretched out his left arm and placed his left hand on my person and commenced rubbing it. I immediately took hold of his left arm, his left hand still being on my person. I said to him 'I am a Police Officer and I am going to take you into custody for indecently assaulting me'. He said 'Not me, you have made a mistake'. I then took the prisoner to Tower Bridge Police Station where he was charged, upon the charge being read to him he said 'You have made a mistake. I left my girl at Long Lane about half-past eleven and went for a walk round, I didn't want to get home too early'.

(PRO MEPO 3/990)

The accused was charged with two offences: indecently assaulting P.C. 528 'M' by placing a hand on his person at a public urinal, contrary to s. 62 of the Offences Against the Person Act 1961, and second that he did commit or attempt to commit an act of indecency with another person, namely P.C. 528 'M', at the public urinal, Contrary to London County Council Bye-Law, 20.3.1900.[18]

While this document refers only to one operation it would appear that the police performance described in this document was not an isolated one. The record notes that since 21 June 1933 similar operations had produced four arrests for indecent assault, a fifth man had been found guilty of importuning and sentenced to three months hard labour, and three men had been found guilty of indecency under the London County Council Bye-Law and fined the maximum amount allowed under the Bye-Law: £5.

While the references to police names and numbers and terms such as 'prisoner' constantly remind us that we are reading of the police presence in this place and thereby of the 'public' nature of the events and of the distance between the police and those events, it is also important to recognize that this police report also describes a private encounter in which the police take part. Of particular interest here is the fact that this report describes a police practice where the agents of the law perform themselves not as outsiders but as insiders. As such they do not so much produce and document the 'public' of this event but rather are shown performing a series of acts that (re)produce the privacy of this event.

Here the police perform the privacy of the event by way of an elaborate choreography, in both the stationary position as well as the movement. They are part of the production of privacy in that they are performed in order to suggest that far from being policemen, that is outsiders, these men are insiders. Their failure to perform the complex rituals of that particular space would have at best suggested that they were strangers or at worst that they were policemen. This would have led to the cessation of all activity and thereby to the impossibility of detection. The police performance of these rituals only comes to an end when they decide to take on another role, that of the agent of the law.

However, these examples provide us with relatively little information about the nature of the techniques that the police must deploy if they are to be successful. If, in order to be successful, the police must mimic or simulate the behaviour of men who seek sex with other men in 'public places', then the research about the nature of the behaviour of these places and the men who go there in order to have sexual encounters might provide a further insight into the nature of these techniques of the law.

Laud Humphreys's work draws attention to various aspects of these encounters. In general, he noted that they appeared to be performed by means of three main roles: players, lookouts (or 'watchqueens') and 'the straight person'. These general categories were further explained and subdivided. However there is a need for caution here. In the context of his study he gives a very specific elaboration of the types of 'players'. In particular in the North American context, he found that the most common sexual practice performed in these 'public' places was fellatio. This is reflected in his description of the sub-categories of 'players': insertee (sucker) and insertor (the one who is sucked or blown). As D.J. West noted in his foreword (West 1970) to the English edition of Humphreys's study, the dominance of this specific practice might be a peculiarity of North America. West suggested, and the reported decisions might add some support to this, that in Britain (mutual) masturbation was the most common sexual practice in this context. As such, in the UK context the 'players' might be more appropriately described as masturbator (the one who masturbates) and the masturbatee (the one who is masturbated).

Humphreys described the 'lookout' or 'watchqueen' as a man who is situated by the door or windows from which he may observe the means of access to the toilet. In general his role, Humphreys explained, is to cough when someone approaches, to nod when the coast is clear or if he recognizes an entering party as a regular (Humphreys 1970: 27).[19] The combination of the watchqueen and player functions, Humphreys suggested, gave rise to three different types of 'lookout': waiters (men waiting for someone with whom they have made an appointment or whom they expect to find at this spot, for a particular type of 'trick'); masturbators (who engage in autoerotic behaviour); and, finally, 'a role superbly suited for policemen and the only lookout role that is not overtly sexual': the voyeur.[20] (Humphreys 1970: 28).

Finally, the third general role, 'the straight person', is the role of one who has come to the toilet for purposes of elimination. This role is one that is relatively remote from the main sexual focus of the event.[21] It also has serious disadvantages as a role for anyone who wishes to observe the behaviour that is taking place in the convenience: 'it is short lived and invariably disrupts the action that the observer has set out to observe' (Humphreys 1970: 28). Such are the demands of privacy in these public places that if those who enter the public facilities wish to be present throughout the course of an encounter then they must perform according to the roles of watchqueen or masturbator/ee (player) or a variation of their combination.

However, the performance of these roles is a complex matter. In particular, Humphreys noted that the exigencies of these interactive encounters demanded a great deal of role flexibility. This 'instability' of role refers to a requirement that participants, 'melt, fuse or drift' from one role to another. The participants step into and out of these roles as the encounter unfolds and as they approach 'the pay-off' (Humphreys 1970: 51–2). Humphreys's research suggested that this feature operated regardless of the role or the participant who might take up that role in the course of an encounter. Neither a prior conscious sense of gender identity, of masculinity or femininity, nor a preference for a particular role in sexual activity (active/passive, top/bottom) worked to counteract this flexibility. It follows that there is nothing masculine about the man who inserts his penis in the mouth or anal cavity of another, and there is nothing feminine about the other, into whose orifice the organ is inserted, nor does it follow that the 'sucker' (masturbator) was the aggressor and the man being 'blown' or masturbated is the aggressee or passive participant (Humphreys 1970: 52). Aggressive or active and passive relate to systems of strategies not types of players. As such a 'passive' player may perform that passivity by means of an 'aggressive' strategy in order to progress the encounter and to secure the completion of the encounter.

Role shifts might occur both during the brief span of a single encounter and over a series of encounters. Proto-players may be transformed into waiters, waiters into voyeurs, voyeurs into players, and players into lookout masturbators, and even straights may be transformed into players.[22] Such is the instability that under normal circumstances the players are identifiable only in the sex act. Nor is this aspect of the roles peculiar to that of the players. In this type of 'living theatre', none of the actors may know his role until the action is finished (Humphreys 1970: 51). This flexibility, he concluded, is due to the fact that the consequences of being caught performing the central roles of insertor/insertee, masturbator/masturbatee are so great that those roles are made manifest only in the final moments of the encounter. Furthermore, because these encounters occur under a great deal of time pressure, participants must be able to step in and out of the parts at will. Humphreys noted that these demands had particular effects. They resulted in a highly standardized but at the same time highly flexible set of roles (Humphreys 1970: 48).

Genital encounters in public conveniences are a form of collective action. As such they depend upon effective communication. Humphreys found that they were non-coercive and non-committal encounters. In order to ensure both progression towards the desired end point, and role flexibility, a skilful performance depended upon the player's ability to convey intentions by means of mutually understood signals, and to receive, interpret, assimilate and act upon the basis of information given by the other participant producing and sustaining reciprocal encouragement

(Humphreys 1970: 59). Failure to perform according to these stringent requirements might signify an outsider and bring the encounter to a premature end.

This analysis of the nature of the encounters in public conveniences has great
importance in developing an understanding of the techniques and performances of
the agents of the law. Agents of social control, if they are to be successful in these
encounters (i.e. invisible), must reproduce these patterns of flexibility, role un-
recognizability, play and non-coercive collective communication.[23] More specifically, Humphreys noted, this might require the police to adopt the roles they are
assigned to eliminate (Humphreys 1979: 55–6).

It is also important, however, to note that encounters that involve agents of social
control differ in a significant way. In this particular version of the 'living theatre',
while the player may still be identifiable in the final instance only in the sex act, it is
the police that name both the moment of that act and the nature of that act when
the agents of social control (re)appear – when disaster strikes.

An important feature of these encounters is silence. Policing techniques are
informed by this requirement and, if they are to be successful, must reproduce it.
The police techniques of collective communication produce policing as a series of
physical movements: a gesture with the hands, motions of the eyes, manipulation
and erection of the penis, a movement of the head, a change in stance, or a transfer
from one place to another. Through these physical performances of the body, the
agents of the law carry the action through stages that, lacking conversation, might
otherwise be awkward. Humphreys provides an inventory of these gestures and
movements, which are organized by reference to the following themes: approaching, position, manœuvring, signalling, contracting, foreplay, pay-off, clearing the
field, and coping with intrusions. They provide a grid by which the techniques of
policing might be further analysed. The inventory of techniques of the body
(somatic techniques) includes the following.

Approaching

The approach to the place of encounter is an important preliminary part of the
performance observed both by those outside the public convenience and where
possible by those already in it. The action of the man outside may communicate a
great deal about his availability for an encounter. For example, a man playing the
role of the 'straight' does not tend to wait outside or circle the place prior to entry.
The role of a straight is to stop, enter, urinate and leave, all in quick succession. For
all prospective participants, two purposes inform the composition of the movements that make up the approach: to look as natural as possible and to take the
opportunity to 'cruise' other prospective players. The particular performance may
take many forms. For example, a person on foot or in a car may circle the area once
or twice, finally stopping in front of the facility. The driver might park a moderate
distance away, to avoid having his car associated with the convenience. If he
remains in the car he may read a newspaper. Sometimes the person will go into the
convenience on the heels of a person he has been watching. Should he find the

occupant of another car interesting, he may decide to enter as a signal for the other man to follow. If no one else approaches or leaves he may enter to see what is going on inside. Some will wait in their car for as long as an hour, until they see a desirable prospect approaching or sense that the time is right for entry. A man who remains in his car while a number of others come and go, then starts for the facility as soon as a relatively handsome young fellow approaches, may reveal both his preferences and his unwillingness to engage in acting with anyone 'substandard' (Humphreys 1970: 61). Whatever his behaviour outside, any man who approaches an occupied public convenience should know that he is being carefully appraised as he strides up the path and enters the building.

Positioning

Once inside, the initial brief passage across the floor to a urinal or a cubicle is an opportunity to 'cruise' those already there. The decision as to which urinal he will use is a tactical consideration. The design of the public convenience is an important factor influencing this tactical decision. In the context of the design commonly found in the facilities Humphreys researched, the building contained three urinals; he noted that if either of the end fixtures was occupied, which was often the case, an entering party who proceeded to take a position at the centre of the three urinals was thought to be precocious – 'coming on too strong'. The occupation of the end urinal is a preferred position as it gives a person more room to manœuvre in the unfolding rendezvous. To take a position at a urinal in the centre is a precocious move – 'coming on too strong'. It is important to recognize that, by the time the person is positioned at the urinal or in the cubicle, the performance is well under way, as much information about his purposes has already been communicated. The performance may then proceed in various ways (Humphreys 1970: 61–3).

Manœuvring

The next step may be, but need not necessarily be, a movement to change one's position in relation to other persons and structures in the room. It is important at this point in the action, first because it indicates a willingness to proceed with the encounter and second because it is a means of suggesting preferences for future roles. Humphreys's evidence suggested that these manœuvres might solidify into standard patterns. For example, a man who moved closer to someone at the urinal might thereby express a preference for the future role of insertee (masturbator). Other manœuvres were also possible. A person may use this stage to move away from someone, or to move closer to someone elsewhere in the room, or to move from the urinal to an unaccompanied stall. All these strategies are incremental but non-essential to the basic action patterns. Again, the design of the public convenience is an important factor influencing the exact performance (Humphreys 1970: 65–6).

Signalling

While for some roles positioning appears to be particularly important, for others signalling is predominant. For Humphreys, signalling concerns movements that relate to the penis. If the new participant stands close to the fixture, so that his front side may not easily be seen, and gazes downward, it is assumed by the participants that he is straight.[24] If he wishes to communicate his willingness to participate further, this may be communicated by means of standing back from the urinal, allowing his gaze to shift from side to side or to the ceiling. This may be followed by allowing his penis to be seen by others. Failure to perform may preclude his involvement in further action at the urinals. At this stage, playing with the penis in what may be called 'pseudo-masturbation' is an important sign.

RESPONDENT   The thing he [the potential insertee] is watching for is 'handling', to see whether or not the guy is going to play with himself. He's going to pretend like he is masturbating, and this is the signal right there . . .

INTERVIEWER   So the sign of willingness to play is playing with oneself or masturbation?

RESPONDENT   Pseudo masturbation.

(Humphreys 1970: 63)

The willing player steps back a few inches from the urinal, so that his penis may be viewed easily. He then begins to stroke it or play with the head of the organ. The eyes now come into play. The prospective partner will look intently at the other's organ, occasionally breaking his stare only to fix directly upon the eyes of the other. Humphreys suggested that no one would be 'groped' or otherwise involved in the directly sexual play of the public convenience unless he displayed this sign.[25] Other signals used by men in the cubicles to attract attention to their interests involve foot-tapping or note-passing. If there is a 'glory hole', it may be used as a means of signalling from the stall. This may be observed in three manners: by the appearance of an eye on the stool-side of the partition (a very strong indication that the seated man is watching you), by wiggling fingers through the hole, or by the projection of the tongue through the 'glory hole'. Occasionally, there is no need for the parties to exchange signals. Others in the room may signal for a waiting person to enter the stall (Humphreys 1970: 63–5).

Contracting

In the positioning, manoeuvring and signalling phases of the game, the participants indicate their intentions. Every move in the encounter is not only a means of bettering one's physical position in relation to other participants but also a means of communication that is essential to moving the encounter along. The emphasis given to certain gestures may change. The contractual phase is a set of gestures concerned with setting both the terms of the later stages of the sexual exchange and as a means of expressing mutual consent.[26] Consent is communicated by means of

152

bodily movements, in particular the exposure of an erect penis. The contracts may be initiated in various ways: for example, by taking hold of another's exposed and erect penis or moving towards one who by means of previous somatic movements associated with approach, positioning, manœuvring and signalling has evidenced an interest in taking the encounter further. The lack of negative response from the recipient is enough to seal the contract. The gradual progression through the various stages and participation in the various roles works to provide enough silent communication to achieve mutuality. The contractual stage merely formalizes this and sets the terms of subsequent activity.

A party's relative aggressiveness or passivity in this phase of the game does not, in itself, indicate the role to be acted out at the climax of the interaction. In connection with the positioning of the first move, however, it does provide an indication of the future role identification. Exceptions make it necessary to withhold judgment as to what roles are being played until the pay-off phase itself (Humphreys 1970: 65–6).

Foreplay

Specific foreplay movements are relatively unimportant. From positioning to pay-off, nearly all players – and some waiters – engage in auto-manipulation. There is little need, therefore, to prepare the insertee/masturbatee for action by any other means of stimulation. Whereas an erection may be an important signal in the early phases of the game, interruptions and repositioning between the contract and pay-off stages occasionally result in the loss of an erection by the prospective insertor (Humphreys 1970: 66–70).

Pay-off

This marks the erotic endpoint of the encounter. Intrusions may temporarily detach the pay-off phase from the action that leads up to it, providing moments of incongruous suspense (Humphreys 1970: 71–5).

Clearing the field

This aspect of the performance is concerned with activities after the sexual exchange has been accomplished. In general, either one or both performers move away from the immediate scene of the encounter, cleaning the penis, rearranging clothing, departing from the scene of the event (Humphreys 1970: 76–7).

Coping with intrusions

The final category of gestures relates to responses to the entry of a new person. Humphreys notes that this nearly always causes a break in the action. The man entering must be legitimized or the game will be disrupted, at least for the duration of his presence. Until the legitimation or departure of the new person occurs, a sort of panic reaction ensues; play becomes disorganized and the focus of strategies shifts from the pay-off to self-protection and then to the appraisal of the new person. Humphreys suggests three chief means of coping with the tension generated by such intrusions into the gaming encounter. The first is the almost automatic and universal response of 'zipping the fly'. At all points where the outer world impinges upon the inner world, zipping the fly is apt to occur. The second common coping mechanism is looking innocent, whereby participants dissociate themselves from the erotic action. This takes the form of a 'huge elaborate disinterest' (Humphreys 1970: 80) and a studied nonchalance. However it is not maintained for long; legitimation never seems to take long. Straights seldom stay for more than two minutes. Waiters appear to play a crucial role in re-establishing the performance. They tend either to begin the opening moves of the game or to re-commence service as lookouts. Where decoys are a known threat, the legitimation process is more elaborate and takes longer. A third means whereby participants cope with intrusions is 'speculative enquiry'. This is a practice of careful observation, by which the participants pick up identification clues dropped by the new arrival (Humphreys 1970: 78–80).

THE SOMATIC TECHNIQUES OF POLICING

These roles and techniques of the body, observed, organized and catalogued by Humphreys, provide a set of tools by which we might analyse police practice. The 1934 report from the Metropolitan Police (PRO MEPO 3/990), which provides one of the most complete descriptions of a police operation in a public convenience, will be the primary focus of attention, though where possible other examples taken from reported cases will be drawn upon to illustrate different somatic techniques of police practice.

The Metropolitan Police statement opens with a description of approaching behaviour:

'At 11.15pm. on the 24th August 1933, I was on duty in plain clothes, accompanied by P.C. 565 'M' Division —— , keeping observation on the public lavatory situated at the junction of Fair Street and Tooley Street . . . - when I saw two men enter the lavatory, they remained there until 11-35pm.'

While this description is rather brief, giving us little information about the detail of the somatic techniques used in the approach, it clearly records that the role the police have adopted at this stage in the surveillance performance is not that of the straight. When before a public convenience the straight does not tend to wait outside or circle the place prior to entry; he stops, enters, urinates and leaves all in quick succession. Here the approach appears to have lasted twenty minutes.[27] In other examples, such as in the case of *Horton* v. *Mead* (1913), police operations evidence a somatic strategy of serial approaches: travelling from convenience to convenience and back again. Again this is always already far removed from the role of the straight. It is important to remember that the somatic practices of policing that are displayed here are performed in order that the presence of the police is rendered illegible particularly by those whom the police want to meet. At the same time, this behaviour must be clearly legible to that same group of people, as the behaviour of any man who approaches an occupied public convenience is being carefully appraised as he moves towards and enters the building. The somatic practices found in *Horton* v. *Mead* ought to be read in that light as both a series of separate approaches by insiders and an extended approach by insiders performed over a much longer period: almost two hours. In other cases, for example in *R.* v. *Redgrave*, the police operation involved five police officers of the local police Vice Squad. We are told of a plain-clothes observation on a public convenience that occurred between 4.45 and 5.00 p.m. Again the duration of the operation draws attention to the fact that the police have already begun to produce the genital male body in its genital relations with other men in performing those somatic practices that may be read as an approach. The case provides us with some more evidence of the somatic practices used by the police during such periods of time. On two occasions an officer entered the public convenience, followed by Redgrave. The law report tells us nothing of the detail of the somatic practices of the police that preceded and made up these two events. However, while the two entries by the police officer and Redgrave might have been random events (and this was part of the argument put forward by Redgrave in his defence), Humphreys's analysis suggests that this is not the only possibility. The joint approach and entry might also be the culmination of a period of intense (albeit brief) communication where by means of various gestures the agent of the law produces and communicates mutually understood signals, and receives, interprets, assimilates and acts upon the basis of information given by the other party, producing reciprocal encouragement and sustaining it.

The police officer's decision to enter may be used as a signal for the other man to follow. As a result, a person might go into the convenience on the heels of a policeman he has been watching. Sometimes the preliminary wait is undertaken to see if a desirable prospect approaches. A man who remains outside, then starts for the facility as soon as a relatively handsome young fellow approaches, may reveal both his preferences and his unwillingness to engage in acting with anyone 'substandard' (Humphreys 1970: 61). In *R.* v. *Ford*, again the approach by the police officer was quickly followed by the approach of another man who was subsequently charged. Thereby in the proximity of the approach the agent of the law performs this male genital body.

Other aspects of the techniques of approach are suggested by this case. The first is that approaches by the police might also involve a car: X said to the policeman, 'I wouldn't leave your car here for very long if I were you, the fuzz come here a lot.' On leaving the facility the police officer sat on a bench outside, eyeing X who had followed him from the lavatory and stood nearby. While these gestures turned out to be a preliminary movement in the unexpected pay-off of criminalization, they might also have been movements that could have turned into the preparation for another approach. What is important is the recognition of the fact that these are the somatic techniques of policing that produce the agent of the law as an insider.

Two purposes inform the composition of all these various movements: to look as natural as possible, and to take the opportunity to 'cruise' other prospective players. The delay in their approach should be recognized not as an absence of action or a denial of an approach but as an important part of the approach. The somatic techniques performed at this moment may be crucial, as the action of the plain-clothes officer outside communicates a great deal about his availability for an encounter to other men outside, whom he has been cruising, or to other men inside who might be watching him and whom he is about to cruise.

As the officer crosses the threshold we can witness the performance entering a new stage: positioning.

> I entered the lavatory and the two men then walked out. A short time later the prisoner. . . entered the lavatory and went to the stall immediately opposite the one in which I was standing. In about a minute later P.C. 565 'M' —— entered and stood in the stall nearest the entrance which was between the prisoner and myself.

Once inside, the initial brief passage across the floor to a urinal is an opportunity to 'cruise' the two men who had inspired the initial entry. The absence of a detailed plan of the convenience makes it difficult to assert with any confidence the tactical considerations that informed the first officer's choice of urinal.[28] It is more apparent in the decision made by the second officer, who installs himself in a urinal at the entrance, and one might presume thereby an end urinal, and (as we later learn) one that is next to the first officer. As Humphreys noted, the tactical occupation of end urinals gives a person more room to manœuvre in the forthcoming play. In this instance, a position by the door would facilitate an arrest, particularly if the arrestee is attempting to escape. Furthermore, it perhaps suggests the preferred future role of this particular officer, that of 'watchqueen', keeping observation not only on those in the convenience but also on those approaching.

His original positioning next to the first officer is also of interest. In this context the officer performs a certain sexual precocity towards the other officer, if not for the attention of the officer himself then for the rest of the audience in the convenience. In *R. v. Ford* we see again the operation of this tactical consideration: '. . . a plain-clothes officer entered a public lavatory and was followed by X, a civil servant, who stood at the other end of the room from the officer'. Here again the design and the manners associated with these particular genital encounters come into play. The officer positions himself in an end urinal (as does X). In this instance, however, it would appear that neither plays the precocious 'coming on too strong' movement by positioning himself at the centre of the urinals, or in close proximity to another in the urinals.

Then, returning to our main drama, the record documents a certain manœuvring:

> After a short time the prisoner left the stall in which he was standing and came round towards me stopping near the stall on my left hand side. I then saw P.C. 565 ——— move round towards the stall which the prisoner had left.

Both the accused and the police engage in the performance of particular manœuvres to change position in relation to other persons and structures in the defined space. In doing so, each engages in body techniques that are designed to indicate both a willingness to proceed with the encounter and (possibly) preferences for future roles: players and/or lookouts.

Again it is important to remember that these events depend upon communication and occur in the context of interaction. In this respect the record is relatively impoverished. We are told little of the somatic practices by means of which these movements are negotiated. However, the fact that these manœuvres occur suggests that both police officers are performing their roles well, appearing as insiders rather than as outsiders.

The encounter continues:

> The prisoner then said to me 'Will you give me a light please?' He then walked behind me and took up a position in the stall immediately on my right, which P.C. 565 ——— had previously occupied.

This aspect of the police performance is of particular interest. It would appear to involve a violation of what Humphreys suggests is a taboo of speech associated with these encounters. This might be interpreted in various ways. It might be interpreted as the behaviour of a 'straight' or a novice, which might threaten to bring the proceedings to an early end. It might also be interpreted in this instance as a signal used to elicit whether the other person is willing to participate further, as evidenced in the manner of the response, which in this instance we never know.

Throughout this performance of surveillance the police officers who entered the convenience formally appear to be passive. However, as Humphreys has suggested, there is a need to be cautious in attempting to make sense of such behaviour. Within this context, Humphreys reminds us, aggressive or active and passive relate to systems of strategies not types of players. Thus a person may perform passivity by means of an 'aggressive' strategy in order to secure the offence. The speed with which the encounter appears to unfold might suggest that in this instance the immobility demonstrated by the first officer ought to be recognized as an aggressive practice.

The performance then reaches its climax:

> After a few minutes the prisoner made a half-turn towards me, stretched out his left arm and placed his left hand on my person and commenced rubbing it. I immediately took hold of his left arm, his left hand still being on my person. I said to him 'I am a Police Officer and I am going to take you into

custody for indecently assaulting me'. He said 'Not me, you have made a mistake'.

Here the police report documents a contracting gesture, 'he placed his hand on my person', and the unexpected pay-off, the arrest.

Using Humphreys's work it becomes possible to map some of the bodily techniques that the police deploy in this particular type of surveillance and examination procedure.[29] His work also draws attention to the limitations of the police accounts of these investigations. In general, the collective nature of the communication by which the encounters unfold in these situations draws our attention to the fact that the police report, while being exceptional in the detail it provides of the police practices in this context, is an impoverished description of events. For example, we learn little of the behaviour of the first officer as the performance progresses. In taking up the key role of narrator he appears to write his own passivity and exteriority into the text. This is in stark contrast to what is demonstrated in Humphreys's work about these encounters. His work would suggest that the progression that is documented in the officer's statement depends at least upon reciprocity and communication. In order for the performance to take place, the first police officer must necessarily be implicated in the communication event, receiving and transmitting information. As the encounter is dominated by silence this must have been done by movements of the body, hands, head, eyes, and so on. Body and hand movements carry the action through stages that, lacking conversation, might otherwise be impossible or at best awkward. There is no suggestion here that the unfolding event was awkward. The narrative evokes the opposite, emphasizing the speed of the encounter. Nor do we learn much of the somatic performance of the second officer. Even the second officer's own statement appears to narrate the story of the encounter from the perspective of the first officer.

In both statements the position of the narrator is of particular interest. The story that the narrator tells of his own role in this event is that of the 'watchqueen' and, more specifically, the voyeur. It presents police practice as passivity and, as Humphreys has noted, suggests that the police role is one that is not overtly sexual.

All these factors work to produce a document that has interesting characteristics. Not only is the detail relating to events central to the unfolding performance of a criminal act omitted, but there is also little detail of other events that are thought to be marginal to that event but central to generating a wider ambience of privacy and security, and are thereby central to it. For example, while there is an instance of an interruption in the officer's report: 'Two other men then entered the lavatory, one of them behind P.C. 565 —— and came around to the vacant stall directly on my left, the other man remaining near P.C. 565 —— ', we are told little either about the behaviour, if not of the police then maybe of the accused, that followed in order to establish the legitimacy of these newcomers, or of their exit prior to the climax of the encounter. The statements appear to erase the fact that the agents of the law, whose object is to secure a conviction, must either work the roles to ensure that they move towards becoming a player and more specifically that they must become a very particular player or in the final instance ensure that the narrative they construct for the court represents them as the 'passive victim': at best the voyeur or at worst the masturbatee or the insertor.

At best the statements record the event in retrospect. During the encounter, role flexibility and role drift make it difficult to determine roles. Humphreys's analysis draws attention to the fact that the roles taken up by the police (and the accused) solidify only in the moment of arrest or in retrospect, in the moment of their narration in the statement (Humphreys 1970: 49). In the narration the roles that crystallize in the endpoint, dictated by the agents of social control, are projected back into the event and organize it.

All these factors suggest that the report of the incident is far from a verbatim account of the somatic performance of all concerned. The documents attached to the statements also evidence an awareness of the problematic nature of this story and in particular the problem of police 'passivity'.

The point is raised by the Magistrate W.H.S. Oulton, Esq., at Tower Bridge Police Court (who would eventually deal with the prosecution arising out of the police operations documented in the statements). On the first appearance of the accused before the magistrate, bail was granted. Between this first appearance and the trial, a memorandum was produced and circulated to the police relating to some observations made by this magistrate dealing with the police practices used in this campaign. A denominator common to the surveillance operations and arrests was the fact that all the offences had been committed against plain-clothes police officers in circumstances similar to those outlined in the statement above. The magistrate drew particular attention to the third prosecution, which was heard just before the trial arising out of the incident documented in the statements above.

Here the accused, like the two defendants before him, had been charged with committing the offence of indecent assault under the Offences against the Person Act 1861 and with committing an act of indecency as under the London County Council Bye-Laws. Both charges referred to the accused placing his hand on the person of the police constable in a public urinal. At the hearing the first charge was not proceeded with. The accused was found guilty of the second charge. After passing sentence, the magistrate made the following remarks about the policing practices that had generated the charge and the court proceedings:

> In this class of offence I would protest against the method of obtaining evidence that is sometimes used. Whilst appreciating the difficulty of securing reliable testimony and the personal sacrifice of those obtaining it, it is in my opinion a sacrifice that a Police Officer should not be required to make. To invite and endure an insult to his manhood of a gross character, his own self esteem must suffer and it effects [sic] the dignity of the Force. I sincerely hope it will end.

> (PRO MEPO 3/990)

The magistrate issued a copy of these comments to a press reporter. They were also forwarded to the police by the chief clerk to the court and were reported back to the police through a report made by a police inspector on duty at the court.

The fourth accused detected by means of these plain-clothes policemen was to appear with his lawyer before the same magistrate the following day. In order to meet the possibility of a hostile reception from the magistrate, the police prepared a memorandum about the policing practices relating to these new proceedings and a copy was sent to the prosecuting solicitors.

The particular problem appears to relate to the fact that the police 'invite and endure' these acts of indecency. While 'endure' suggests that police participation might still be characterized as a passive practice (a certain unwillingness), in the final instance this fails to counteract the importance of the suggestion that the police play an active role in these encounters: they invite the unlawful act. In the suggestion that, as a result of this police practice, the officers' own self-esteem will suffer as will as the dignity of the Force, the magistrate appears to suggest that these practices not only invite perversion but the loss of esteem and dignity suggests that through these practices the officer and the Force might become perverted. Thereby involvement appears to raise serious problems of individual and institutional integrity. It appears to be a problem of how to fabricate a world but not to be in or of that world (see Humphreys 1970: 26–7).

The responses from the police confirm that it is this active or aggressive aspect of the police practice that is problematic. All stress the importance of passivity as evidenced in the fact that the police operations arise out of complaints by the public. However, thereafter this passivity becomes more difficult to maintain. A divergence in the description of the policing practice emerges. For example, the inspector on duty at the court merely describes the operation in the following terms: ' . . . of late a number of persons have been arrested and convicted on the evidence of Constables who have entered the urinal in plain clothes and have been indecently assaulted'. Here police practice is presented as benign or *ad hoc*. Likewise 'A/Superintendent' 'M' states that:

> At no time have any specific Police Officers been directed to pay special observation to detect offences at this lavatory and none of the Officers in these prosecutions have been concerned in more than one case.
>
> The result of Police activities show that the complaints were well founded.
>
> (PRO MEPO 3/990)

These observations are to be contrasted with the description of the operations offered by 'A/Superintendent'. He describes the operation in slightly different terms:

> [A]ll police especially those employed in plain clothes have been instructed to give the matter every attention with a view to detect and arrest offenders. Plain clothes officers in the ordinary course of their patrol have kept

observation on the urinal and enter it on occasion, with the result that several arrests have been made and convictions obtained.

Here the operation is presented as both special and routine. First, the special nature of the operation is emphasized. However this is swiftly disavowed in a declaration that it was routine. The latter is reinforced in a further observation that, 'In the present case the evidence was to the effect that the P.C. entered the urinal to relieve himself when the prisoner caught hold of his person, was arrested and charged with the offence.' Finally, 'D.A.C.4' offers the following description: 'As a result of complaints of acts of indecency between males taking place in this urinal, Police in uniform and plain clothes, have been directed from time to time to pay special attention to put a stop to this objectionable practice.' Here the special nature of the operation is routinized by way of 'from time to time'.

The final response to the magistrate's comments is contained in a the following policy statement produced by the Metropolitan Police:

'Confidential memorandum'

Numerous complaints have been received at a Police Station that a certain urinal was being frequented by perverts and that acts of indecency in it were of common occurrence, the attention of all ranks was drawn to the matter by means of remarks in the Rough Book by various officers (including the Sub-divisional Inspector) and Police were instructed generally to make special efforts to put a stop to the evil, no orders being given in regard to the nature of the action which should be taken. This resulted in four arrests and convictions, in each case the Police Constable in plain clothes being the object of an indecent assault. To obtain evidence, in each case the Police Constable elected to loiter in the urinal and to this extent to adopt the role of an agent provocateur.

When offences of this nature are complained of at any particular place, they must be put a stop to, but Police must not use methods which, in effect, provoke the commission of such offences. It is degrading to the individual officer and derogatory to the good name of the Force that Police officers should be permitted to lend themselves to such procedure.

Such offences can best be prevented by the activities of uniform police. Definite orders should be given by the S.D. Inspector to individual Uniform Patrols to visit frequently the place which has been complained about so by their visits to prevent any further complaints. It is better to prevent offences than to arrest.

Should it prove necessary in exceptional cases to employ men in plain clothes, Superintendents should see to it that suitable men are selected and that they are warned to avoid acting in such a manner as to lay themselves open to the suspicion of inviting the commission of an indecent assault.

(PRO MEPO 3/990)

Again, throughout the emphasis is upon the passivity of police practices. In the exceptional situation where plain-clothes officers are deployed their practice is to be confined.

Various features of this dialogue between the police and the magistrate are of interest. The first is the revelation by the magistrate, and the recognition by the police, that these police practices may not only involve the active promotion of genital encounters between men but more specifically require police officers to take part in these acts. The threat of perversion is based upon the fact that somatic practices of policing produce perversion; through the techniques of policing, perversion is first produced within the law in order that it may be detected outside the law, made an object of the law and made subject to the law. Thereby the supposed distance between perversion and the norm is threatened.

The second point of interest is the magistrate's demand that policing take a passive role. The various responses by the police officers demonstrate that this is an important requirement that not only helps to organize the way in which these police practices are to be made intelligible to the police but also is central to their public display. Finally, the 'confidential memorandum' draws attention to the techniques through which that passivity is to be achieved. In the first instance it is to be achieved by an emphasis upon prevention rather than detection. Second it is to be achieved by means of uniform patrols rather than plain-clothes operations. Third, where plain-clothes operations are to be used it is to be achieved by (unspecified) limitations upon police behaviour.

Many of these points were first made in two Royal Commission reports: the *Report of the Street Offences Committee* (Street Offences Committee 1928) and the *Report of the Royal Commission on Police Powers and Procedure* (Royal Commission 1929). Both reports concluded that the offences relating to the solicitation of men by men belonged to a different and much graver types of social offence than the solicitation of women by men (Royal Commission 1928: 13, para. 21) and that the police practices used to investigate and detect them, the use of plain-clothes officers, were particularly problematic. Here the nature of the risk was said to be in the fact that the police may become *agents provocateurs* and engage in entrapment (Royal Commission 1929: para. 201).

Starting with the assumption that the use of *agents provocateurs* was a rare practice,[30] the Royal Commission of 1929, drawing on the work of the 1928 Royal Commission, proceeded to develop an analysis of the problem and to propose general guidelines and to suggest some special measures to deal with the police practices in these cases. They noted that offences of public indecency gave the police general problems. The Royal Commission found that it was difficult for the police to adopt a passive stance with respect to these offences. On the one hand offences were being committed. On the other hand, even if members of the public had taken the step of complaining to the police they were apt to withhold their names and addresses, be extremely reluctant to give evidence in such cases and expect the police to act without their evidence. The result was that the law creating these offences would be almost a dead letter if cases were not decided on police evidence alone. Another problem related to the fact that the law relating to public indecency was to some extent designed to reflect the degree of public condemnation attaching to the particular conduct in question, in the light of the manners of the time. In their attempts to enforce the law without the active support of the public there was a danger of the police acting in some cases as arbiters of contemporary morals. They concluded that it was not the duty of the police, and that it was not right that any section of the public should impose such responsibility upon them. For this reason, they concluded, the police, so long as they were not supported by the active co-operation of individual citizens who were prepared to give evidence of annoyance, should not be expected to enforce any standard of decency that was not in accord with public opinion (Royal Commission 1929: 78–9, para. 208). As such, the Commission concluded that the police had no alternative but to take upon themselves the burden of proving public annoyance where the offence was flagrant and open (Royal Commission 1929: 77, para. 199). However, they went on to say that the police should confine themselves to dealing with offences of this kind that come to their notice when they are passing though places that are frequented by the public.

In general proceeding to investigate and detect such offences and thereby enforce these laws, the Royal Commission concluded, police practice should proceed on the basis that it is the primary duty of a constable to *prevent* the commission of crimes and offences (Royal Commission 1929: 6, para. 13). This was to be best secured by the use of uniformed police (Royal Commission 1929: 76, para. 204). Beyond that, the key issue relating to plain-clothes operations was what action, if any, a policeman may properly take beyond concealing his identity and observing what goes on (Royal Commission 1929: 41, para. 106).

The Commission was presented with different views on this point. One school of thought held that the duty of the police should be strictly confined to observation only and that they should not participate in the offences committed. To go beyond observation might induce a person to commit an offence that he would not otherwise have done. The other school of thought suggested that it was necessary that the police should participate in offences, although they should not in any event initiate them. This view was presented by a number of chief constables. One example of this type of police practice was given by the late Commissioner of Police of the Metropolis. It related to policing violations of licensing laws. In such situations, he concluded, if the police did not order drinks, 'they might just as well ring the bell and say who they were. No one could go into a night club and sit down at a table and not order any drink' (Royal Commission 1929: 41, para. 106). In this example he draws attention to the importance of the need to act like 'insiders', because to act otherwise than according to the dictates of the cultural context in which the police operations were taking place would be to reveal those officers as 'outsiders'. The Royal Commission suggested that neither of these two schools of thought lent any countenance whatever to a police practice of initiating offences with a view to enticing or entrapping members of the public into committing breaches of the law. Any such action, they concluded, would at once meet with the strongest disapproval (Royal Commission 1929: 41, para. 107).

As a general rule, they concluded, the police should observe only without participating in the offence (Royal Commission 1929: 42, para. 108). An exception would arise in a certain type of case in which observation without participation was, owing to the nature of the case, impossible (Royal Commission 1929: 42, para. 109). As an exception, participation could be resorted to only on the written permission of the Chief Constable (Royal Commission 1929: 42–3, para. 110). They recommended that more instruction should be given to constables by their superior officers as to the case with which these delicate duties should be carried out. In dealing with solicitation cases they recommended that when first discovered the offender should be warned. An arrest should follow subsequent incidents (Royal Commission 1929: 24, para. 55).

They also suggested that special provisions should be made to deal with plain-clothes operations. First, as policemen employed in plain clothes expose themselves to greater risk of temptations then when they are in uniform, plain-clothes officers should act in couples. Second, as a prolonged partnership of the same two officers would largely nullify the safeguards that the presence of a second officer affords, they also recommend that the men so employed should have their districts frequently changed. Finally, there should be an absolute prohibition of the use of plain-clothes police for the final step of arresting or taking the names of persons to be charged with indecent conduct. The use of plain-clothes police officers in this connection increases the risk of persons posing as police officers in plain clothes, in order to levy blackmail, and also affords special opportunities for bribery and corruption of the police themselves (Royal Commission 1929: 79). If adopted, full publicity should be given to this requirement so that the members of the public should be less liable to be imposed upon by blackmailers posing as police (Royal Commission 1929: 79).[31]

While the demand for uniformed operations and an emphasis on observation are offered as somatic practices remote from the sexuality of perversion and thereby safer practices of policing, in the return to accepting the somatic practices that are plain-clothes operations, the main general concern evidenced in these proposals appears to be the need to manage, and thereby provide better control of, those somatic practices. More specifically it appears to generate proposals for the further institutionalization of these somatic practices.

The statements of 1934 suggest that the reports had a very particular impact upon the practice of policing. They provided some of the key elements by which policing practice would now present itself; re-citing the formal complaint in its absence; emphasizing the police role as 'watchqueen'; writing the accused according to the needs of the aggressive player.

Many of these points are addressed in another Metropolitan Police document of the period (PRO MEPO 3/987). After hearing evidence at the Marylebone Street Police Court against X for persistently soliciting, the Magistrate Ivan Snell discharged the accused and made the following remarks about the investigative and recording practices of the police:

In this case, a difficulty has arisen, and I hope that what I am about to say will have no repercussions. This was the fourth case of the kind that had recently been before the Court, and in all, if I remember rightly, the evidence was similar. There is always one thing that happens – that during the course of observation, the chief officer, as a rule, goes upstairs and has a few minutes conversation with the one of the persons who is supposed to have been importuned down below, but in no case has that person ever been brought before me to corroborate the story of the police. That is in four cases recently. There are others further back. Each time I have thought to myself during the conduct of the case, 'Well, if they can bring that witness, that clinches the matter. It is a great disappointment, and I am thrust back on the situation of having to judge these cases on the word of two Police Officers, which was strenuously denied by the accused. Another very curious coincidence has happened in these four cases. It appears that in every case, the man was always doing exactly the same . . . as this man was doing. For a long period of time, he remained apparently with his penis in a state of erection, and was masturbating himself, and he called attention to it, during a period of nearly always about 20 minutes, to the persons to the left and right. Sometimes in some of the cases, it was to the Police Officers themselves, who were being importuned. In none of these cases did I hear of any person taking such a dislike to being importuned in that way that he struck, or made a remark to the person. I feel that the ordinary person who went into the lavatory and found a man masturbating, and turning towards him smiling at him, would take one of three courses. He would either call him names and say 'You dirty something', or laugh and tell somebody else of the amusing thing it was, doing such a thing, or he would encourage the man to do it, so as to accept the invitation. Curiously enough, in the four cases we have had in this short period of time, I do not think a man has taken any of these three courses. The only evidence was, that the man who was importuned frowned, or scowled, and then went away. These are curious coincidences. It is disappointing not to get something a bit different. I came to the conclusion yesterday that the next case I had, unless there were some other facts which were more definite, apart from the clear word of the Police Officers, I should have to insist that there must be something, because there is beginning at the back of my mind, a certain amount of suspicion. These two Officers have been watching in this lavatory, and have told me a story. I cannot say for one moment that they are not telling me a true story. But I was disappointed in not hearing something that would establish in my mind, that would make it stronger, and differentiate it from other cases. In these circumstances, you are going to have – perhaps you are lucky – the benefit of the fact that I have not had something more in this case stronger than the case against you. I know it is a very difficult thing. Police Officers are put there, and people won't come and help them. That is how the matter stands today, and you will be discharged.[32]

These observations draw attention to the way in which the statements and the evidence given to the court relating to police investigations in public conveniences tend to follow a particular formula. First the narrative emphasizes the passivity of the police. This takes various forms. The narrative is inaugurated by a complaint from 'a member of the public'. Thereafter the story focuses upon the aggressive actions of the accused and the passivity of all the other characters involved. Within this scheme of things the police emerge as the 'watchqueen' or voyeur. The magistrate's comments, however, draw attention to the problematic nature of this narrative, particularly if it is to be taken as an accurate representation of the event. In general, the magistrate's attention is drawn to the statement/evidence because it appears to be formula driven. As such he notes the repeated absence of the complainant who provoked the inquiry. He questions the repeated passivity of the other parties in the convenience encounter. Finally, he questions the passivity of the narrators, the police, in the production of the narrative. At the same time, ironically, he reinforces the demand for passivity that he has revealed is so problematic. Here the constant repetition of the narrative of passivity merely serves to reveal the aggressive practice of passivity.

CONCLUSION

This chapter has attempted to undertake an exploration of those police practices that are concerned with the legal production of the bodies and desires of men who have genital encounters with other men as homosexual (and previously as pervert and invert). The analysis has suggested that this homosexual (and the pervert and invert before it), rather than being something that is outside police practices, a disquieting enigma that always hides, an insidious presence that speaks in a voice so muted and often disguised that the police will remain deaf to it, and thereby a presence that might evade detection, is the product of these technologies and practices of the law. At best the silence that is connected to the homosexual in order to make its sense and nonsense is a requirement and an effect of the technologies of its production. This silence forms a part of the very mechanics of incitement and production that generate the homosexual in law. This requirement of silence is a prerequisite, generating a requirement to speak about the male genital body. As such, silence is indispensable to the proliferating economy of the discourse on this homosexual of the law. Through the principle of silence (and invisibility) that is installed in the machinery of policing is made the necessity of elaborate police practices and procedures to extract the truth of sex through the technique of surveillance and confession. In law, this male genital body is imagined as a body that is difficult to speak in order that it might be forced to speak (Foucault 1981a: 66). At the time of writing, the lesbian and gay press suggests that these practices are far from being a thing of the past.

The analysis draws attention to the fact that the truth of this male genital body as homosexual(ity) in law does not reside solely in the subject who, by confessing, would reveal it wholly formed. It is constituted, in law, in the final instance, not in the one who acted or spoke but in the one who assimilates and records it: the agents of the law. It is the latter's function to generate the science of this body of law: to catalogue its form, map its movements, verify its obscure truth through practices of surveillance and examination. Thus the machinery of policing is a machinery dedicated to producing the truth of the male genital body in law, where that body is but a sign, an obscure mark that had to be ferreted out and read or listened to (Foucault 1981a: 66–7). What is peculiar about these practices of the law is not that they consigned sex to a shadow existence but that they are dedicated to speaking of it and performing it with great zeal. Both making it the secret and exploiting it as the secret (Foucault 1981a: 35). The repeated assertion of the urgency with which these practices must be at best eradicated and at worst controlled, and their repeated return, suggests that they have a particular importance in the constitution of the culture of social order as a genital order and that the agents of the law have an important role in the production and transmission of that culture of social order as a genital order.

The analysis has drawn attention to the fact that these techniques of investigation are composed of a complex set of practices. They take the form of the production of an absent presence, by way of the construction of secret cupboards, the installation of fibre-optic technology and the construction and maintenance of 'glory-holes'. The cases and documents studied here also draw attention to a distinctive set of police practices or somatic techniques: police officers' endless cruising; the performance of a particular set of bodily gestures, such as the movement of the hands, the eyes, the head, the body in its relation to the urinal and to other bodies; the adoption of specific erotic sartorial codes, such as the ripped T-shirt, blue jeans, plaid shirt. Humphreys's work gives us an insight into the nature of these techniques. These police practices of the body are of particular importance. They draw attention to the importance of the production of the homosexual(ity) of law within police practices (and as such within the law) as a prerequisite to the production of homosexual(ity) as that which is outside the law. Here, in the name of eradicating homosexual(ity), policing as participant observation threatens to intensify and amplify the presence of homosexual(ity). This is confirmed by reference to the recent history of policing. Since the late 1940s, in the UK these police practices of homosexuality, largely confined to the police forces of England and Wales and more specifically to the police practices of the metropolis, have flourished and indeed become more and more insistent.[33] So those police practices formally dedicated to diminishing homosexual practices have been implicated in producing their increased social visibility.

But there is a need for caution here. Humphreys's analysis draws attention to the fact that the production of this male genital body by way of its male genital encounters in the text of the law is also a representation of this body that is profoundly impoverished. It is a body that is represented and recorded according to particular narratives. Thus, as the earlier analysis has demonstrated, while the machinery of policing documents various aspects of the silent ritual that escalates towards the climax demanded by the agents of the law, this documentation must tell

167

a particular story that marginalizes the productive nature of the law in general and the performance of homosexual(ity) by the agents of the law in particular.[34] These narratives are produced according to particular considerations of intelligibility that install a certain systematic blindness, a refusal to see and to understand the nature of the encounter, a refusal concerning the very thing that was brought to light and whose formulation was urgently solicited (Moran 1995). Choosing not to recognize appears here as yet another vagary of the will to truth (Foucault 1981a: 55).

The smiling plain-clothes policeman who engages in (pseudo-)masturbation (Crane 1982: 49) has only recently begun to appear in the texts produced by those organizations who work outside the parameters of the criminalizing and patholo-gizing frames of reference that organize the narration of these encounters. Their appearance draws attention to the way in which the agents of the law provide a hierarchy of personnel who keep watch, organize, provoke, monitor and report. They are an immense apparatus for producing truth. The police practices operate as a continuous incitement to discourse and to truth even if this truth were to be masked at the last moment (Foucault 1981a: 56). They are a machinery of law that makes legal practice a practice of voyeurism. They institutionalize a set of practices that install legal practice as a certain exhibitionism.[35] Thereby the male genital body in its male genital relations is produced as a specific homosexual(ity) of law and it is by these mechanisms and practices that this body of law is kept alive. Police practices in the twentieth century suggest that there was undoubtedly an increase in effectiveness and an extension of this domain of production.

8

THE USES OF HOMOSEXUALITY
Rights, victims and parliamentary reform

The headlines in the media in general, and in the lesbian and gay press in particular, suggest that contemporary law and legal practice in the United Kingdom has a lot to say in general about genital relations between persons of the same sex and in particular about genital relations between men. They point to the significance of same-sex genital relations in the context of the regulation of the workplace, in legal relations concerned with the family, in housing, in pensions rights and interests, in the regulation of communications and the media, in the administration of the law, and in the context of the legal powers of local government. Last but not least, many of the headlines draw attention to the importance of genital relations between men in the criminal law and those laws governing the various institutions that administer the criminal justice system. All in their different ways suggest that the current law has a lot to say about homosexuality.

However, a survey of the legal rules contained in Acts of Parliament and the Common Law rules, made by the judiciary and found in the text of their judgments, gives a very different picture of homosexual(ity) in the law. Neither 'homosexual' nor 'homosexuality' appears in any law relating to employment matters, family legislation or pensions law. Nor are these terms to be found in laws dealing with the media. Neither the law that regulates prisons nor the law that creates and regulates the administration of justice resorts to them. Even the criminal law, which has for so long and so extensively provided the material for the headlines, still has only one formal reference to homosexual: the Sexual Offences Act 1967.

A search through the law reports, which contain a selection of judicial pronouncements relating to the interpretation of statute law (otherwise silent with respect to homosexual(ity)) and statements of the rules of judge-made law, produces a slightly different picture of the place of homosexual(ity) in the law. These reports provide a richer source of references to homosexual(ity) and in part they can provide an insight into the disjunction between the apparent high profile of the concern with genital relations between persons of the same sex in contemporary law suggested by the lesbian and gay press and the poverty of references to homosexual(ity) in the formal collection of the law.

This chapter seeks to explore this state of affairs. In undertaking this exploration the chapter will also be concerned with a more specific issue: the uses of 'homosexual(ity)' in the law subsequent to the reforms of the Sexual Offences Act 1967. These matters will be pursued by way of a series of case studies. The first case studies will consider the introduction of 'homosexual' in the context of rules that are silent on that matter. One of the cases considered, *Knuller* v. *DPP*, allows us to consider the significance of the Sexual Offences Act 1967 in this context. Thereafter the case studies focus upon three important instances where homosexuality has been addressed. The first deals with the interface between homosexuality and human rights. The second considers the interface between homosexuality and law in the context of a dispute that arose out of a recent large-scale police operation code-named 'Operation Spanner'. Here the courts were required to return to the meaning of the phrase 'homosexual acts' in the context of what were described in the proceedings as acts of 'homosexual sado-masochism'. The final example to be considered here will address the debates about homosexuality that led to the most recent reform of the law on homosexuality in the UK: an amendment to the 1967 Sexual Offences Act to reduce the 'age of consent' from 21 to 18.

READING 'HOMOSEXUAL' INTO THE LAW

The first case study focuses upon the reported decisions in two cases: *Masterson* v. *Holden* (*Masterson* 1986) and *Knuller* v. *DPP* (*Knuller* 1971, 1972). Each deals with the way in which 'homosexual' might be read into the law in a different context. The first case deals with reading 'homosexual' into statute law that is otherwise silent on the matter of homosexuality. The second explores the addition of 'homosexual' in the context of law made by the judges, case law. The second case is of significance in another way. It provides an opportunity to consider the interface between these practices of reading 'homosexual' into the law and the 1967 reforms found in the Sexual Offences Act of that year, which formally introduced the term 'homosexual' into the law.

The law reports reveal that, with the exception of the Sexual Offences Act 1967 and s. 28 of the Local Government Act 1988, in the context of statute law, 'homosexual(ity)' is always read into a written law that is otherwise silent on the matter. One example will be taken to illustrate this aspect of the legal practice of homosexual(ity). The case report of *Masterson and another* v. *Holden* (*Masterson* 1986) relates to an appeal from the South Westminster Magistrates Court. The appeal arose out of a prosecution brought under s. 54 of the Metropolitan Police Act 1839. So far as is material the section provides that:

> Every Person shall be liable to a Penalty... who, within the Limits of the Metropolitan Police District, shall, in any Thoroughfare or public Place, commit any of the following Offences.... Every Person who shall use any threatening, abusive or insulting Words or Behaviour with intent to provoke a Breach of the Peace, or whereby a Breach of the Peace may be occasioned...

Masterson and Cooper were found guilty of this offence. The criminal proceedings related to an incident in the early hours of the morning on Oxford Street, in central

London. Masterson and Cooper, we are told, were seen 'to be engaging in overt homosexual behaviour' (*Masterson* 1986: 39). The magistrates found that this 'homosexual behaviour' took the following form. Cooper, we are told,

> ...rubbed the back of Masterson with his right hand and later Cooper moved his hand from Masterson's back and placed it on Masterson's bottom and squeezed his buttocks. Cooper then placed his hand on Masterson's genital area and rubbed his hand around this area. The defendants continued kissing and cuddling.
>
> (*Masterson* 1986: 40)

While homosexual(ity) does not appear in the formal words of the statute it appears twice through the legal practices that are central to production of the final decision of the tribunal. First, 'homosexual' is used once in making the sense (and nonsense) of the behaviour of Masterson and Cooper in the legal proceedings. It is used a second time in making the sense (and nonsense) of the key statutory phrase 'insulting behaviour'. Here, in the final instance, a particular sense and nonsense of 'homosexual' is installed in the law. The sense and nonsense of this 'homosexual' of law is made as insulting behaviour. In turn the legal sense (and nonsense) of 'insulting behaviour' is made through this 'homosexual' of law. Here homosexual(ity) is made in the law by means of a legal practice of interpretation. That practice of interpretation is a practice of representation that not only relates to the formal language of the law 'insulting behaviour' but is also a practice of imagining the body and more specifically imagining the male genital body in its male genital relations. These two instances of representation are intimately connected. The two bodies of Masterson and Cooper as male genital bodies are imagined or represented in the law in a particular way; as homosexual where homosexual is insult. In turn, the law, 'insulting behaviour' is made in the image of these two male genital bodies: as 'homosexual'. Thereby the sense (and nonsense) of the two bodies concerned is made in the law and the law is made in an image of their two bodies.[1]

Case reports also draw our attention to the uses of homosexual(ity) within the context of a second source of law; the unwritten rules of law or judge-made law. Like statute law, the reports demonstrate that homosexual(ity) appears despite the formal absence of a concern with such matters in the common law. An example of the place of homosexual(ity) in the context of these judge-made rules can be found in the legal proceedings brought against the publisher and staff of a magazine, *International Times*. The legal proceedings are known by the title *Knuller* v. *DPP* (Court of Appeal, 1971, and the House of Lords, 1972).

The case related to a prosecution under two judge-made rules; of conspiracy to corrupt public morals (a common-law offence the existence of which had only recently been confirmed by a majority decision in the highest tribunal in the UK, the House of Lords, in the case of *Shaw* v. *DPP* (*Shaw* 1962)) and conspiracy to outrage public decency.[2] Knuller, the publisher of *International Times*, and various individuals who were the directors, editor and writers on the magazine were charged with these judge-made offences. The offences related to the publication of a number of contact advertisements by men for men. All the defendants were found guilty. The company was initially fined £1,500 and required to pay £500 costs. The other three defendants were each sentenced to concurrent terms of imprisonment of eighteen months and twelve months suspended for two years. Each was ordered to pay £200 towards the costs of the prosecution.

In the first instance, 'homosexual' is again notable by dint of its absence from the law as demonstrated by the description of the offences. In the counts that set out the detail of the offences charged, the advertisements that are the object of attention are described as 'advertisements for the purpose of sexual practices taking place between male persons... with intent thereby to debauch and corrupt the morals as well of youth as of divers other liege subjects' (*Knuller* 1971: 316), and 'lewd, disgusting and offensive advertisements' (*Knuller* 1971: 316). These charges draw attention to the absence of 'homosexual' from the law's formal vocabulary. At the same time, they remind us of the fact that this absence does not necessarily inhibit either the inauguration of proceedings in particular or attempts to imagine the male genital body in its genital relations with other male bodies in the law. Law proceeds to represent the male genital body in its genital relations by way of its idiosyncratic lexicon.

While 'homosexual' is formally absent it does appear in this case. In fact it is central to the determination of the tribunals whose judgments are recorded in the law reports. 'Homosexual' appears in the attempts to make the sense (and nonsense) of the contact advertisements for the law. Evidence of its use is found in the judgments. Here the advertisements are described in terms slightly different those found in the formal charge. Here they are described as advertisements for the purpose of inducing or encouraging homosexual acts. In the Court of Appeal, Lord Justice Fenton Atkinson described one of the advertisements in the following terms:

'Young gay [and 'gay' in this context means homosexual] male desperately needs to earn £40 as soon as possible. Will do anything legal. Genuine replies only please.'

(*Knuller* 1971: 317)

Later he explained that the advertisement, 'Gay active bodybuilder required for a very lucrative weekend', was 'a financial inducement being held out in return for homosexual services' (*Knuller* 1971: 317). In these examples, Lord Justice Fenton Atkinson translates the advertisements from one vernacular, that of the magazine subculture in general and a sexual subculture in particular, into the vernacular of another culture for a different purpose, that of the law. His insistence upon the use of 'homosexual' (in contrast to 'gay') is of particular importance. Here, he demonstrates the way in which contemporary legal practice not only resorts informally to 'homosexual' but also makes that informal use of 'homosexual' compulsory in order to conquer other possible meanings and reduce them to a meaning dictated by and through the law. Thus in making sense and nonsense of these advertisements as references to the male genital body in its male genital relations, those bodies and relations must be imagined in and for the law by way of homosexual(ity).

'Homosexual' appears a second time in the legal practices through which sense (and nonsense) of the law is made. In this instance, the sense of the law had to be made formally by way of the phrase, 'conspiracy to corrupt public morals'. The judgments demonstrate that homosexual(ity) is central to the making of a sense of that phrase. In the text of the judgments, the significance of homosexual(ity) in the making of this sense is emphasized in part because this dispute arose after the Sexual Offences Act 1967, which formally introduced 'homosexual' into the domain of law. On the one hand counsel for the defendants had argued that the 'homosexual' introduced by the 1967 Act installed that term in law with a specific meaning. It was introduced to designate certain acts that are no longer to be subject to prohibition through the criminal law. Counsel concluded that, by reason of that Act of decriminalization, the homosexual(ity) of law should no longer be read as corruption (or corruption as homosexual(ity)).

Both the Court of Appeal and the House of Lords rejected that attempt to attribute a meaning to 'homosexual' in law. In response to this argument, in the Court of Appeal, Lord Justice Fenton Atkinson reproduced two extracts from the judgments of Lord Simonds and Lord Tucker, who had given judgments in the earlier case of *Shaw* v. *DPP.* In both of the extracts from that case, which related to the publication of a directory of female prostitutes, these judges had resorted to 'homosexual' as a metaphor for extreme corruption. In turn, both quotations were used to suggest that this particular representation of 'homosexual' would persist beyond any reform of the law that might decriminalize certain homosexual practices between consenting adult males in private. Thus, for Lord Justice Fenton Atkinson, the formal introduction by Parliament of 'homosexual' to refer to a category of acts that were no longer to be designated criminal by virtue of the Sexual Offences Act 1967 did not alter the possibility of 'homosexual' being deployed in law as a metaphor of extreme corruption. He concluded that 'the fact that Parliament has now said that acts of this kind between adults in private shall not be a crime does not carry with it in our view the consequence that such conduct may not be calculated to corrupt public morals' (*Knuller* 1971: 319).

In part, the judges explain the continuation of the capacity of 'homosexual' to represent extreme corruption by reference to the role of the jury; it is up to the jury to decide what is and what is not corrupting. However, the role of the jury should be placed in the context of the fact that the judge must direct the jury as to the parameters of corruption and Parliament may determine what is or is not capable of signifying corruption.

In the House of Lords, Lord Reid explained the continued capacity of homosexual(ity) to stand for corruption by resort to the 'homosexual' of the Sexual Offences Act 1967. He concluded that there was:

> . . . nothing in the Act to indicate that Parliament thought or intended to lay down that indulgence in these practices is not corrupting. I read the Act as

saying that, even though it may be corrupting, if people chose to corrupt themselves in this way that is their affair and the law will not interfere. But no licence is given to others to encourage the practice.

(*Knuller* 1972: 904)

In that event, he concluded, it was still possible for a homosexual(ity) of the law to signify the male genital body as extreme corruption and was thus within the parameters of this homosexual(ity) of the law for a jury to proceed on the basis that homosexual(ity) is corruption within the law. Thus the sense of the legal rule of conspiracy to corrupt as homosexual(ity) is made in making a sense of homosexual(ity) as corruption in law.

These two cases also have a wider significance. Both provide an insight that can help to explain the gap between the formal absence of references to homosexual(ity) in the law and the law's wide-ranging concern with inter-male genital relations. First, in both instances they draw our attention again to the fact that same-sex relations might be produced within the law not by way of a language of law dominated by a homo/heterosexual binary opposition but by means of the idiosyncratic lexicon of archaic terms remote from the language of sexuality: insulting, conspiracy, corruption. While much of this study has focused upon an analysis of the place of one specific archaic term, the cases of *Masterson* and *Knuller* suggest that the analysis that has been undertaken in that specific context could be pursued in the context of a wider range of archaic terms. These might include assault, attempt, blasphemy, conspiracy, corruption of good manners, deprave, disgraceful conduct, disorderly conduct, gross indecency, importune, immoral purpose, indecent, infamous manner, injure the public interest, insulting behaviour, obscenity, outraging public decency, rogue, scandalous actions, solicit, uncleanness, unreasonable behaviour, vagrancy. Each might provide a different context in which the male genital body might be represented in the law but not one that is necessarily remote from that explored in the context of buggery. Second, these cases draw attention to the fact that, in the absence of specific references to homosexual(ity) in the statutes and judge-made rules of law, a homosexual(ity) of the law might be produced in contrast to the archaic terms, through the legal practices of reading and interpretation and in the practices of the administration of the law.[3]

HUMAN RIGHTS

The second case study looks at the interface between law and homosexual(ity) in the context of litigation about human rights. In the conjunction between homosexual(ity) and rights – and more specifically in calling these rights 'human rights' – a very particular strategy is embarked upon. Here the politicization of a specific identity and desire is conjoined with a distinctive juridical agenda that has been described as 'one of the monumental legacies left by the Enlightenment' (Gaete 1993). Here 'homosexual' is mobilized in intimate association with juridical themes of authenticity, final truth, rationality, humanity and legitimacy. My study involves the analysis of a particular judgment of the Court of the European Convention of Human Rights that deals with the homosexual(ity) of the law found in the 1967 Act as a human rights issue: *Dudgeon* v. *United Kingdom* (1982).

Dudgeon v. *United Kingdom* is a dispute that is of particular interest. The case frames the conjunction between homosexual(ity) and human rights in a specific context, Article 8[4] of the European Convention of Human Rights. By way of Article 8, Dudgeon claimed that the total criminalization of homosexual conduct carried out in private between consenting adults was an interference with the right to respect for private life and not justified as necessary in a democratic society. The European Commission of Human Rights (*Dudgeon* 1981) and a majority of the European Court of Human Rights (*Dudgeon* 1982) agreed. The decisions of these two bodies have a particular connection with the Wolfenden review in various ways. First, Dudgeon's claim was for the application of the Sexual Offences Act 1967 to Northern Ireland. Second, in concluding that the 1967 Act should be applicable to Northern Ireland the result of the case effectively mimics the Wolfenden reform proposals to decriminalize certain genital acts between men. At the same time, however, the decisions produced by these institutions of the European Convention of Human Rights differ from the Wolfenden review and the 1967 Act in a radical way, in that they frame that project of decriminalization as a project of recognition and respect for human rights, a matter that had been directly addressed and specifically dismissed in the course of the Wolfenden review (Moran 1996). The focus of analysis here is to begin to understand how the sense of the conclusions arrived at in the European Court of Human Rights becomes not only thinkable but thinkable in such a way as to render other solutions difficult if not impossible. The particular motif that I want to focus upon is the idea(s) of homosexual(ity) invoked by the use of 'homosexual' in these proceedings. This will be pursued by way of an analysis of the judgments of the Court.

In the majority opinion in support of Dudgeon's application we find the deployment of a particular idea of 'homosexual'. Its use is illustrated in the following examples:

> The applicant has, on his own evidence, been consciously homosexual from the age of 14.
>
> (*Dudgeon* 1982: para. 32)

> ... his private life (which includes his sexual life) ... he is disposed by reason of his homosexual tendencies ...
>
> (*Dudgeon* 1982: para. 41)

> The Convention right affected by the impugned legislation protects an essentially private manifestation of the human personality.
>
> (*Dudgeon* 1982: para. 60)

Judge Walsh (a dissenting judge) draws attention to the particular characteristics of the 'homosexual' that is articulated in these examples. He explains it in the following terms:

> However it is to be acknowledged that the case for the applicant was argued on the basis of the position of a male person who is by nature homosexually predisposed or orientated. The Court, in the absence of evidence to the contrary, has accepted this as the basis of the applicant's case and in its Judgment rules only in respect of the males who are so homosexually orientated (see for example paras 32, 41 and 60 of the Judgment).
>
> (*Dudgeon* 1982: para. 12)

Here Judge Walsh draws attention to the way in which 'homosexual' is used to represent identity as a conscious awareness of self that is long-standing. It is made to stand for the applicant's very personality. As such this 'homosexual' has a strong ontological focus. More specifically this 'homosexual' imagines this male genital body as congenital. In articulating the ontological and aetiological themes of 'congenital' it is also important to note that this assertion is not so much a manifestation of 'homosexual' that directly addresses and resolves or refuses the possibility of other ideas of 'homosexual', in particular one that emphasizes the pervert as an acquired ontological condition, but is an instance of a use of 'homosexual' where those other themes have at best been displaced, and more specifically displaced in a particular way. In fact, in *Dudgeon* these other ontological and aetiological themes of 'homosexual' are displaced from the majority judgments only to return with vigour in the 'homosexual' of the dissenting judges. The judgment of Judge Walsh provides a clear example of the use of this other idea of 'homosexual' for human rights.

It appears in the following extract:

> The fact that a person consents to take part in the commission of homosexual acts is not proof that such person is sexually orientated by nature in that direction. A distinction must be drawn between homosexuals who are such because of some kind of innate instinct or pathological constitution judged to be incurable and those whose tendency comes from a lack of normal sexual development or from a habit or from experience or from other similar causes but whose tendency is not incurable.
>
> (*Dudgeon* 1982: para. 12)

The significance of 'homosexual' as this dichotomy is explained in the following terms:

> It is not essentially different to describe the 'private life' protected by Article 8(1) as being confined to the private manifestation of the human personality. In any given case the human personality in question may in private life manifest dangerous or evil tendencies calculated to produce ill-effects upon himself or upon others.
>
> (*Dudgeon* 1982: para. 8)

A stark contrast is drawn here between Judge Walsh's use of 'homosexual', where the ontological and aetiological themes of acquired/pervert is celebrated, and the 'homosexual' of the majority with its emphasis on the congenital. Here Judge Walsh not only introduces the 'homosexual' in terms of a dichotomy, of pervert–invert, acquired–congenital, but also maps that dichotomy according to a logic of good and evil. For Judge Walsh, 'homosexual' is mobilized to name an ontology and aetiology of danger and evil. Here Judge Walsh engages in a celebration of 'homosexual' that has particular characteristics. On the one hand, it demands the congenital as it is the congenital that stands for the original evil and corrupt state. By way of the congenital the possibility of the acquired state as future corruption is given meaning. Here this male genital body as homosexual is imagined as corruption and contagion. Another image of corruption haunts his imagining of homosexual. It is presented in the following terms:

> It is known that many male persons who are heterosexual or pansexual indulge in these acts not because of any incurable tendency but for sexual excitement.

Here corruption is shown to haunt the imagination of Judge Walsh in a more pervasive way. It is imagined as being more closely aligned with desire itself and with pleasure in general and not with a specific identity or a specific genital body. This homosexual(ity) as corruption appears to be transformed into the figure of the heterosexual or the pansexual who may engage in male-to-male genital relations for sexual pleasure. Here corruption is a universal potential and homosexual(ity) is nothing more than an acquired state.

It is important to recognize that this is another 'homosexual' for human rights. In its conjunction with human rights it produces that rights project as a very specific project. This is a rights project framed by demands for treatment and eradication. This is explained by Judge Walsh in a particular way. He explains it in the following terms:

> So far as the incurable category is concerned, the activities must be regarded as abnormalities or even as handicaps and treated with the compassion and tolerance which is required to prevent those persons from being victimized in respect of tendencies over which they have no control and for which they are not personally responsible.
>
> (*Dudgeon* 1982: para. 12)

Here 'homosexual' is used to imagine a sense of self that is, in essence, 'victim'. In this instance, homosexual(ity) is made victim by an anonymous actor. Judge Walsh then proceeds:

> However, other considerations are raised when these tendencies are translated into activities. The corruption for which the Court acknowledges the need for control and the protection of the moral ethos of the community

177

referred to by the Court may be closely associated with the translation of such tendencies into activities.

(*Dudgeon* 1982: para. 12)

Here the male genital body in its male-to-male relations as homosexual is victimized a second time. This is the legitimate victimization of State-sponsored control. Here homosexual(ity) is used to imagine a victimization in the name of human rights and for human rights.

These observations draw attention to the fact that two very different but related ideas of homosexual(ity) might be put to work in the various opinions dealing with the fabrication of a connection between homosexual (and we might add gay and queer) and human rights. If there is this ambivalence in the connection between homosexual and human rights how might we explain the nature of the connection that is made between the various different ideas of homosexual in the *Dudgeon* decision and their connection with human rights in the majority opinion?

Again we might start with an astute observation made by Judge Walsh. He suggested that:

The judgment of the Court does not constitute a declaration to the effect that the particular homosexual practices which are subject to penalty by the legislation in question virtually amount to fundamental human rights. However, that will not prevent it being hailed as such by those who seek to blur the essential difference between homosexual and heterosexual activities.

(*Dudgeon* 1982: para. 19)

Judge Walsh is right to point out that in general the citation of 'homosexual' in the judgment of the majority, and the success of Dudgeon's demand for decriminalization in the name of human rights, need not be read as a declaration of a necessary or inevitable connection between homosexual (or gay or queer) and human rights. More specifically it need not be taken as a use of 'homosexual' to name a subject who might claim human rights in the name of that subject. The latter outcome might be explained in various ways. The juridical subject of human rights in general, and in particular of the human right to respect for private life, might not be a juridical subject as homosexual subject, but might merely be a juridical subject as human subject. Some support for the conclusion that the subject of human rights is only ever the human subject might be found in Article 14 of the Convention, which suggests that the juridical subject of the Convention is neither sexed, gendered, raced, nor to be defined over against any other of the categories of otherness listed therein. As the judgment of the Court in *Dudgeon* suggests (in their rejection of an argument based upon Article 14) the juridical subject of Article 8 has not been divided by way of homosexual(ity) as a category of the other. There is no need to give specific attention to homosexual(ity) as a violation of the prohibition that is placed upon any attempts to fragment the ontology of the juridical subject.

On the other hand, the use of 'homosexual' as congenital does appear to have some particular significance in the majority judgments. While the particular ontological and aetiological claims, as the natural and the inborn, might not ultimately form the formal juridical subject of human rights, they do have a particular resonance within the context of the rhetoric of legal humanism through which the juridical subject of human rights is imagined. Here the juridical subject of human rights is imagined as a subject position in law grounded in the true self, and in an idea of authentic identity, the congenital self.[5] The use of 'homosexual' to imagine the embodied subject as an authentic subject precedes and conditions the formation of that subject as a juridical subject of human rights (Gaete 1993: 19). Within this scheme of things, the *Dudgeon* decision demonstrates that the 'homosexual' as congenital is of some importance, as it is in this use of 'homosexual' as authenticity that the male genital body is always already the embodied subject of human rights.

Judge Walsh's observation perhaps has another significance here. The homosexualization of human rights that Judge Walsh recognizes as a possibility arising out of the *Dudgeon* decision might also be the end of homosexualization, in that the juridical subject that is imagined there in the success of the claim is not a sexualized subject. Judge Walsh seeks not only the power to name the authentic subject of human rights but also seeks the capacity to determine the condition under which that name is used. However, his comments draw our attention to the problematic nature of such attempts at mastery; it is impossible to sustain that kind of mastery over the trajectory of categories within (legal) discourse. Finally, Judge Walsh's observation draws attention to the fact that the subject position is that which must precede not only the subject but also the moment of its citation.

In the connection of authenticities, of human and homosexual, lies both the impossibility and possibility of homosexual rights. That possibility and impossibility are not only repeated in the imaginings of those outside the law that cite the 'homosexual' of *Dudgeon*, but are also a part of the practices of the Court in subsequent judgments, such as those of *Norris v. Ireland* (*Norris* 1989) and *Modinos v. Cyprus* (*Modinos* 1993). But the *Dudgeon* decision also demonstrates something more. The connection between homosexual and human rights is not exhausted in securing a subject position for rights. Another intelligibility of 'homosexual' is also imaginable and always already installed in the conjunction of homosexual and human rights. This produces very different effects. Here 'homosexual' is not so much the subject of human rights but a possible victim for human rights and thereby the limits of human rights.[6]

The conjunction of homosexual and human rights is of particular interest in various ways. It draws attention to the fact that resort to 'homosexual' (and in turn 'gay' and 'queer') for a juridical agenda is to engage in an act of naming that is always already an engagement with the histories of usage that one never controlled, that constrain but also create the very possibility of emblematizing subjectivity both within the law and beyond. It is also of interest in the way that the majority decision in *Dudgeon* inflects the 'homosexual' of the law found in the Sexual Offences Act 1967 in a way that is remote from that which informed its production in that Act. Thus while the 'homosexual' of *Dudgeon* might in the first instance appear as a mere repetition and thereby a re-production of the same, the analysis suggests that when produced in the context of a human rights provision its repetition is far from being a re-production of the same. In the context of the conjunction of homosexual and human rights, it preserves its ambivalence and at the same time it is given a very specific inflection. In this instance the ambivalence is inflected by way of particular ontological and aetiological themes. The ambivalence draws attention to the need to take account of the production of 'homosexual' within this particular juridical context. In each moment it is a contingent way of imagining the male genital body as a final or absolute representation of that body as object and subject in law. As such, 'homosexual' works as both a present (and future) possibility and a limit. Finally, it is important to recall that the interpretation of the 'homosexual' of the Sexual Offences Act 1967 is a use of 'homosexual' for human rights, which is a radical departure from the logic of 'homosexual' that informed the process and proceedings though which 'homosexual' entered English law.

THE HOMOSEXUAL OF SADO-MASOCHISM

The next example of a use of 'homosexual' to be considered here emerged in the context of an extensive police investigation, code-named 'Operation Spanner', which began in 1987[7] and proceeded to haunt the domestic legal system, as *R. v. Brown*, until 11 March 1993, when the Judicial Committee of the House of Lords sitting as the final court of appeal in England and Wales published a collection of opinions dealing with charges that raised questions about the legality of certain acts between men.[8] Through these various encounters, over forty men were arrested. Sixteen men were charged and found guilty. As a result of the criminal proceedings fourteen of the sixteen defendants lost their jobs, several lost their homes and some lost their good health (Kershaw 1992; *Brown* 1992a: 310). The original sentences imposed upon the individuals who performed these consensual acts included terms of imprisonment of over four years. Homosexual(ity) was made to occupy an interesting place in the course of these lengthy proceedings. On the one hand, the 'fact' of homosexual(ity) dominated the proceedings. Lord Lane, who gave the judgment for the Court of Appeal, explained the consensual acts by men with other men performed in private homes that were the object of these proceedings in the following terms: 'The appellants belonged to a group of sado-masochistic homosexuals' (*Brown* 1992b: 495). In turn, this was repeatedly asserted in the House of Lords.[9] The suggestion that these sado-masochistic acts are 'homosexual' acts is of particular interest. On the other hand, the men were formally charged and, by means of a majority of the judges in the House of Lords (three to two), finally found guilty, not of 'homosexual acts' or 'homosexual offences' but of wrongful acts that were named in law as acts of unlawful violence, being assaults occasioning actual bodily harm or acts of unlawful wounding.[10] The judiciary in both appeal courts work to produce the 'truth' of these acts and the 'facts' of these bodies and their desires. The appearance and disappearance of homosexual from the representation of these bodies is the focus of this analysis.[11]

The application of 'homosexual' to these men and these practices is of interest in various ways. First, the deployment of 'homosexual' was not a practice peculiar to the prosecution or unique to those giving judgment against the men. 'Homosexual' was invoked in this instance by the defendants.[12] They argued that as 'homosexual acts' their sado-masochistic performances were protected from prosecution both by virtue of the formal definition of 'homosexual offences' in the Sexual Offences Act 1967, which decriminalized certain 'homosexual acts' between men in limited circumstances, and by virtue of the decision of the Court of the European Convention of Human Rights, *Dudgeon* v. *United Kingdom* (1982), which outlawed the criminalization of certain 'homosexual acts' as contrary to human rights, in particular contrary to Article 8 of the European Convention of Human Rights, which seeks to secure respect for the individual's private life. The judges were forced, thereby, to address the 'homosexual' of these acts and persons.

In response to these formal arguments, which sought to deploy 'homosexual', Lord Lane, in the Court of Appeal, and the majority of the judges in the House of Lords (*Brown* 1994: 233–4, 245–6, 256 B–D) concluded that the defendants were not entitled to the protection afforded either by the 'homosexual' of the Sexual Offences Act 1967 or under the European Convention of Human Rights. In short, they concluded that homosexual sado-masochistic acts were not formally homosexual acts.[13]

In part the judicial conclusion that these acts of homosexuals were not homosexual acts might be explained by reference to the formal definition of 'homosexual acts' found in the law in s. 1(7) of the Sexual Offences Act 1967, which states that:

> a man shall be treated as doing a homosexual act if, and only if, he commits buggery with another man or commits an act of gross indecency with another man or is a party to the commission by a man of such an act.

As none of the acts related to either acts of anal penetration or acts preparatory to such penetration between men they were not 'homosexual offences' by way of buggery. However, this formal argument fails in the context of gross indecency.[14] Lord Jauncey in the House of Lords noted that the activities before the court were 'necessarily' acts of gross indecency, being an exhibition that had some proximity or reference to the genitals performed by two or more male persons in the presence of each other. As such these acts were capable of being formally defined as 'homosexual acts' under the 1967 Act and thereby potentially protected from prosecution.

However, ultimately this did not prevent the judges in both the Court of Appeal and in the House of Lords rejecting the argument that the acts that were the object of attention were 'homosexual acts'. In general, the reason given in support of the rejection of the defendants' resort to 'homosexual' is that these acts were not homosexual acts but acts of violence.[15] Thus these acts were to be given a very specific formal meaning. Once named the acts of homosexuals, the (homo)sexual[16] was to be displaced and the acts were to be named merely as acts of violence.

However, at the same time that the 'homosexual' was to be denied by the judges, the judges repeatedly asserted it in persisting with the idea that these acts were performed by homosexuals.

One explanation for the determination to name these 'homosexual acts' of gross indecency as acts of violence might be found in the tactical factors that informed the decision of the police and prosecution not to charge the men with acts of gross indecency. The Sexual Offences Act 1967 imposes a time limit on prosecutions.[17] Section 7 of the 1967 Act states that no prosecution may be commenced more than twelve months after the date on which the alleged offence was committed. Some of the charges before the court related to incidents that had, at the time of the House of Lords appeal, occurred fourteen years previously.[18] Naming the genital sado-masochistic acts of all male encounters not as 'homosexual acts' but as acts of violence enabled the police and prosecution to avoid these restraints on the production of 'homosexual' in law.[19]

The reference to the *Dudgeon* decision raised slightly different issues. While the effect of the decision in the UK appears to have limited the meaning of 'homosexual acts' to the narrow statutory meaning enacted in the 1967 Act, this meaning of 'homosexual' does not necessarily apply to the provisions under the European Convention of Human Rights or the jurisprudence that interprets the convention. For example, the *Dudgeon* decision could support a wider definition of homosexual acts, and thereby a more generous protection from criminalization, than that found in the 1967 Act.[20] Any consideration of this possibility was avoided not only by Lord Lane in the Court of Appeal but also by the judges in the House of Lords. Again this outcome was achieved by naming the sado-masochistic acts between men not as 'homosexual acts' but as acts of violence (*Brown* 1994: 236–8, 255–7).[21] In naming these acts 'acts of violence' the judges sought to place the acts within paragraph 2 of Article 8 by stating that:

> There shall be no interference by a public authority with the exercise of his right except such as is in accordance with the law and is necessary in a democratic society in the interests of natural [*sic*] security, public safety or the economic well-being of the country, for the prevention of disorder or crime, for the protection of health or morals, or for the protection of the rights and freedoms of others.

The judges concluded that this would allow the State to impose a criminal restriction on acts of violence performed in private in order to protect the wider interests of the public.[22]

This formal rejection of 'homosexual' is realized in the detail of the judgments in the Court of Appeal and in the majority decisions in the House of Lords where the bodies, desires, practices and pleasures of the men who became the object of the law's interest were represented in the law by way of elaborate expositions on violence. More specifically, the judgments seek to make sense and nonsense of these male bodies, desires and pleasures according to a specific logic of violence.

In general, these bodies, desires, practices and pleasures are portrayed either as an unruly and contagious violence in opposition to the law as order, predictability, reason, rule, control and limit or as bad violence in contradistinction to the good violence of the law (Sarat and Kearns 1991: 221–4; Derrida 1992: 39; Girard 1979: 37).

The representation of the male genital body by way of this economy of dual violence is of particular significance. As bad violence, this male genital body is imagined as either a greater violence or a violence with the potential to generate greater violence (a contagious violence) and thereby is more destructive than the violence of the law. It is in the context of these two logics of violence that 'homosexual' returns and that sense and nonsense of that 'homosexual' is made. More specifically, the sense and nonsense of this 'homosexual' of law is made as bad violence in opposition to law as good violence. It is to the fabrication of this 'homosexual' by way of the idea of law as good violence that we must now turn.

This violence of the law is a violence perpetrated in the name of the community (Devlin 1965: preface and ch.1) in order to protect that community. This violence not only protects the community from the violence that is located outside the community but is also said to channel and redirect other violence that is scattered throughout the community. As such it protects the community by providing a substitute for the violence within the community (Girard 1979: 8–10, 1986). Thereby it is a violence that creates the bonds of community rather than being a violence that destroys community. Finally, the violence of the law is public vengeance. It differs from the private vengeance that is associated with bad violence in that the latter is characterized by its capacity to escalate, to generate further violence. The violence of public vengeance is presented as a violence without reprisal or reciprocal vengeance: a violence without escalation. The violence of the law does not suppress violence; rather it purports to limit it effectively to a single act of reprisal, enacted by a sovereign authority specializing in this particular function, thereby bringing violence to an end (Girard 1979: 13–16). It is named the lesser evil: legitimate violence (Sarat and Kearns 1992: 4). As such it is a curative violence. It is a violence that is said to rationalize revenge, limiting and isolating its effects in accordance with social demands. The violence of the law is said to be a practice that offers to treat the social disease of unruly, escalating violence without fear of contagion, and presents itself as a highly effective technique for the cure and, as a secondary effect, the prevention of violence (Girard 1979: 22).

This characterization of law's violence is of particular interest. Girard draws attention to the fact that these characteristics of the law in general and the judicial system in particular have a form and function similar to the institution of sacrifice.[23] As a sacrificial practice, legal practice is not merely a practice of violence but a practice of violence that requires a particular object of that violence: a victim. It is in the context of the social need for a victim that we can begin to understand the contradiction between the repeated naming of these male sado-masochistic bodies as homosexual and the repeated assertion that the homosexual is irrelevant. It is in the social need for a victim that this 'homosexual' is made in the law.

In order to understand how the homosexual is made victim it is necessary to consider the requirements according to which, in general, the victim of sacrifice is produced. This body as victim is imagined as a body without social bonds. It is imagined as a body without the capacity to establish the same. It is a body that is imagined as exterior and marginal to the community. These attributes are important, as they suggest that the physical or civil death of the victim will not automatically generate a reciprocal act of revenge (Girard 1979: 13). Here the violence of the law demands the marginality and vulnerability of the body that is to be the object of violence so that the violence might be exercised without fear of reprisal. In order to represent that marginality, the victim is made to depict characteristics of physical and/or moral monstrosity. While this is an essential requirement of the constitution of the sacrificial victim, the production of marginality also threatens to frustrate the sacrificial rites.

If sacrifice is to be successful there must also be a substitution; the victim must be made to stand as a substitute for the members of the community who are the actual possible objects of intra-community violence, serving as the one against whom violence is channelled in the name of protecting the community from its own violence. If this is to succeed, the body that is to be made the object of collective violence must also be imagined as a body that is the same as those that are to be named the community: its double (Girard 1979: ch. 6). It is their interchangeability that makes possible the act of sacrificial substitution.

This draws attention to various fundamental requirements that must be satisfied in the production of the body as sacrificial victim. The body must be imagined as both the double and the monster. While the final representation will tend to emphasize only one aspect (usually the monstrous aspect) in order to minimize the other, this ought not to detract from the requirement of both aspects.

This also draws attention to the fact that sacrificial substitution implies a degree of misunderstanding. Its vitality as an institution depends on its ability to conceal the displacement upon which the rite is based: from intra-community violence to a violence that threatens from outside the community and from the victim as one within the community to the victim as one outside the community. Once attention is focused on the sacrificial victim, the individuals of the community who were originally singled out for acts of intra-community violence fade from view. However, sacrifice must never lose sight entirely of the original object, or cease to be aware of the act of transference from that object to the surrogate victim; without that awareness no substitute can take place and the sacrifice loses all efficiency (Girard 1979: 5).

The 'sado-masochistic homosexual' as victim is a double body. First, as sado-masochism, the sense and nonsense of this body is made as an unruly contagious violence. It is also an embodied violence that is imagined as being outside the community. Second, as homosexual, this body is at the same time imagined not just as a male genital body in its male-to-male relations but more specifically as a male genital body as unruly contagious violence. As such, this double body has been made to appear according to a very particular narrative of law and violence.

The whole process of the production of the 'sado-masochistic homosexual' is dominated by the requirement that this body must appear as a monstrous double. It is made in the image of moral monstrosity in its representation as unruly (bad) violence in contrast to the rule bound rationality (good violence) of the law. It is made in the image of physical monstrosity in its representation as scarred and broken bodies, as open and weeping wounds.

It is also as violence that 'sado-masochistic homosexual' is produced as the same as (the double of) a violence that lies elsewhere. The appeal decisions evidence the place and nature of this other violence. It is revealed in the analysis of the distinction that is drawn in the judgments between the impossibility of consent in the context of 'sado-masochistic homosexual' and the possibility of consent as a defence in the context of other acts of violence: 'contact' sport, boxing, and rough horseplay. The judges note that an ethos of physical contact is deeply entrenched in each. More specifically, they demonstrate how each involves deliberate bodily contact of particular force. Thus 'contact' sport may involve 'what would otherwise be a painful battery... conceivably of sufficient severity to amount to grievous bodily harm' (*Brown* 1994: 266). In boxing, 'each boxer tries to hurt the opponent more than he is hurt himself, and aims to end the contest prematurely by inflicting a brain injury serious enough to make the opponent unconscious, or temporarily, by impairing his central nervous system through a blow to the midriff, or cutting his skin' (*Brown* 1994: 265D–F). Rough horseplay between male youths is explained by reference to *R. v. Terence Jones* (1986).[24] In that case a group of male youths seized two others. In the case report we are told that the latter were grabbed, pulled to the ground, punched, kicked and thrown in the air on three separate occasions. On falling to the ground they suffered substantial injury; a ruptured spleen and a broken arm. Both required immediate and extensive hospital treatment. The activities were described by the court as rough and unruly. The appeal judgment notes that the violence was treated by the defendants as a joke. The protests of the victims and their demands that the violence cease were ignored. The court concluded that consent to these acts of violence was a possible defence that should have been put to the jury. This case is of interest not only because of the way it reveals the degree of male-to-male violence that the law is willing to tolerate, but also because of the court's approach to the matter of consent. The judgment draws attention to the fact that in this instance the law does not require the actual consent of the person who is the object of the defendant's acts. It is sufficient that there be a genuine belief by the defendant. Nor does the law require that the belief be reasonably held. This approach to consent refuses to recognize the importance of the voice of the one who is the object of the defendant's acts and thereby gives greater protection to the one who performs those acts of violence. Here the violence that is later projected onto 'sado-masochistic homosexual' (in the process of its misrecognition), in order to condemn it, is institutionalized, normalized and celebrated: 'as boys do' (*Jones* 1986: 377). Thus at the same time as the judicial exegesis seeks to separate the violence of 'sado-masochistic homosexuals' out from the idea of violence between men in institutionalized sports and other cultural settings, it produces, through that projection, the connection between the two.

The homosexual found in these judgments plays a particularly important role in the production of the sameness of these two violences. A point common to the judicial consideration of all the categories of acceptable violence, though one that is never overtly referred to, is that fact that they are only ever discussed as all male-to-male practices: manly sports. The 'homo' of this homosexual reproduces this man-to-man theme (it appears as its double) in another context: sado-masochism. The importance of the 'homosexual' of the law is that, at the same time that that sameness is produced in the homosexual, 'homosexual' is also an image of monstrosity. In its more familiar manifestation as monstrosity the production of homosexual as sameness (double) is quickly erased.

The formal disavowal of the homosexual and its repeated citation in the judgments is significant in two respects. First, it marks the place of the requirement of a misunderstanding that must accompany the process whereby the victim is made to stand as a substitute for the other men in the community who are the actual possible objects of intra-community violence in male-to-male encounters. That misunderstanding relates to the homosocial[25] nature of the actual intra-community violence. It is in this context that this 'homosexual' of law has special significance. Through the production of the 'homosexual' as unruly contagious violence, homosocial violence is misnamed and the endemic and institutionalized violence of homosociality is displaced onto an idea of the homosexual. Thereby legal practice both recognizes the nature of homosocial violence, which is a violence that requires unwilling victims, uses coercion, refuses to acknowledge the cries of the victim, achieves subordination and produces inequality, and projects it onto homosexual (sado-masochism). In doing so it produces 'homosexual' as the double of homosocial, creating the possibility of the substitution at the same time as it creates 'homosexual' in the law as monstrosity. At the same time it works to install a systematic blindness with regard to the homosexual (sado-masochism), denying it the possibility of being a practice of equal players, where each respects the other, of willing participants, of negotiation, contract and mutual pleasure, or of reason, rule and order (Moran 1995).

In references to violence between men and women in the judgments in *R.* v. *Brown*, the judges draw attention to another site of intra-community violence: heterosocial violence. The homosexual as victim is made intelligible not by way of the violence of homosociality (between men) but also the violence of heterosociality (by men against women).[26] The homosexual as victim might also be put to work as a substitute for the men and women of the community who are the actual possible objects of this homosocial and heterosocial violence. 'Homosexual' acts as the body against whom this intra-community violence is channelled in the name of protecting the community from its own violence. In the process of making 'sado-masochistic homosexual' the monstrous double, the judges demonstrate another feature of sacrificial practice: the production of difference. It is not so much the difference between violence and non-violence or the difference between bad violence and good violence. Here the homosocial and heterosocial contexts draw attention to the fact that these practices of sacrifice are also implicated in the production of the difference between homosexual and heterosexual. As such, the violence of the law is deployed for a particular sex, and a particular sexual and gender hierarchy (Girard 1979: ch. 3; Thompson 1995).

Another important feature of legal practice as a practice of sacrifice that is of significance here is the function of 'guilt'. The attribution of guilt to 'sado-masochistic homosexuals', which henceforth passes for the 'true' of those bodies, desires and practices, differs in no way from those attributes that will henceforth be regarded as 'false', except that, in the case of 'true' guilt, no effective voice is raised to protest any aspect of the charge. Through 'guilt', a particular version of events succeeds in imposing itself. It loses its polemical nature in becoming the 'truth' itself. In 'guilt', one voice alone makes itself heard (Girard 1979: 78). Through 'guilt', the machinery of legal practice as a sacrificial practice disappears from sight. The attribution of 'guilt' also works to conceal – even as it reveals – the resemblance of legal practice to acts of vengeance. In fact, the system functions best when everyone concerned is least aware that it involves retribution (Girard 1979: 21–2). In this respect *R. v. Brown* is a particularly interesting and important case. In *R. v. Brown*, rather than covering over the sacrificial nature of legal practice, the 'guilt' of the defendants works to reveal the sacrificial nature of legal practice. It also works to reveal law as a practice of vengeance and, in particular, it suggests that the production of a homosexual in law might also be read as an act of vengeance. In *R. v. Brown*, 'guilt' is problematic, because the actions of the defendants were all consensual act. As such, the acts generated no victims. The absence of victims is also represented in the fact that, in *R. v. Brown*, all the sado-masochistic practitioners are before the law. If there are victims in this case then they are made victims only by the law and for the law.[27] The production of the guilty as victims in this case draws attention to the role of law in the production of public vengeance and to recognition of the practice of law in general and of this 'homosexual' of law as a sacrificial practice. It is as sacrificial victim that the monstrosity of 'sado-masochistic homosexual' is celebrated so loudly by the judiciary as contagion (a violence that is both an essential part of the identity of those subjected to the law and a sort of fluid substance that flows everywhere and impregnates on contact) and infection (with particular reference to HIV and AIDS; see *Brown* 1994: 246A–B), as a practice of escalating vengeance, at the same time that its manifestation as none of these is passed over.

The homosexual of 'sado-masochistic homosexual' is also of interest in another way: it provides a challenge to the law. The homosexual(ity) that is so regularly recited and denied in *R. v. Brown* raises the spectre of an erotics of male-to-male relations that is denied in homosociality (cf. Deleuze 1989). More specifically, homosexual as consensual genital relations between men raises the spectre of a homoerotics that provides a critique of homosocial violence. The violence of the decision in *R. v. Brown* as represented in the arbitrary nature of the legal reasoning and in the severity of the prison sentences originally imposed upon the accused points to the troubling proximity and radical difference of another 'homosexual'.

The investigation, trial and appeal proceedings have produced and organized an immense verbosity about 'sado-masochistic homosexuals'. The exorbitant history of the Operation Spanner investigations and court proceedings suggests that all responded with enthusiasm to the contiguity of sado-masochism, homosexual and the law. The representation of 'sado-masochistic homosexual' in the law is the effect of various practices of the police, prosecuting authorities, defence lawyers, and judiciary, which have extorted admissions and confidences, accumulated endless details through examinations and insistent observation: 'contacting bodies, caressing them with their eyes, intensifying areas, electrifying surfaces, dramatizing trouble moments, wrapping these bodies' in the law's embrace (Foucault 1981a: 44). What had prior to these events been a minority practice, performed within a limited closed community, largely invisible to all including the various practitioners of the law, has been made public and been given a public potential that had been largely absent prior to the Operation Spanner investigations and the *Brown* proceedings. The exorbitant nature of the proceedings shows a determination to speak publicly of homosexual sado-masochism and to hear it spoken about, and to cause it to speak through explicit articulation and endlessly accumulated detail. Through these practices, these male genital bodies, desires, practices and pleasures were made sense and nonsense of according to the same logic: as unruly and contagious.[28] These bodies and desires have been made to appear according to a very particular narrative of law and violence. The appearance of these bodies and desires through the practices of law is an effect of censorship (the prohibition of an unconscious wish), and the imposition and enforcement of a very particular interpretation. Rather than bringing meaning to an end, this censorship has been central to the construction of meaning. It has been put to work upon a mass of material to authorize and enforce a particular arrangement of things. Elements of a situation are selected, added to, (re)organized. Thereby the portrait of these male genital bodies as 'sado-masochistic homosexual' is fabricated according to a particular comprehensibility, by way of a particular scenario, that organizes details producing a particular spurious unity, a connectedness, an idiosyncratic intelligibility within the field of law (Laplanche and Pontalis 1988: 65–6, 314–19, 412). Thereby the homosexual is made to appear as victim. Here the homosexual is celebrated as monstrous double and at the same time is made in the image of (as the double of) a violence that lies elsewhere. This is both a homosocial and a heterosocial violence that is endemic to the community and the violence of the law. In the final instance, the distinction that produces 'homosexual' as a body apart from the community is an effect of the violence of the law itself, as the imposition and enforcement of a particular meaning, that bestows the attribute of victim on these male genital bodies and desires. This homosexual is made for sacrifice.

Two events subsequent to the final judgment in *R. v. Brown* are of importance. The first event occurred on 16 May 1993,[29] a little over two months after the House of Lords decision. The *Pink Paper*, a (UK) national newspaper for lesbians and gay men, reported that thirty-eight men had been arrested in a police swoop on a gay party in Hoylandswaine, a small village in the north of England. The raid, conducted by twenty-six police officers in a squad of nine police cars and vans, followed an anonymous tip-off that men had been seen entering and leaving a house with large bags. Having, on the basis of this information, obtained a warrant to search for stolen goods, the police entered the property. There they discovered a party. The party host described the scene immediately prior to the arrival of the police as 'merely a party for my gay friends', where the guests were standing around chatting and drinking. As a result of the raid all the party-goers were arrested and taken to the police station. All were subsequently released on bail. At the time of the report, none of the men had been charged. When asked what the charges against the men might be, a chief inspector with the South Yorkshire Police informed the newspaper that 'the charges being brought would depend on "what the men said"'.[30]

R. v. *Brown* seems to have been of particular significance in this intervention and temporary incarceration. Various factors suggest that the activities of the police were in some way informed by and invested with the recent judgment of the House of Lords. First, the Hoylandswaine investigation has an interesting history. We are told that it was inaugurated by an anonymous telephone call, not to the local police – the South Yorkshire force – but to the Metropolitan Police. In the first instance, a call to the Metropolitan Police about an incident relating to the handling of stolen goods taking place in a village several hundred miles away from their jurisdiction makes little sense. It makes more sense when set in the context of the police investigation that gave birth to the *Brown* proceedings: Operation Spanner. The surveillance and investigation of the men that took place under Operation Spanner were in part inspired and largely conducted by the Metropolitan Police (Obscene Publications Squad). Second, in sharp contrast to the description of the party given by the party host, the police tell a very different yet specific story of the party scene they apparently discovered upon their arrival. For the police it was not so much a party where men stood around chatting and drinking but one where some men were tied up, some were handcuffed and some wore masks. Third, as a result of the raid for stolen goods the police seized particular items: leather jackets, leather and rubber trousers, sex-toys, masks and a sling. Under English law, any lawful seizure depends upon a connection being made between the items seized and a criminal offence. None of the items seized appeared to have been stolen, the original justification for the search. Nor is it an offence in itself to possess or wear leather jackets or leather trousers within the context of an all-male gathering. Nor, after R. v. *Brown*, is it specifically an offence to wear such items as part of a sado-masochistic performance, provided that there is consent and those act amount to no more than common assault. The seizure, however, if it is to be lawful, suggests that the leather jacket, leather and rubber trousers, mask, sex toy, and sling had to be paraphernalia of unlawful practices. As such they might be read metonymically; each alone and together are made to stand for an illegality that is elsewhere. The decision in R. v.

Brown makes these items capable of being read as signs of an illegal practice. That the legal practices performed by way of the police seizure might have given a meaning to these items that deployed the sense and nonsense of the body and desire so insistently demonstrated in *R.* v. *Brown* is shown in one observation made by the police: that decisions relating to any charges and prosecutions flowing from the raid would have to take account of the *Brown* decision.

Other factors suggest that the raid might evidence another aspect of the post-*Brown* practice of the law. When set in the context of evidence of the history and current practice of police harassment of gay men, be it in the specific form of raids on gay parties or in other forms,[31] the Hoylandswaine raid does not suggest any particular connection between the police action and the *Brown* judgment. The raid can be read as just another example of the routine policing of gay men. In turn it is important to recognize that the artefacts seized as a result of the raid have long been encoded as metonyms of perverse and thereby illegal sexual practices. Thus when placed in the context of a group of gay men these items might be read as the trappings of unlawful (homo)sexual practices in general. This possibility is evidenced in the Hoylandswaine incident in the reported suggestion that the men might be charged with the homosexual offence of conspiracy to commit gross indecency. As such, the seizure of these items might be read merely as part of the routine of policing sexual relations between men.

As meaningful elements that signify unlawful acts, the items seized are capable of at least two readings: one that relates to sado-masochism in particular and one that relates to unlawful (homo)sexual practices in general. On the one hand, it is important to recognize the gap that separates the two expressive systems through which the leather jacket and other artefacts may evidence illegal activity. On the other hand it is also important to recognize their proximity. The signs of different illegalities are capable of being produced through the same paraphernalia. The homosexual and sado-masochism may function as one and the same representations of perverse sexualized bodies and desires (Stychin 1995). This draws attention both to the way that illegal homosexual relations might be read as separate from sado-masochism, and at the same time might also be read as the same as sado-masochism. The similarity between the portrait of homosexuality that haunts the imagination of the Common Law and the portrait of sado-masochism suggests that the former may well be reduced to the latter in the wake of the House of Lords decision. As such, *R.* v. *Brown* may work in general to re-criminalize sexual relations between men as it works to name sado-masochism as unlawful violence and to equate homosexuality to sado-masochism. The raid on a bungalow in Hoylandswaine is perhaps a pertinent reminder of this aspect of *R.* v. *Brown*.

The Hoylandswaine incident also problematizes one of the attributes said to be associated with the good violence of the law: that it brings violence to an end. The Hoylandswaine incident suggests that the violence of the law performed in the trial and appeal procedure is not so much brought to an end in those decisions but institutionalized. The invasion of the party by the police and the incarceration of the party-goers is the repetition of that violence. Thus the violence of the law is not so much an act of violence to end violence but an act of violence to inaugurate a new regime of lawful violence.

A second series of events[32] also problematizes the suggestion that the violence of the law brings other violence to an end. Subsequent to the *Brown* decision there has been an escalation in violence towards gay men. In particular, during the summer of 1993, several gay men were murdered (Stychin 1995). Between 1992 and 1993 the number of acts of extreme sexual violence (male rapes) against gay men reported to the London police doubled (*Pink Paper*, 1 April 1994). This evidence draws attention to the problematic nature of any suggestion that the measured violence of the law will end violence within the community, or channel it through the law. Here the violence of the law in *R. v. Brown* appears more as an invitation to channel violence against gay men in the community and an invitation that is regularly taken up.

PARLIAMENTARY REFORM: 'AGE OF CONSENT'

The final instance of the use of 'homosexual' that will be considered here comes from recent attempts to reform the Sexual Offences Act 1967. In part these reforms were a success, being enacted in the Criminal Justice and Public Order Act 1994. They are the first substantive reform of the 1967 Act that has taken place since 1967.[33] The analysis here will focus upon one aspect of that reform.[34] In the 1967 Act, only those men over the age of 21 who performed homosexual acts in private were to be placed outside the criminalizing practices of the law. The most recent reform proposals sought to reduce this 'age of consent' to 16. The reform demands were only marginally successful: 21 has now been replaced by 18. The focus here is upon the debates that related to the proposals to amend that aspect of the 1967 Act. The specific objective is to analyse the themes according to which the male genital body in its male-to-male relations was imagined in the connection made between age and homosexual(ity) in the recent reform debates, in order to develop an understanding of the particular intelligibilities that have been put to work to make sense of that body by way of the phrase 'age of consent', and to explore the shifting terrain of controversies relating to genital relations between men, law reform in general and decriminalization in particular.

The conjunction of age and homosexual(ity) made in the reform proposals brought before Parliament in February 1994, initially promoted by Stonewall, a lesbian and gay law reform organization, were framed by reference to the phrase, 'the age of consent'. This phrase is important in various ways. While age has always been a significant factor in imagining the male genital body as homosexual, and in particular in the context of the production of that body for the purpose of its criminalization and decriminalization, the history of the production of that criminal and decriminalized body attests to the novelty of current attempts to formulate the conjunction of age and homosexual(ity) as 'the age of consent'. Earlier conjunctions of age and homosexual(ity) have been produced through different terms. For example, in the context of the Wolfenden review the conjunction was undertaken by way of 'adulthood'. In the more recent review undertaken by the Policy Advisory Committee on Sexual Offences (1980: 14, para. 35; 1991: 11) and the Criminal Law Revision Committee (1984: 51–5), it was conducted by way of 'minimum age'.[35] In both of these instances, the terms used to produce the male genital body in its genital relations with other male bodies were set up in contrast to 'age of consent', which was said to be a phrase exclusive to the body in its cross-sex genital relations. Over against the 'age of consent', 'adulthood' and 'minimum age' were vehicles whereby the male genital body in its genital relations with other male bodies might be represented as a body that was not only different from but also less privileged than the body in its cross-sex relations.

In the recent reform debates, the phrase 'age of consent' was transformed. It worked as a symbol of a common boundary marking an attempt to imagine a male genital body in its genital relations between men as a full genital subject. 'Age of consent', as a common term, was put to work to represent the male genital body by way of an important motif: equality. This is confirmed in the detail of the parliamentary debates. Edwina Currie, for example, who introduced the reform proposal to terminate criminalization at 16 into the House of Commons, presented that proposal in the following terms. The reform proposal, she declared, 'was not after gay rights but equal rights for everyone' (*Hansard*, House of Commons, Vol. 238, 1993–4, col. 78; see also col. 81).[36] Tony Blair (at present head of the Labour Party in opposition) presented the theme of equality by giving a slightly different inflection to the 'age of consent': 'It is not an issue of age but of equality' (*Hansard*, col. 97).[37] Through the deployment of a term that is presented as being indifferent to the hetero–homo divide – age – the male genital body is made to represent equality.

Such was the success of this motif that those who argued against the proposal sought to refuse the conflation of the 'age of consent' with equality. For example, Michael Howard, the current Home Secretary, argued for a reduction in the limit of criminalization to 18 in the following terms: 'Equality of treatment under the law between homosexuals and heterosexuals does not . . . represent an end in itself' (*Hansard*, col. 95; see also col. 97).

The male genital body as equality was also made proximate to another theme. This appears in the following assertion that 'age of consent' represents 'equal rights under the law and for the same law for everyone' and 'equality before the law' (*Hansard*, Currie, col. 81, and Kinnock, col. 86). Here the male genital body in its inter-male relations is to be imagined not only by way of equality but by reference to a very particular equality: equality in the law. More specifically, 'age of consent' is presented as a new calibration of this male genital body as a full genital subject, organized by way of an attempt to recuperate the law. This theme is given significance in the difference between the gendered and sexualized chronology of maturation of, on the one hand, the male genital body in its same-sex relations, 21, and, on the other hand, the male genital body in its cross-sex relations, 16. This division of bodies was represented as a mark of the corruption of the law.

Again this theme can be seen in operation in the detail of the arguments. In

Stonewall's document in support of reform, *The Case for Change* (Stonewall 1993), the distinction between 16 and 21 is imagined as a manifestation of the weakness of law: the arbitrariness of law; law as threat; law as an abuse of power, law beyond accountability; law as wilfully blind; law as political rather than principled; law as something always already rotten: 'The law has mouldered on the statute book for 25 yrs'. In addition, to draw the male genital body's boundary between immaturity and maturity at 21 was presented as a division of bodies that evidences law as a practice that distorts and destroys the body[38] rather than a division that produces the embodied legal subject as a symbol of law's fairness. As such, the division of bodies in the distinction between 21 and 16 was presented as a boundary that represented the failure of law: the failure to deter; the failure to enable each to exercise individual responsibility; the failure to protect the young who are vulnerable, in particular the failure to protect them against sexual violence and the failure to protect their health and sexual welfare through education. The fragmented body inscribed through the existing different calendars of immaturity and maturity was presented as being a manifestation of the law as prejudice, the law as bigotry made legitimate. As such, this unreformed body as homosexual, in its difference, represented the body as degraded by law: a body with a second-class status. Finally, Stonewall presented this division of bodies as a negation of all that should be celebrated: the consensual, the loving and the caring.

These themes also dominated the pro-reform parliamentary speeches. Thus for Edwina Currie, the status quo represented law as an erratic practice. Here law made itself appear as fear, enforced silence, compulsory inhibition, abuse, harassment, blackmail and extortion. As such, the image of the body divided was put to use to express the idea that: 'the law has the opposite effect of what many Honourable Members want' (*Hansard*, col. 77). The law was also said to be compromised by the 'homosexual' of the Sexual Offences Act 1967. This 'homosexual' was presented as a way of making sense of the body as prejudice and by way of discrimination.[39]

In contrast, those that advocated the status quo or a reform to 18 celebrated these characteristics of the law in general and the 'homosexual' of the 1967 Act in particular. Here the prejudice and discrimination of the law were represented as a form of 'guidance' that was both 'helpful' and 'protective' (*Hansard*, col. 101).[40] Michael Howard suggested that these attributes of the criminal law reflected 'a public understanding of the difference between homosexuality and heterosexual activity' (*Hansard*, col. 96).

The reform battle also produced other themes whereby sense and nonsense of the male genital body were to be made for and against reform. Of particular importance was the representation of the body as nation. For example, for Stonewall the divided mature male genital body (21/16) symbolized the unfairness of the nation (a denial of pluralism). This divided body was imagined as a nation uncivilized and idiosyncratic. The often referred-to suggestion that the division represented the need to give special protection to the young was presented as a perversity of nation and as the nation as idiosyncrasy: 'a particularly English concern'. The male genital body in its male genital relations was also produced by way of a comparison with other European nations. Twenty-one (the highest age of consent in Europe) was presented as the nation as aberration, and the nation as symptomatic of a certain backwardness and a certain tyranny: 'The British law is now totally out of line with that of most other Western democracies . . . . The only other countries with a harsher criminal code than the United Kingdom are Bosnia, Macedonia, Rumania, Serbia and Bielarus' (Stonewall 1993).

The body as nation recurs in the argument that the division of the mature male genital body between 21 and 16 represented a threat to sovereignty and to national integrity in that it exposed the nation to the scrutiny of the Commission and Court of the European Convention of Human Rights. Here the boundaries of the body and the integrity of the body are the boundaries and integrity of the nation (*Hansard*, col. 96). Both would be restored through a reform that enacts the nation as the institution of equality.

In Parliament, the mature male genital body as 21 was imagined as a certain geography: a boundary (between immaturity and maturity) that designated a nation that was not at ease with itself (*Hansard*, col. 75). The divided mature male genital body as 21 and 16 was a bounded body that represented the nation as undemocratic (*Hansard*, Kinnock, col. 86, and Smith, col. 111).

The parliamentary debates also demonstrate that the sense and nonsense of this male genital body as nation might perform another function, this time at the service of those who opposed the Currie amendment. Here the idiosyncrasies of the boundary of the body (between immaturity and maturity at 21 and 16) represented and celebrated the autonomy of the nation. This was presented in the following terms: 'We are still a sovereign state and this Parliament must take the decision – not people sitting in Brussels or anywhere else' (*Hansard*, col. 88), and: 'If we are unusual in Europe in respect of our age of consent for homosexuals and we are satisfied that there is good reason for us to do so, we are entitled to maintain that position' (*Hansard*, col. 97).

The sense and nonsense of this male genital body as nation was also produced in conjunction with another theme: health. The connection is most obvious in references to a government publication, *The Health of the Nation*. Here it was noted that 21 was a factor reflected in the fact that the nation has one of the highest rates of suicide in the world and that it had witnessed an escalation in the rates of HIV infection (*Hansard*, Currie, col. 78). Health is also used to make sense and nonsense of the male genital body in a conjunction with the theme of the law. Thus the law as fear, enforced silence, compulsory inhibition, abuse and harassment work against the dissemination of health advice and good sex education (*Hansard*, cols. 77, 78, 81, 84 and 85).

All these themes make the sense and nonsense of the male genital body as 'homosexual' by way of age. 'Homosexual' also plays an overt or a formal role in the struggles to install a new idea of the male genital body in the law. In these debates, 'homosexual' formally appeared in a particular context: it was invoked by those who argued against reform. It was also deployed according to the requirements of a very specific sense and nonsense of this male genital body. Here homosexuality was equated with buggery: 'She [Edwina Currie] is seeking to persuade Honourable Members to vote to legalise the buggery of adolescent males' (*Hansard*, col. 60). As has already been noted, Sir Nicholas Fairbairn brought the debate to an abrupt halt with his observation 'that the committee will not be misled by the fact that heterosexual activity is normal and homosexual activity, putting your penis into another man's arsehole, is perverse' (*Hansard*, col. 98).[41] Here the reduction of the act of homosexual buggery worked to produce 'homosexual' as a sign of a wrongful (and still criminalized) act and at the same time as a sign of some imagined inner essence. More specifically it is a sign of that inner essence as the unnatural, corruption and perversion.[42] Buggery was also given another significance. It is to be found in the following contribution to the parliamentary debate:

> The average age for the first anal intercourse among homosexuals – I use a more discrete euphemism than —— is 20.9 yrs. That form of intercourse is profoundly relevant to the possibility of acquiring AIDS. That mean age is so close to the prescribed age in law of 21 as to suggest that it is not without its relationship to the existing age boundaries. If the boundary is moved down to 16, there is a risk that the average age for that AIDS-inducing form of sexual intercourse may move down into the more vulnerable age group.
>
> (Alison, 21 February 1994, *Hansard*, col. 102)

Here the male genital body in its inter-male relations as buggery is imagined according to a complex web of associations. In general, buggery imagines this male genital body as a diseased body. In the conjunction between anal intercourse (buggery) homosexual and AIDS, that inner being is also imagined as not only a diseased state but also a contagious condition. Here AIDS itself is imagined as a symbolic extension of that inner being (Watney 1987).

These debates draw attention to the fact that by way of age homosexual is deployed to make sense and nonsense of the body as a boundary: between immaturity and maturity; between the disqualified subject and the full subject. But it would be wrong to conclude that homosexual as age is a boundary that is merely concerned with the division of time. It is not a simple matter of duration, of years and months. In general, age as maturity might best be described as a point within an expressive calibration (Barthes 1977). Furthermore, age is a calibration of the body that produces the body by way of many different boundaries that represent many different themes. Some calibrations seek to plot development. Others represent the body as a natural order. Others are calendars and boundaries of the body that are overtly cultural. Here chronology as a boundary operates as a technique of measurement that inscribes social rank, economic hierarchy, national divisions, moral classification, genital rank. Together these factors draw attention to the fact that the boundary between immaturity and maturity in law is neither a mere chronological division nor a single or uniform division. Age is a complex fragmented matrix of multiple calibratory schemes that seek to plot privilege and disability, responsibility and capacity. It is a complex of calibrations that map the boundary not only of the full legal subject but also of the various degrees of subjection to the law. This draws attention to the fact that age is always already a complex matter of significance, not only to offences in general but in particular to those relating to genital relations between men. In the conjunction of homosexual as age this matrix of themes and values is deployed to make the sense and nonsense of the male genital body in its male genital relations. In the final instance, Parliament voted to limit criminalization to the age of 18. Thereby they agreed to institutionalize a (new) sense of homosexual in the law and thereby to continue the project of homosexual as a way of imagining the male genital body in its genital relations as discrimination between 'hetero' and 'homo' in the law.

The case studies undertaken in this chapter draw attention to the fact that the post-1967 landscape of 'homosexual' in the law is diverse and complex. In some respects, the meanings that give form to and might be spoken through the 'homosexual' of the law are monotonous. On the other hand, it is important to recognize the richness and diversity of matters that are articulated by way of this 'homosexual'. These case studies merely provide a series of snapshots of the struggles that have taken place, and continue to take place, in and through the 'homosexual' of the law. While this analysis seeks to point to their connectedness, it is also important to recognize the individuality of each instance. Both aspects of the event need to be retained in order to understand the interface between homo-sexuality and the law. Both must be taken into account in order to understand the nature of the engagement with the law.

Any engagement with 'homosexual' will necessarily be an engagement with not merely the themes and values that are deployed for the strategic purposes of intervention but, potentially, with the whole matrix of meaning that is condensed in the term. While this may be thought of as a problem for any strategy of intervention, it ought also to be considered as an asset for those who seek to intervene in the name of the homosexual, gay or queer subject, as this multiplicity is not merely the limit of intervention and reform it is also its very possibility.

9

CONCLUSIONS

D, while waiting for a friend, noticed a young man walking towards him. The young man was smartly but casually dressed, wearing a personal stereo and headphones. The young man walked past him, made eye contact, smiled and proceeded to walk down the promenade in the small seaside town of Morecambe. As he walked away he repeatedly turned and re-established eye contact with D. D followed at a distance. Some way down the promenade the young man sat down on a bench. He continued to turn his head towards D, make eye contact and smile. Before D arrived at the bench the young man began to retrace his steps. He walked past D, looked him in the eye and smiled. D turned and followed, watching as the young man turned periodically to look at him. The young man then proceeded to enter a nearby public toilet. D followed but left when he discovered that the young man had entered a cubicle. A short time later the young man came out of the toilet and proceeded to sit nearby. D joined him and began a conversation. They talked for some time about the young man's career, his likes and dislikes. He was a chef; he lived at home with his parents, lived a dull life in a small town. D asked if he would like to go for a drink. The offer was declined. D asked again; again it was declined. The young man suggested that they take a walk down the promenade. D thought this odd, became suspicious and declined the invitation. He then proceeded to leave, to return to his car. The young man followed. He caught up with D as they approached a bus stop. There they were joined by four other people, two men and two women. At that point, the young man announced that he was a member of the police force and introduced the others as police colleagues. They proceed to question D about his behaviour and his intentions. They suggested to him that he was trying to make sexual advances of a criminal kind (importuning and soliciting) to the young constable. They told D that his name and address would be recorded in a book at the local police station.

About the same time, September 1995, Angela Mason, the current Director of the lesbian and gay parliamentary reform lobby organization, Stonewall, was addressing the first lesbian and gay law conference in the UK, 'Legal Queries', at the University in the nearby town of Lancaster. She commented that there is new momentum and opportunity for law reform. At the same time, the lesbian and gay press was reporting that Parliament had recently discussed a law reform proposal to make discrimination in the workplace, against lesbians and gay men, illegal. The Courts were considering the exclusion of lesbians and gay men from the military. The political party then in opposition, the Labour Party, was developing a lesbian and gay rights agenda.

This study is an attempt to explore the connection between these various incidents and developments relating to the law as it impacts upon same-sex genital relations and the distance that separates them. In the first instance, the police seek to perform 'homosexual' as an object of the law: as a form of deviance, a pathology in need of detection, and correction. At the same time they also perform 'homosexual' in another sense. In acting as a pretty policeman, the police officer performs 'homosexual' as the subject of law enforcement. Here, in performing 'homosexual' in order to criminalize, the agent of law forgets his own criminal practice of 'homosexual'. The law reform examples are also connected to the deployment of 'homosexual' but in a different way. Homophile law reform connects to 'homosexual' by way of its capacity to articulate demands for rational approaches to law and social order, for respect and recognition and its capacity to express defiance and indignation.

This study argues that the 'homosexual' that connects and separates these incidents is not so much a reference to a forbidden act or a criminalized identity but a set of technologies of production and a means of articulating a complex matrix of values. The legal use of the term 'homosexual' involves a struggle over the entire framing of knowledge about the body as the human subject and its juridical capacities, desires, pleasures and practices. The various encounters with the terms that make up the lexicon of the law, be it the archaic terms 'importuning', 'soliciting', 'buggery' or the more recent 'homosexual', are encounters with a complex culture of representation. Each in different ways draws attention to the fact that the representation of the body in law is a matter of signs (of metaphor) and as such a matter of multiple and shifting meanings and of conflicting and enduring traditions. This study has explored the 'homosexual' of law as a terrain across which the male genital body might be imagined in a multiplicity of ways producing different effects in law; as mere object of law or both full genital subject as well as a privileged and disqualified subject.

The 'homosexual(ity)' that was explored through the Wolfenden review and formally installed in the law in the Sexual Offences Act 1967 is a way of imagining the male genital body in its genital relations with other male bodies that has a certain ambivalence. On the one hand, this 'homosexual' is formally introduced into the law as a new term though which a particular male genital body, its acts, desires and pleasures, might be imagined in the law in order that this body may no longer be an object of the law – decriminalized. Here the reform resorts to 'homosexual' in order to bring the appearance of 'homosexual' to an end. 'Homosexual' is to be silenced as it must disappear into a narrowly defined private space. At the same time, 'homosexual' is given a new presence. It is formally added to the law as a new term though which that body might be re-imagined as an object of the law, re-criminalized for a new project of eradication.

As this study seeks to demonstrate, this ambivalence with regard to the representation of the male body in its genital relations with other male bodies is neither a recent invention nor a state of affairs generated by or peculiar to this institutionalization of 'homosexual' in the law. The ambivalence echoes the juxtaposition of the injunction to silence, and the coextensive compulsion to speak. This is a dynamic that is deeply implicated in the production of the male genital body in its genital relations with other male bodies over a long period of time.

While drawing attention to the durability of this dynamic, at the same time this study draws attention to an important moment in its modernization: from 'buggery' to 'homosexual'. In general it seeks to explore its contemporary idiosyncrasies and its current operation, creating both the possibility and the impossibility of new juridical relations.

In focusing upon the law as a complex of practices whereby sense and nonsense of the male genital body is made and installed, institutionalized and enforced, this study challenges certain assumptions and ideas about the law and legal practice. My analysis seeks to add a new dimension to the particular debates about law and law reform that focus upon law as a matter concerned with rules and rationality. It seeks both to enrich these debates and challenge their terms and objectives. In providing such a challenge, my focus on 'homosexual' seeks to draw attention to the importance of considering law and legal practice as not only a matter of rules but also a matter of representation. The various examples considered in this study can all be read as disputes that relate to the interface between competing ideas of the male body in its genital relations with other male bodies. This analysis suggests that these exchanges are best understood as a struggle over competing intelligibilities and unintelligibilities of the body and its pleasures, each undertaken within an idiosyncratic context. Engagement with or intervention in the law is primarily not so much an engagement with rules and rationality but more an engagement with the dynamics of representation.

One factor that connects the two sets of events that open this chapter is the repetition of 'homosexual(ity)'. Its repetition in very different places at the same time, and in different places over a period of time, should not be understood as a manifestation of the singularity or fixity of the meaning of the term 'homosexual(ity)'. Repetition should not be taken to signify the ability of the term 'homosexual(ity)' either to capture the fixed essence of the phenomenon that it purports to name or to be read as a sign of its ability to define exhaustively the thing it represents in the same terms on each occasion. The multiplicity of meaning that might be made present through 'homosexual' suggests that its ability to be repeated in different places at the same time, in the same place at different times, and in different places at different times points more to the impossibility of singularity, fixity, essence. Its success lies in its very ability to be repeated in different contexts in different times and through the complex matrix of values that make the sense and nonsense of homosexual, to represent different things. At best, 'homosexual(ity)' should be understood as expressive of a rich shifting matrix of cultural and temporal concerns.[1] This draws attention to the need to take seriously the possibility of deploying the term beyond the cultural and temporal specificity of its immediate production and deployment.[2]

At the same time, this study draws attention to some of the limits of an engagement with 'homosexual' in the law. For example, while the formal introduction of 'homosexual' into the law through the Sexual Offences Act 1967 modernized and expanded the lexicon of the law, it is important to note that at the same time the introduction of 'homosexual' into the lexicon of the law might have the opposite effect. It also works to contract the lexicon of the law. It formally achieved this in the statutory redefinition of 'buggery' and 'gross indecency', which gave these two terms a new common denominator, 'homosexual', and thereby reduced them to a single phenomenon in law, 'homosexual offence'. As the cases of *Masterson* and *Knuller* demonstrate, its contracting force might also operate at an informal level. At this level it might have a more dramatic effect within the law. It may reduce any unlawful act that relates to genital relations, past, present or future, between persons of the same sex to 'homosexual'. A wide variety to terms, such as indecent, assault, soliciting, importuning, insulting behaviour, breach of the peace, conspiracy, corrupt and deprave (to name but a few), might henceforth be named 'homosexual' in the law. More generally, an engagement with the homosexual(ity) of law is also an engagement with the intelligibilities and unintelligibilities that create the possibility of the sense and nonsense of the male genital body in law. These may in turn impoverish our understanding of the body in general and of genital relations in particular.

In attempting to understand the novelty and the particularity of this homosexual(ity) of the law, it is important to locate the rise of homosexual(ity) as a particular way of making the sense and nonsense of the male genital body and male identity, both outside the law and within it, in the context of other terms and schemes of sense that have been and continue to be used to name this body, its desires, practices and pleasures. These different ways of making sense and nonsense of this embodied subject are to be found in terms such as bugger, sodomite, hermaphrodite, Uranian, invert, pervert, the third sex, pansy and queer. The continued legibility of many of these terms, outside if not within the law, draws attention not only to the need to pay particular attention to the distinctive inflections produced through them but also to the need to be sensitive to the distinctive inflections of meaning that are generated through the deployment of the term 'homosexual(ity)' as a privileged and distinct practice of subjection in the law. It also draws attention to the need to pay particular attention to the connections made between homosexual(ity) and these other sensibilities of the male body. Their connection with other terms in law, such as human rights, the legal subject and legal personality, may generate a range of distinctive inflections of meaning that provide a radical departure as well as a repetition of the same.

Finally, the analysis of the law's silence and the recent meeting between 'homosexual' and 'sado-masochism' in the law draw attention to another important point. They demand that we acknowledge that any struggle over representation in the law takes place in the context of the violence of the law. Furthermore, they demand that we recognize that the violence of the law has particular qualities. The law's violence is concerned with coercion, terror, fear, domination, hostility, subordination, silence and inequality. In *R. v. Brown*, the 'homosexual' of law takes on an important role. It provides a means whereby a critique of the violence of the law, and in particular displays of the ethical impoverishment of certain legal practices, might be staged. More specifically, it raises questions about the nature of law's violence, and about the relationship between law's violence and desire, pleasure, dialogue, participation and consent. Where law's violence is denied, all ethical considerations of law's violence are silenced. A recognition of law's violence opens up a new ethical space in law (Douzinas and Warrington 1994). As such, a recognition of the law's violence is to be welcomed and not to be denied. Unless those who wish to engage with the law in general and modern legal scholarship in particular can cope with the fact that retaliatory vengeance, ritual sacrifice and legal punishment are capable of intersecting in legal practice as a practice of representation, little light will be shed on the ethical questions of violence, law and the body. The problem of homosocial and heterosocial violence will remain invisible, and particular bodies and desires will be sacrificed in the name of law and order.

In the final instance, in drawing attention to all these factors, this study seeks to promote a renewed engagement with the law: 'knowledge is not made for understanding; it is made for cutting' (Foucault 1977: 154).

Any engagement with the 'homosexual' of the law will necessarily be an engagement with not merely the themes and values that are deployed for the strategic purposes of intervention but, potentially, with the whole matrix of meaning that is condensed in the term 'homosexual'. While this may be thought of as a problem for any strategy of intervention, it ought to be taken to be an asset for those who seek to intervene in the name of homosexual, gay or queer. This multiplicity is not only the limit and problem of any intervention; it is also central to its very possibility. Out of that multiplicity will come change and the limits of change at any one time.

The main focus of this book has not only been to develop an analysis of the terms of the Sexual Offences Act 1967 and the reform debates that preceded it, or the statutes and judge-made rules that impact upon the lives of those who perform genital acts with persons of the same sex, but also to develop a more general analysis of the law and the emergence of a particular way of imagining the male body in general and the genital male body in its genital relations with other male bodies in particular within the law. In pursing this agenda, this study seeks to break out of the traditional parameters and approaches in work that considers the interface between law and homosexuality. In addressing this wider agenda, the analysis has pursued those values through which sense and nonsense of this body of the law has been and continues to be made. Furthermore, it begins an exploration of a range of those meanings in the context of a critical analysis of those contemporary techniques and practices through which that imagined body is made and becomes installed within the law as homosexual.

APPENDIX OF CASES

Aitken (1992) *R.* v. *Aitken* [1992] 1 WLR 1006
Audley (1631) *Lord Audley, Earl of Castlehaven* (1631) 3 State Trials 401
Bowers (1986) *Bowers* v. *Hardwick* (1986) 478 US 186, 106 S. Ct 2841 (1986)
Brown (1992a) *R.* v. *Brown* (1992) Cr App R 302
Brown (1992b) *R.* v. *Brown* [1992] 1 QB 491
Brown (1994) *R.* v. *Brown* [1994] AC 212
Clarence (1888) *R.* v. *Clarence* (1888) 22 QB 23
Court (1987) *R.* v. *Court* [1987] QB 156
Courtie (1984) *R.* v. *Courtie* [1984] 1 All ER 740
Crook (1966) *Crook* v. *Edmondson* [1966] 2 QB 81
Donovan (1934) *R.* v. *Donovan* [1934] 2 KB 498
Dudgeon (1981) *Dudgeon* v. *United Kingdom* (1981) 3 EHRR 40
Dudgeon (1982) *Dudgeon* v. *United Kingdom* (1982) 4 EHRR 149
Ford (1978) *R.* v. *Ford* [1978] 1 All ER 1129
Gray (1982) *R.* v. *Gray* (1982) Cr App R 324
Hickman (1783) *R.* v. *Hickman* (1783) 1 Leach 277
Hornby (1946) *R.* v. *Hornby and Peaple* (1946) 32 Cr App R 1
Horton (1913) *Horton* v. *Mead* [1913] 1 KB 154
Howells (1976) *R.* v. *Howells* (1976) Cr App R 28
Hunt (1950) *R.* v. *Hunt* [1950] 2 All ER 291
Jones (1775) *R.* v. *Jones* (1775) 1 Leach 139
Jones (1986) *R.* v. *Terence Jones* (1986) 83 Cr App R 375
Kirkup (1993) *R.* v. *Kirkup* [1993] 2 All ER 802
Knewland (1796) *R.* v. *Knewland* [1796] 2 Leach 721
Knuller (1971) *Knuller* v. *DPP* (Court of Appeal) [1971] 3 All ER 314
Knuller (1972) *Knuller* v. *DPP* (House of Lords) [1972] 3 All ER 898
Lemon (1978) *R.* v. *Lemon* [1978] 3All ER 175
Lemon (1979) *R.* v. *Lemon* [1979] 1 All ER 898
Masterson (1986) *Masterson and another* v. *Holden* [1986] 3 All ER 39
Modinos (1993) *Modinos* v. *Cyprus* (1993) 16 EHRR 485
Norris (1989) *Norris* v. *Ireland* (1989) 13 EHRR 186
Reakes (1974) *R.* v. *Reakes* [1974] Crim LR 615
Redgrave (1981) *R.* v. *Redgrave* (1981) Cr App R 10
Rowed (1842) *R.* v. *Rowed and another* (1842) 3 QB 180
Shaw (1962) *Shaw* v. *DPP* [1962] AC 220
Wiseman (1718) *R.* v. *Wiseman* (1718) Rep. 91

NOTES

1 INTRODUCTION: BRIEF ENCOUNTERS

1 This law applies directly to England and Wales. Scotland and Northern Ireland have different but closely related legal systems.
2 For example, see Symonds 1928.
3 Throughout the book homosexual(ity) is used to represent both homosexual and homosexuality.
4 The problematic nature of this particular history is raised in Copley 1989.
5 The term 'Uranian' is located within the theme of celebrating a present by reference to a past, in that it invokes a particular aspect of an icon of Greek culture, the philosophical writings of Plato, more specifically the *Symposium*, and writes and deploys that as a way of naming genital relations between men.
6 For a slightly different narrative of the genesis of 'gay', see Bristow 1990.
7 In the UK, the Gay Left Collective was prominent in the genesis and circulation of such ideas. An excellent example is to be found in Gay Left Collective 1980.
8 See, for example, Watney 1980.
9 See Watney 1981; Fernbach 1980.
10 Another term used by Krafft-Ebing is 'antipathic sexual feeling'. Other categories are also found operating within Krafft-Ebing's scheme of things, such as 'neuropathic' and 'psychopathic'.
11 The congenital acquired dichotomy is echoed in the nature/nurture debate within lesbian and gay politics. A particularly interesting analysis of this dichotomy is to be found in Dollimore 1991 and Fuss 1989. For an application of these debates in the context of the jurisprudence of the USA see Ortiz 1993.
12 Krafft-Ebing described it as 'an abnormal condition natural to him', and 'from his [the homosexual's] morbid standpoint, it is natural' (Krafft-Ebing 1948: 382).
13 'Homosexual rights', 'gay rights' and 'queer rights' have come to assume particular importance. Each of these phrases, in its way, can be understood as an attempt to turn ways of imagining and celebrating the same-sex genital relations and its pleasures to a particular way of imagining juridical relations – rights talk. This connection has particular significance. In their conjunction with rights, and more specifically in calling these rights 'human rights', a very particular strategy is embarked upon. Here the politicization of a specific identity and desire is conjoined with a distinctive juridical agenda that has been described as 'one of the monumental legacies left by the Enlightenment' (Gaete 1993). Thereby 'homosexual', 'gay' and 'queer', as practices of indignation, defiance and celebration, are mobilized in intimate association with juridical themes of authenticity, final truth, rationality, humanity and legitimacy.

14 For a similar development in the context of race and rights, see Williams 1991.
15 Feminist legal scholarship has also explored this conjunction. See for example Edwards 1981 and Smart 1989.
16 The exception to this rule is the USA, where about half the State jurisdictions have criminal laws that purport to be or have been found to be gender neutral and thereby have been found to criminalize genital relations between women (Robson 1992: ch. 3; Hart 1994). If consensual genital relations between women were known to the English criminal law then it was by reference to different offences. Hart suggests (Hart 1994: 3–4) that there criminalization might have taken place by way of offences relating to prostitution (but cf. Crompton 1980). A recent case in the UK, *R. v. Saunders*, where a woman was found guilty of an indecent assault against another woman, drew attention to the possibility of the criminalization of this female body in terms that mimic the homosexual (male) body of the criminal law (see also Robson 1995).
17 See PRO HO 345/9, CHP/93, which provides a summary of a discussion between certain members of the Wolfenden Committee and Professor Alfred C. Kinsey (Weeks 1977; Lauristen and Thornstad 1974).
18 For reference to the consideration of other reform initiatives in Holland, Scandinavian countries and Germany as part of the Wolfenden review, see, for example, PRO HO 345/9, CHP/100, CHP/101, CHP/102, CHP/103 and CHP/109.
19 The post-decriminalization developments in Canada are explored in Herman 1994a.

2 NOVELTY AS THE TRADITION OF LAW: BUGGERY AS HOMOSEXUAL

1 The formal appearance of 'homosexuality' is more recent. It was introduced in 1988 by s. 28 of the Local Government Act, which inserted a new section 2A into the Local Government Act 1986. The section states that:

(1) A local authority shall not
  a) intentionally promote **homosexuality** or publish material with the intention of promoting **homosexuality**;
  b) promote the teaching in any maintained school of the acceptability of **homosexuality** as a pretended family relationship;
(2) Nothing in subsection (1) above shall be taken to prohibit the doing of anything for the purpose of treating or preventing the spread of disease.
(3) In any proceedings in connection with the application of this section a court shall draw such inferences as to the intention of the local authority as may reasonably be drawn from the evidence before it.

'Homosexuality' is here used not to regulate individuals but to regulate the actions, powers and responsibilities of specific institutions and local government. In part this use of homosexuality is a response to a wider deployment of homosexual and homosexuality in the generation of administrative policies and practices of certain public authorities that attempted to establish a new, post-1967 politics of identity within local government (Cooper 1994). More specifically, the 'homosexuality' of the Local Government Act 1988 was installed in the law to designate acts that are a prohibited politics of representation. It was introduced to regulate the resort to an identity politics and thereby to regulate the representation of same-sex genital relations by certain public authorities (Colvin 1989; Smith 1990, 1995; Thomas and Costigan 1990; Cooper 1994). It was also a rhetorical figure within an anti-left politics and a politics of centralization. It is important to note that it does not outlaw an identity *per se* but rather outlaws acts that seek to represent that identity in a particular way.

2   In Scotland and Northern Ireland the introduction of 'homosexual' is more recent still. In Scotland the decriminalization provisions were introduced in 1980 (s. 80(7) Criminal Justice (Scotland) Act). It was introduced in Northern Ireland in 1982. The provisions were applied to the Channel Islands in 1990 and the Isle of Man in 1992.

3   By virtue of s. 145 of the Criminal Justice and Public Order Act 1994, this subsection has been amended and now reads: 'have attained the age of eighteen years'. These reforms also apply to Scotland and Northern Ireland.

4   Buggery is declared an offence by virtue of s. 12 of the Sexual Offences Act 1956. Section 12(1) (as amended by the 1994 Criminal Justice and Public Order Act) declares that:

> It is a felony for a person to commit buggery with another person, otherwise than in the circumstances described in subsection (1A) below, or with an animal.

Throughout this study the analysis focuses only upon that aspect of buggery that relates to genital relations between men. While a study of heterosexual buggery and buggery that involves genital relations between humans and animals would have a connection with the present study in the interconnection between same-sex buggery it would also have a very different history, which is beyond the scope of the present text. Heterosexual buggery has never been an offence in Scotland (see Gordon 1978). Its existence in English law seems to have been uncertain until the case of *R.* v. *Wiseman* (1718). The Criminal Justice and Public Order Act 1994 decriminalizes consensual heterosexual buggery where it takes place in private and where both parties have attained the age of 18. This is achieved by way of the addition of s. 1A to the Sexual Offences Act 1956.

5   The offence of gross indecency was introduced into the law by way of s. 11 of the Criminal Law Amendment Act 1885 (48&49 Vict. c 69) in the following terms:

> Any male person who, in public or private, commits, or is a party to the commission of, or procures or attempts to procure the commission by any male person of, any act of gross indecency with another male person, shall be guilty of a misdemeanour, and being convicted thereof shall be liable at the discretion of the court to be imprisoned for any term not exceeding two years, with or without hard labour.

The offence is now to be found in s. 13 of the Sexual Offences Act 1956.

6   Coke writes one of the earliest and most extensive meditations on buggery in the early seventeenth century, in Chapter 10 of *The Third Part of the Institutes of the Laws of England* (Coke 1628), which he entitled 'Of buggery or sodomy'. His work suggests that the two are synonymous. While this may be true in certain contexts, there is ample evidence to suggest that the two terms when used in different contexts have generated slightly different meanings. Sodomy, with its Old Testament origins, has wider meanings than buggery, which has its roots in medieval heresies. The latter refers to any anal penetration and man-to-animal penetration. Sodomy, in the USA, includes genital relations between women, which buggery has never done. Buggery/sodomy has dominated the production of the male genital body in its genital relations with other men in law in the wider family of common-law legal systems. Thus it has had considerable significance in jurisdictions such as Scotland, Ireland, Canada, the USA, New Zealand and Australia (though at times 'sodomy' has been used as an alternative to 'buggery').

7   Bracton noted that the law required that sodomites be burned.

8   The history of the phrase 'gross indecency' is both shorter than and different from that of buggery. (See Weeks 1977, 1981; Brown 1993; Cohen 1993; Hyde 1970, 1973, 1976; Simpson *et al.* 1976; Walkowitz 1992.)

9　The discrimination and prejudice that is performed in and through the production of the male genital body in its same-sex genital relations in the law represents that body by way of a chain of associations that connect 'sodomy' ('buggery') to 'homosexual' and more recently to the terms 'lesbian' and 'gay'. In making this chain of associations each term is made to stand for the other. More specifically, through this connection the always already criminal of sodomy (buggery) is displaced and reconfigured as the always already criminal of homosexual, and more recently gay and, in the USA, lesbian. These themes are explored in detail in Chapters 3 and 4 of this study.

10　More recently the importance attached to this particular relationship has been an important theme of legal scholarship in the USA. This matter has assumed particular importance in the wake of the 1986 Supreme Court decision of *Bowers* v. *Hardwick*, which joined 'homosexual' to 'sodomy' in its conclusion that under the US constitution a fundamental right did not extend to 'homosexual sodomy'. (See Halley 1990, 1993a, 1993b.)

11　Drs Curran and Whitby had also been responsible for gathering the data that had been presented to the committee on homosexuality. They presented the information in a Memorandum (PRO HO 345/9, CHP/107).

12　It would be wrong to conclude that these extreme punishments were always carried out. In English law they represent the maximum that might possibly be imposed through the secular jurisdiction. Greenberg suggests that they were rarely carried out in practice. This emphasizes the symbolic significance of the formal statements of the maximum punishments (Greenberg 1988: 273–4).

13　A summary of the statistical evidence dealing with these points was presented to the committee in a 'Note by the Secretary on recidivism' (PRO HO 345/9 CHP/104). At the end of the summary he concluded that the tables 'suggest that the extent of recidivism amongst homosexual offenders is significantly less than among offenders as a whole'.

14　The potential for the retention of the distinction between act and identity and the conflation of act and identity in the buggery–homosexuality association might be demonstrated by way of a consideration of the operation of the sodomy–homosexual distinction in the US Supreme Court in *Bowers* v. *Hardwick*. (See Halley 1993a, 1993b and 1994.)

15　It is of interest to note that a preference for buggery is conceptualized here as a practice between men. Why should it only be homosexual buggery that mimics normal heterosexual intercourse? Various answers might be suggested. One answer might be that to suggest that heterosexual buggery mimics normal heterosexual intercourse would have been more accurate. Such an argument would distance homosexual buggery from normal heterosexual intercourse and would thereby have exposed the false association between heterosexual intercourse and male-to-male buggery. It ought not to be forgotten that the purpose of naming buggery as an imitation of normal heterosexual intercourse is to ensure its position as a threat to social order. On the question of the forgetfulness of the law on heterosexual buggery (sodomy), see Halley (1991, 1994) and Thomas (1993). All these materials address the matter in the context of the USA. The decriminalization of heterosexual buggery in the Criminal Justice and Public Order Act 1994 brings cross-sex and male same-sex buggery together. The anomaly of the distance between the two was a major argument for reform. Sodomy between men and women is not an offence in Scotland.

16　The importance of the collection and the presentation of this data should not be underestimated, as in the context of the Wolfenden review it drew attention to the fact that the foundations of the law's concern with buggery and the status attributed to it point to the importance of myth in legal cultural practices. Other scholars have already documented the general history of these myths and their performance through a wide range of cultural practices. (See for example, Boswell 1980; Greenberg 1988; Goodich 1979; Bray 1982.) See Brundage (1987) for the practice of these myths within the European legal tradition.

17 In making these proposals the committee did not propose to retain a category of punishment that would equate particular acts of buggery with rape. Buggery without consent would under these proposals attract a maximum sentence of ten years' imprisonment whereas rape attracts a maximum sentence of life imprisonment. Non-consensual buggery now falls under the definition of rape (see s. 1 Sexual Offences Act 1956 as amended by s. 14 Criminal Justice and Public Order Act 1994).

18 This was a position that had been advocated by contributions by both the Church of England in the memorandum submitted by the Church of England Moral Welfare Council (PRO HO 345/7, CHP/26) and the Roman Catholic Church through the report of the Roman Catholic Advisory Committee (PRO HO 345/8, CHP/76).

19 Earlier in the general argument, the committee had drawn attention to the difficulties associated with the use of the word 'normal'.

> In relation, first to the presence of abnormal symptoms, it is nowadays recognized that many people behave in an unusual, extraordinary or socially unacceptable way, but it seems to use that it would be rash to assume that unorthodox or aberrant behaviour is necessarily symptomatic of disease if it is the only symptom that can be demonstrated. To make this assumption would be to underestimate the very wide range of 'normal' human behaviour, and abundant evidence is available that what is socially acceptable or ethically permissible has varied and still varies considerably in different cultures.
>
> (Wolfenden 1957: 14, para. 27)

The use of 'normal' in the context of sexual intercourse is in sharp contrast to the note of caution in paragraph 27. In the context of sexual intercourse it is used to deny diversity and to impose a singular and an impoverished idea of human sexual practices.

20 This did not exhaust the arguments in favour of the offence. It was also suggested that the retention of buggery would allow the law to retain a category that could signify the law's condemnation of homosexual acts that were similar to heterosexual rape. It is important to note that the abolition of the offence of buggery does not lead to the conclusion that the law could not produce offences that would reflect various degrees of prohibited sexual relations, particularly involving violence. As the dissenting report points out, the removal of the offence of buggery would not render the law incapable of dealing with male rape:

> [T]he general criminal law provides for punishment with imprisonment up to five years for acts causing bodily harm, and up to life imprisonment for acts causing grievous bodily harm. Alternatively, in a prosecution for indecent assault, the question of injury would be taken into account by the court as a relevant circumstance.
>
> (Wolfenden: 1957, 123–4)

The reform of the offence of buggery between men in the Sexual Offences Act 1967 produced a situation where non-consensual buggery (male rape) was punished less severely than cross-sexual rape (McMullen 1990). This situation was changed with the redefinition of rape to include anal penetration without consent in the Criminal Justice and Public Order Act 1994.

21 In this respect, s. 3 does not go as far in its reform as the Wolfenden Committee proposed. In particular the maximum penalty for gross indecency remained two years' imprisonment.

22   The one offence referred to here is the offence of buggery as an unlawful act performed by one man with another. Even prior to the 1967 Act, buggery also related to an offence performed by a man and a woman and an offence performed by one person with an animal.

23   The connection between homosexual, buggery and tradition that is produced in the Wolfenden Report rehearses the US Supreme Court's connection between homosexual, sodomy and history (see Goldstein 1988, 1993).

3 BUGGERY: A SHORT HISTORY OF SILENCE

1   The interface between genital relations and silence is multiple and complex. This chapter focuses upon the place of silence in the context of the representation of genital relations between men. See Hart (1994: ch. 1) for a discussion of the place and nature of the silence that is put to use in the representation of genital relations between women.

2   On the importance of the riddle in the generation of narrative in general and of legal narrative in particular, see Barthes (1990) and Moran (1991a).

3   Silence has also played a role in the representation of genital relations between men in other common-law jurisdictions where buggery or sodomy have had a lively history. For example, a recent reference to the riddle of silence in the USA is to be found in *Bowers* v. *Hardwick* (Bowers 1986). More generally on the USA see Katz (1983), Goldstein (1988, 1993) and Halley (1993a, b). With respect to Australia see French (1993). While the focus of this analysis is the deployment of silence in the English common-law tradition, the chapter has wider significance as it provides an insight into the practices of silence in other common-law jurisdictions.

4   It first appeared in Coke's *A Booke of Entries: Containing Perfect and Approved Presidents* (Coke 1614). The text includes a precedent for an indictment, a formal written accusation required in order to initiate a trial, for sodomy. As a precedent, the indictment suggests that the 'abominable sin of Sodom, called in English Buggarie...ought not to be named among Christians' (quoted in Smith 1991: 51). While the edition referred to here was published in 1628, the materials upon which it is based may have been circulated earlier, reflecting an earlier practice of silence (see Pluknett 1942; Baker 1972).

5   The conjunction of buggery and sodomy in the title of Coke's meditation is of particular significance. It draws attention to a point of connection between the sodomitical legal tradition of the USA and the English legal tradition of buggery. The remainder of his meditation privileges the term used within the English legal system, buggery. In Scotland the term used is sodomy (see Hume 1986; cf. McKenzie 1688, where buggery is the term used).

6   Latin original.

7   The current requirements for the indictment for buggery require a statement of the offence, 'Buggery contrary to section 12(1) of the Sexual Offences Act 1956', and a statement of the particulars of the offence such as, 'A.B. on the — day of ——, committed buggery with X a male person.' The particulars must specify the age of the other party, the presence or absence of consent and, where both parties are over 18, the fact that it was committed otherwise than in a private place. See *R. v. Courtie* (1984).

8   Buggery was also the topic of another popular pamphlet during this period concerned with proceeding brought against John Atherton (Atherton 1641; Bray 1982).

9   Bray also notes that this is outside the Christian order of things.

10   Another example is to be found in the nineteenth-century writings of H.J. Stephen, in his *Commentaries on the Laws of England* (Stephen 1845). When dealing with the offence of buggery he declares:

We will not act so disagreeable a part as to dwell any longer upon a subject, the very mention of which is a disgrace to human nature. It will be more expedient to imitate in this respect the delicacy of our English law, which treats it in its very indictments as a crime not fit to be named.

(Stephen 1845: 62)

Note how his text mimics that of Blackstone, creating the illusion of continuity.

11   See Garland (1985), Smart (1989) and Bell (1993). All develop the theme of the interface between law as a specific domain of truth and the truth claims generated in other contexts by other disciplinary practices. My work suggests that their periodization of law's intertextuality with respect to the body is problematic.

12   It is important to note that, in this instance, sodomy does not refer to anal intercourse but has a much more diffuse meaning.

13   This conclusion is graphically followed in *R.* v. *Knewland* (1796), where Judge Ashurst observes:

The bare idea of being thought addicted to so odious and detestable a crime, is of itself sufficient to deprive the injured person of all the comforts and advantages of society: a punishment more terrible, both in apprehension and reality, than even death itself. The law, therefore, considers the fear of losing character by such an imputation as equal to the fear of losing life itself, or of sustaining other personal injury.

(*Knewland* 1796: 78)

14   It is interesting to note that, at the time, both buggery and robbery were capital offences. However, unlike buggery, when the accused was found guilty of robbery the sentence of death was rarely carried out. In *R.* v. *Hickman* the accused was found guilty and sentenced to death. However, the sentence was never carried out. Hickman was reprieved and, at the end of the April Session 1784, received his Majesty's pardon on condition of being transported to Africa for fourteen years.

15   These cases also illustrate the potential for the commodification of silence. Here silence is for sale (Isenbergh 1993).

16   Lord Alfred Douglas's phrase is of particular interest. It demonstrates the way in which the social that lies in the shadow of law's silence may represent itself as the silence that operates within the law. So the silence outside the law is not a silence that marks the absolute limit of discourse on the male genital body in its genital relations with other male bodies. It is a silence that creates the possibility of imagining this male genital body and these male genital relations. Here the naming of the body as silence is the very possibility of its representation.

17   He was also subject to civil proceedings relating to his debts and his marriage (Wilde 1972).

18   Other defences are also available, such as absolute and qualified privilege, fair comment, and rebuttal of prima-facie case of publication by an agent.

19   This refers to Wolfenden's meeting with Sir Maxwell Fyfe referred to in Chapter 1.

20   Silence continues to inform the review in that the transcripts of the discussions and meeting remain secret and will continue to be unavailable until well into the twenty-first century.

21   Blackmail had a particularly high profile during this period, owing in part to the Cold War. Homosexuality was seen as a threat to national security because the homosexual was open to blackmail. In a debate on the Atomic Energy Bill on 29 April 1954, the Lords considered a provision to allow an appeal against a decision to dismiss an employee from the United Kingdom Atomic Energy Authority (UKAEA). The provision was limited to those who might be dismissed on the basis of their political affiliations. The Minister accepted that political affiliation was not the only grounds for

dismissal on the basis of national security. Another threat to national security was moral turpitude, which, the Minister explained, meant homosexuality. In response the Minister was asked, 'Is he saying that a homosexual is automatically now considered to be a security risk?' In reply he declared, 'I should like to take advice on that but my impression is that the answer is "Yes". It certainly is in America. It is the result of the law as it now stands' (*Hansard*, House of Commons, Vol. 526, 1955–6, col. 1866–7). For a more general analysis of the relationship between homosexuality and national security, see Moran (1991b).

22 In a debate in the House of Commons on 29 April 1954, the Minister of Works had said, 'if a man is a homosexual he is much more easily blackmailed, owing to the law being what it is at present, than almost anybody else' (*Hansard*, House of Commons, Vol. 526, 1955–6, col. 1865).

23 See PRO HO 345/8, CHP/51, CHP/59, CHP/68 and CHP/69.

24 The committee found that in the three years prior to the inauguration of the review, 1950–3, almost 50 per cent of all the known blackmail cases reported to the police in England and Wales were connected with allegations of homosexual practices (Wolfenden 1957: 39–40, para. 110).

25 Perhaps the most important aspect of the Labouchere reform relates not so much to the inauguration of a new offence through the introduction of the phrase 'gross indecency' into the law but in the reference to 'in public or in private'. This draws attention to the fact that the law itself knows no place from which a duly authorized speaker may imagine the male body and perform that body in law. Through this phrase the law declares its unbounded operation. As there is no place from which the authorized speaker might be formally excluded the phrase signifies the general availability of terror and the threat of violence. The description of the Labouchere amendment as 'blackmailer's charter' perhaps first recognizes this always already unbounded characteristic of the law as problematic. But at the same time it marks its further institutional formalization and entrenchment in the 1885 Act. Thereby the 1885 amendment amplifies the law's economy of silence and thereby amplifies the violence of the law and the terror associated with the law's economy of silence. But it is also important to recognize that in naming it 'blackmailer's charter' that terror is also named a form of terror that must be controlled and in certain instances brought to an end. Furthermore, while the 'private' of s. 11 is a reference to the unbounded nature of law's operation, this 'private' also formally heralds the possibility of imagining within the law its opposite, a silence potentially outside the law: the private. In the name 'blackmailer's charter' is perhaps both a recognition of a certain violence in the law and the beginning of another politics, which seeks to bring that violence to an end.

26 The witness goes on to draw attention to another manifestation of blackmail. Blackmail has long justified the exclusion of homosexuals from the Civil Service in general and the Foreign Office in particular (see Moran 1991b).

27 An example of the state practice of blackmail against homosexuals by the British government might be found in the case of Sir Roger Casement (see Hyde 1964). A more recent example of its use is suggested by the incidents surrounding the Kincora Boys Home in Northern Ireland (see Foot 1990). Such a practice is not exclusive to the British government; an example of its use by other states can be found in the *Report of the Tribunal Appointed to Inquire into the Vassall Case and Related Matters* (Vassall Tribunal 1963), which deals with the state use of blackmail by the USSR.

28 Two Royal Commissions, the Street Offences Committee (1928) and the Royal Commission on Police Power and Procedure (Royal Commission 1929) had noted the proximity of law and blackmail in the proximity of plain-clothes police practice and the practice of blackmailers. They proposed to establish a distance between them by reducing the resort to plain-clothes police operations.

29 The film provides another instance of the use of silence in the naming of the wrongful act. Throughout the film, no mention is made of the act that the blackmailee has committed. This silence symbolizes the enormity of the act.

30 It is interesting to note that the one position that might give the homosexual a position of power, being a blackmailer, is not a position that is thought to be available to him; it will also lead to his downfall.

31 Gordon Westwood's survey on the lives of male homosexuals in Great Britain, first published in 1960, found further evidence of the intimate connection between the terror of the law and that of the blackmailer:

> After the case [against the blackmailer] the detective who had held the money paid to the blackmailer spoke to the contact: 'He suggested that we go to the lavatory, where he gave me back the money. Then he said that as he' d kept me out of the case, he ought to have some of it, so I gave him five pounds.'
>
> (Westwood 1960: 141)

Westwood found that, while a relatively small percentage of his sample had been blackmailed (13 per cent), almost all were affected by the possibility of blackmail. Fear of blackmail was not the only fear. Westwood also found that over 75 per cent of his sample feared the police to such an extent that they would not report the crime of blackmail against them to the police for fear of further victimization at the hands of the police:

> I used to say I'd go to the police but I've heard of a bitch who went to them and they locked her up, so I don't know what I'd do now.
>
> (Westwood 1960: 149)

32 In this respect the barrister Melville Farr is in an interesting position. He is not only the victim but he is also an agent of the law. In his role as agent of the law he also takes up the position of avenging angel and voyeur.

33 More recent research undertaken into levels of violence against lesbians and gay men draws attention to the continuing importance of the fear of the police that many gay men and lesbians live with. For example, one of the most recent surveys that provides evidence of relations between lesbians and gay men and the police is a survey undertaken by the Edinburgh Gay and Lesbian Switchboard in 1992. They found that only a small minority of those who had been subject to violence and harassment because of their sexuality had contacted the police and none of the sample expressed satisfaction with the treatment that they had received at the hands of the police (Edinburgh 1992).

34 In the course of the debate, forty-two MPs made a contribution to the debate. Eleven MPs gave full speeches on the topic of reform (the rest made brief contributions by way of short comments or questions). Of the eleven that made full speeches, ten spoke in favour of reform, though four of the eleven spoke for alternative reform proposals (two spoke and voted in support of a proposal to reduce the age of consent to 18 years and one in support of a proposal to reduce it to 17 years and initially voted for reform to the age of 16). Two spoke against reform, only one of whom eventually voted against all the proposals to reform the law. At one point, towards the end of the debate, one MP, Mrs Teresa Gorman, raised a point of order in the following terms, 'I know you to be a fair and balanced Chairman of the Committee, but may I point out that throughout the three-hour debate, one Member only has been called, my right hon. Friend the Member for Selby (Mr Alison), who has made the case against either of the clauses? I am sure that you would wish there to be balance in the argument' (*Hansard*, House of Commons, Vol. 238, 1993–4, col. 113).

35 Both MPs voted against all the reform proposals. Mr Walker acted as a teller for the Noes.

36 Mr Marlow voted against all the proposals for reform.
37 It is wrong to conclude that the public law and private law are separate domains in the USA. For example, the private-law claims of defamation and invasion of privacy by making public a private fact have to be read in conjunction with the first amendment, which seeks to protect freedom of speech. At best the legal closet is contingent. In the UK only the civil actions of defamation and breach of confidence might be invoked. A public-law dimension might arise by virtue of article 8 of the European Convention on Human Rights, which seeks to protect an individual from interference with his or her privacy by the state. It has been used against signatory states to achieve limited decriminalization of genital relations between men when those relations have been subject to total criminalization (see *Dudgeon* 1982; *Norris* 1989; *Modinos* 1993).
38 Gross also draws attention to the compulsory nature of privacy: 'The right to privacy is a double-edged sword. Privacy can be *enforced* as well as pursued' (Tucker quoted in Gross 1993: 164).
39 Also on homophobic violence, see Comstock (1991) and Blumenfeld (1992).

4 MAKING SENSE OF BUGGERY

1 See Halley (1993a, b) and Goldstein (1988, 1993), who discuss other aspects of this curious history in the context of the USA.
2 In medieval texts, reference is made to sodomy. In *Fleta* it appears in Chapter 35, 'Of Arson' (*Fleta* 1955). The chapter deals with the burning of houses as well as the burning of bodies as a form of punishment. Sodomy appears in the latter context:

> Apostate Christians, sorcerers and the like should be drawn and burnt. Those who have connection with Jews and Jewesses or are guilty of bestiality or sodomy shall be buried alive in the ground, provided they be taken in the act and convicted by lawful and open testimony.

> In the *Mirror of the Justices*, sodomy appears in Chapter 5, 'Of the Sin of Laesa Majestas', in the section of the text headed, 'Of Sins against the Holy Peace'. The crime of *laesa majestas* is described in the following terms:

> . . . a horrible sin committed against the king, and this may be against the king of heaven or earth. Against the king of heaven in three ways: by heresy, apostasy, and sodomy; against the earthly king in three ways: by those who kill the king or compass his death; by those who disinherit him of his realm, or betray his host, or compass to do so; and by these avowaters who defile the king's wife or his eldest legitimate daughter before her marriage, she being the ward of the king, or the nurse suckling the heir of the king.
>
> (*Mirror* 1983: 15)

> No mention is made of buggery in Sir William Staunford's Elizabethan text, *Les Plees Del Coron* (Staunford 1557).

3 It also provides a commentary on the same.
4 The full description offered by Coke (1628: 57) reads as follows:

> Deodands when any moveable thing inanimate, or beast animate, doe move to, or cause the untimely death of any reasonable creature by mischief in any county of the realm (and upon the sea, or upon any salt water) without the will offence or fault of himself or any person. They being so found by lawful inquisition of twelve men, being precium sanguinis, the price of blood, are forfeited to God, that is to the king, Gods lieutenant on earth, to be distributed in works of charity for the appeasing of Gods wrath.

5 The editor to Cobbett's *State Trials* notes the context of the enactment in his observations that the legislation was introduced about six years after Henry VIII had begun the suppression of the Monasteries and at about the time when their suppression seemed to have been taken up as a general policy. He also notes that the enactment coincides with an escalation of monastic suppression.

6 The theme of the relationship between buggery and treason is developed further by Coke in the chapter on buggery in his Law Reports (now to be found in the English Reports). In the extract, 'Beggary' (sic), he refers to the *Mirror of the Justices* and notes that in that text:

> the crime ... is called *Crimen laesae Majestatis*, a sin horrible, committed against the King of Heaven: and this is either against the King celestial or terrestrial in three manners: by heresy, by buggery, by sodomy.

This transcription of the *Mirror* is interesting in various ways. First, it is true to say that the *Mirror* asserts that the crime of *laesa majestas* may be committed against both heavenly and earthly kings. However, unlike Coke, the *Mirror* states that the prohibitions that are crimes against the heavenly king differ from those acts that are crimes against the earthly king. Thus, in the *Mirror*, the crimes of *laesa majestas* relevant to the king of heaven are threefold: heresy, apostasy and sodomy. The crimes of *laesa majestas* against the earthly king are not, as Coke suggests, the same crimes. The *Mirror* describes them in the following way: crimes committed by those who compass the death of the king; those who disinherit him of his realm, or betray his host or compass to do so; and by those who defile the king's wife, or his eldest legitimate daughter before her marriage or the nurse suckling the heir of the king. In his rewriting of the *Mirror*, Coke elevates the earthly king to the position of the heavenly king. A second change made by Coke in the process of transcription is to be found in his description of the three crimes against the celestial king. Rather than heresy, apostasy and sodomy, Coke transcribes them as heresy, buggery and sodomy. This slip of the pen is of interest in that it transforms the offence of apostasy, which is one of abandoning the religious orthodoxy, into the offence of buggery. As such, Coke reveals that buggery is a crime of religious heterodoxy, or more specifically the abandonment of or non-adherence to the new orthodoxy of the Protestant/Tudor revolution. Furthermore, Coke's slip marks the great importance of buggery as a signifier of the crime of dissent within the contemporary Protestant universe as it appears a second time in his accurate transcription in the third crime of sodomy. In transcribing the *Mirror*, Coke translates the ancient text according to the obsessive requirements of a particular contemporary politics and thereby transforms the earlier text. He translates the reference to sodomy in the *Mirror* where it is a sin against God alone, repeats it in the mistranslation of apostasy to buggery and rewrites it, in the name of the Protestant ascendancy where Church and State are one, as a sin against God and the king. Thereby buggery is made treason. In doing so, Coke writes the past according to the needs of his own time. He invents a new historical fact and puts it to the service of a contemporary and future politics of the new Protestant state. Thereby the *Mirror* can more easily work in conjunction with the other sacred texts of the common law to symbolize continuity.

7 This is further emphasized in writing, 'Buggery or Sodomy', as an offence that is immemorial within the specific legal tradition of the common law. As a manifestation of that legal tradition, the prohibition of buggery is given a particular temporality: without time. As part of the common law, Coke writes buggery or sodomy not only into the heart of his seventeenth-century idea of a legal culture but also into the heart of a legal culture that is defined by way of a specific geopolitical sensibility – Englishness (Goodrich 1990, 1992). The lofty position within Coke's taxonomy of

wrongs again suggests that buggery or sodomy did occupy a position at the heart of these things.

8 In addition, other factors that are not referred to in the Proemium also appear to have some significance. In particular, the texts appear to be organized by reference to a distinction between person and property, where the former has been given priority over the latter.

9 The taxonomy found in Hale's earlier text, *Pleas of the Crown*, does differ in some respects. Here the taxonomy opens not with a general exposition on capital punishment and the criminal capacity of the subject but with the distinction between offences immediately against God and offences immediately against man. As such, the ecclesiastical is given priority over the secular. Thereafter the priority is much the same as in the *Historia*, producing a similar taxonomy.

10 It is also important to recognize that factors that may inform the work of an author may change over time. Hale's work is of particular significance in this respect. Also Hale's two texts draw attention to the fact that different requirements of intelligibility may produce similar effects, as demonstrated by the common distribution of buggery within the two texts. Thus what appears to be a repetition may be the expression of different themes.

11 He then proceeds to non-capital offences against God at common law and statute, dealing first with common-law offences then with statutory offences. He then refers to the category of specific offences against religion: offences against the established Church; offences that concern all persons in general; and finally those offences relating more immediately to persons of the popish religion. Thereafter he deals with those offences more immediately against man, first more immediately against the king, second against the subject. The latter is then dealt with according to whether the offence relates to the life of man or his goods and habitation.

12 In part, this shift echoes Blackstone's taxonomy produced in *The Commentaries on the Laws of England* (Blackstone 1769). The four volumes of this work respectively deal with: the nature of laws in general; the rights of things; wrongs or civil injuries; and public wrongs, or crimes and misdemeanours. Buggery appears in Volume 4, Chapter 15: 'Of offences against the persons of individuals'. It appears as rape and assaults, batterings and woundings.

13 See *R. v. Court* (Court 1987, 1989).

14 In the offence of buggery, *both* parties are guilty of an offence, though only a man can be the one who penetrates.

15 Statutory taxonomies also feed back into further attempts by legal scholars to produce taxonomies. A good post-1956 example is to be found in the text of A.C. Smith and B. Hogan, *Criminal Law* (Smith and Hogan 1992). While their text incorporates the sexual as an organizing category of the law, it also mediates it, giving it a certain novelty. As such they rewrite and reorganize matters according to their own particular concerns. First, they use the category 'sexual' in a new way, expanding its parameters with the inclusion of indecent exposure. As such, their work points to the usefulness and the increasing valorization of the sexual. Furthermore, the distinction between natural and unnatural gains significance. For Smith and Hogan, all matters sexual are first distributed according to this division. For example, they separate out those assaults that relate to natural offences from those that relate to unnatural offences. Further-more, all matters relating to natural offences are made to precede those relating to the unnatural. Finally, they use the unnatural in completely novel ways, for example, bringing solicitation, which the Sexual Offences Act merely names as a kindred offence, exclusively within the boundaries of the unnatural.

5 THE ENIGMA OF 'HOMOSEXUAL OFFENCES'

1 One of the few references to this 'homosexuality' as a reference to female-to-female genital relations is found in a letter from Roberts, the secretary to the committee, to Wolfenden, dated 30 September 1954. Having pointed out that the memorandum from the Home Office mentions that homosexual acts between women are not punishable, he continues:

> I mention this deliberately so as to provide an opportunity for those members wishing to raise the point . . . to do so.
> It is quite possible that at some stage of our proceedings we shall be forced squarely with the question whether what is sauce for the gander ought not to be sauce for the goose.
> (PRO HO 345/2, Letter from Roberts to Wolfenden, 30.9.54)

2 The government also directed the committee to consider a second issue: the law and practice relating to offences against the criminal law in connection with prostitution and solicitation for immoral purposes.

3 'English law' refers to the law applicable to England and Wales. The review did include a consideration of the law in Scotland but not in other parts of the UK, in particular Northern Ireland, the Isle of Man or the Channel Islands. Its initial proposals for reform of the law applicable to homosexuality applied only to England and Wales.

4 For example, the first memoranda received by the committee from the Home Office (PRO HO 345/7, CHP/2) and the Scottish Home Department (PRO HO 345/7, CHP/4) deployed the phrase 'homosexual offences' as an organizing category. The Home Office document declared that, 'The following offences known to English law may be regarded as "homosexual offences" . . . ' (PRO HO 345/7, CHP/2: 1). The use of 'may' and the quotation marks that frame 'homosexual offences' draw attention to the problematic and tentative use of the term, but at the same time the text demonstrates the legibility of that phrase and its use as a citation that is deployed to produce a list of offences.

5 Papers submitted to the Wolfenden review that addressed the question of the nature and causes of homosexuality include: PRO HO 345/7, CHP/30, 36, 37; PRO HO 345/8, CHP/42, 57, 67, 84; PRO HO 345/9, CHP/86, 90, 95, 107.

6 See Curran and Parr (1957). In the final instance, the committee was much more optimistic about the possibility of abstinence. It observed that, 'Many persons, though they are aware of the existence within themselves of the propensity, and though they may be conscious of sexual arousal in the presence of homosexual stimuli, successfully control their urges towards overtly homosexual acts with others' (Wolfenden 1957: 12, para. 23). As such, the homosexual condition never manifests itself in overtly sexual behaviour. This, the committee concluded, was due to various factors: 'ethical standards, or fear of social or penal consequences . . . a happy family life, a satisfying vocation, or a well-balanced social life' (ibid.). However, it went on to conclude that, 'Our evidence suggests however that complete continence in the homosexual is relatively uncommon – as indeed it is in the heterosexual – and that even where the individual was by disposition continent, self-control might break down temporarily under the influence of factors like alcohol, emotional distress or mental or physical disorder or disease' (ibid.).

7 While the main thrust of the argument was that homosexual acts were the manifestations of homosexuality, the committee also noted that this might not always be the case. Homosexual persons have heterosexual intercourse with or without homosexual fantasies. As such, homosexual persons may perform heterosexual acts (Wolfenden 1957: 11, para. 19).

8 ̃ As an example they refer to 'the well known case of Lord Castlereigh', who developed a paranoid melancholia in which he believed he would be caught and imprisoned for homosexual offences and which led to his suicide.

9 Some members of the committee met Professor Alfred C. Kinsey in 1955. His work proposed a heterosexual–homosexual rating scale. The memorandum of Dr Kinsey's meeting with members of the Wolfenden Committee can be found at PRO HO 345/9, CHP/93.

10 See for example PRO HO 345/7, CHP/2, CHP/4; and PRO HO 345/9, CHP/95.

11 By way of the Criminal Justice and Public Order Act 1994, the offence of lewd and libidinous practices between men has been added to the list of 'homosexual offences' in Scotland that are decriminalized under the application of the Sexual Offences Act 1967 to Scotland.

12 Both the Home Office and the Scottish Home Department had noted that 'homosexual acts between women are not criminal offences' (PRO HO 345/7, CHP/2, CHP/4).

13 While this definition does not appear in the final report of the Committee, it does appear in a proposed amendment to an early draft of Part 2 – Homosexual Offences, Chapter 1 General Considerations, submitted by Dr Curran. (See PRO HO 345/11, CHP/DR/3.)

14 Gross indecency (in identical terms) is now to be found in s. 13 of the Sexual Offences Act 1956.

15 On gross indecency, see *R. v. Hornby and Peaple* (1946), *R. v. Hunt* (1950). On indecency see *R. v. Court* (*Court* 1987, 1989; Moran 1989b).

16 For an excellent discussion of the incidents that gave rise to the legislation, see Walkowitz (1992). For other histories of s. 11 see Smith (1976), Weeks (1981: ch. 6).

17 Immoral Traffic (Scotland) Act 1902, s. 1.

18 This has been amended by s. 143 of the Criminal Justice Act 1994, which decriminalized certain offences of cross-sex buggery. In order to fall within the scope of decriminalization, the act of buggery must take place in private, as defined by the act, with consent, and both parties to the act must have attained the age of 18.

19 As amended by the Criminal Justice and Public Order Act 1994.

20 Janet Halley has also noted, in the context of the USA, that buggery is sexualized in a very particular way by the courts so as to render heterosexual buggery invisible. (See Halley 1991, 1994, 1993a and b.)

21 The offence applicable to acts of indecency between women does not prescribe the gender of the wrongdoer.

22 In part this is very surprising, especially having regard to the fact that in the nineteenth century 'self pollution' had been named as the 'cause' of homosexuality as well as the cause of other sexual perversions (see, for example, Krafft-Ebing 1948). Nor can it be explained by the public–private distinction. None of the offences incorporated in the list work with that distinction as a limit to the criminalizing potential of the law. The idea of privacy as a limit to the criminal law applicable to genital relations between men is an idea that entered the law of England only in 1967 with the Sexual Offences Act.

23 On amnesia and the law see Moran 1993.

24 As Foucault notes, this does not lead to the conclusion that the object of consideration must remain mute or the unconscious object of attention but he must speak according to a particular code: 'a certain reasonable, limited canonical and truthful discourse' (Foucault 1981a: 29). See also Halley (1993a: 82).

25 See Foucault (1979: 17).

26 It is important to note that the Admiralty fleet orders do not talk about 'homosexual offences' or 'homosexual acts'. The offences and acts are variously referred to as 'unnatural acts', 'unnatural vice', 'unnatural offences' and 'offences of immorality'.

The orders were submitted as an appendix to the 'Memorandum from the Admiralty...'. In that memorandum the offences are referred to as 'homosexual offences'. This draws attention to the fact that in some instances, such as this, papers were presented in response to requests from the committee. In making such requests the phrase 'homosexual offences' was invariably used. Responses worked to that agenda even though this was a departure from their existing classificatory practice.

27 There is an interesting disjunction at this point between two schemata of knowledge at work in and through the examinations. This is demonstrated in the importance that is given to the signs that are to be taken as evidence of buggery. The law takes the sign of penetration as the requirement of buggery. The medical examination takes the presence of semen as the sign of buggery.

28 The offences of sexual immorality between males that Naval Officers may be called upon to investigate are: (1) Buggery; (2) Assault with intent to commit buggery; (3) Indecent assault; (4) Act of gross indecency with a male person; (5) Procuring the commission of an act of gross indecency with another male person; (6) Attempts to commit offences (1),(4) and (5) above; (7) Inciting to commit either (1), (3), (4), or (5); (8) Uncleanness, or other scandalous action in derogation of God's honour and corruption of good manners.

29 Michel Foucault also makes the point:

> ... 'crime' the object with which penal practice is concerned has profoundly altered: the quality, the nature, in a sense the substance of which the punishable element is made, rather than its formal definition. It is these shadows [such as perversions] lurking behind the case itself that are judged and punished.
>
> (Foucault 1979: 17)

30 Ellis had been Clinical Psychologist at the Mental Hygiene Clinic of the New Jersey State Hospital at Greystone Park, and Chief Psychologist of the New Jersey State Diagnostic Center and of the Department of Institutions and Agencies.

31 Dr Snell notes that the category of pseudo-homosexual is probably composed of those who have outwardly, and in the absence of stress or contingency, developed normal heterosexuality; their earlier homosexual urges are but feebly repressed, their veneer of heterosexuality is thin. It is in this group that the denial of heterosexual opportunity, for example, among seamen, prisoners of war and occasionally in our own establishments, results in homosexual behaviour.

32 Other examples are to be found in the Wolfenden papers: PRO HO 345/9, CHP/86: Appendix 1 and 4 (both relate to different classificatory schemes deployed by medical officers in the Prison Medical Service); PRO HO 345/9, CHP/95 (British Medical Association memorandum, Appendix A), and PRO HO 345/9, CHP/84 (Dr Sessions Hodge, of the Neuro-Psychiatric Department, Musgrove Park Hospital, Taunton, who offered an analysis of fifty cases that he had seen in his criminological practice).

33 See Foucault (1982: 208–26; 1979: 135–95).

34 Other papers presented to the Wolfenden Committee draw our attention to the wider dispersion of sites of production both in the law and beyond the law.

6 POLICING AND THE PRODUCTION OF THE HOMOSEXUALITY OF LAW

1 In its final report, the committee made several conclusions. First, it found that this dramatic change had peculiar characteristics. For example, it was a dramatic increase that had a specific geographical locus, being confined to England and Wales (Wolfenden 1957: Appendix 1, Table 1). While these statistics were widely believed to evidence a great increase during the previous fifty years, not only in the prevalence of homosexuality but also in homosexual behaviour in England and Wales, they

concluded that there was little evidence to support this. They suggested that the belief that these statistics inevitably represented an increase in homosexuality and homosexual behaviour reflected the fact that the whole subject of homosexuality was much more freely discussed than it was formerly and public interest in the subject had undoubtedly increased, with the consequence that court cases were more frequently reported and that responsible papers and magazines gave considerable space to its discussion. Further support for this conclusion, they suggested, was to be found in Scotland, where there were similar beliefs about the rise in homosexuality and homosexual behaviour, even in the absence of any statistical evidence of any increase in offences known to the police (Wolfenden 1957: 19, para. 42).

The committee then went on to offer a more detailed explanation of the statistical picture. Through a comparison of the statistical picture between, on the one hand, England and Wales and, on the other hand, Scotland, the committee drew attention to various important factors that were at play in the statistical representation of homosexuality and homosexual behaviour known to the police. For example, the dramatic differences between the appearance of homosexuality produced in the statistics for England and Wales and its production in those that related to Scotland was in part a manifestation of some fundamental differences in criminal procedure in these two jurisdictions. Various factors were isolated. For example, the statistics represented different prosecution practices and procedures. In Scotland 'homosexual offences' were prosecuted not, as in England and Wales, by those who conducted the investigation and performed the acts of detection, the police, but by a separate public prosecutor, the Procurator Fiscal. The Procurator Fiscal determined which offences were to be prosecuted by way of a duty to initiate and conduct proceedings in the Sheriff's Court in any case in which he considered that the public interest warranted such action. This appeared to have generated particular effects in the statistical representation of homosexuality by way of 'homosexual offences'. For example, in England and Wales many of the offences recorded as known to the police, and many that appeared in the statistics of prosecutions, related to events that had taken place several years prior to police intervention. In Scotland such incidents rarely appeared in the statistics. In large part this was due to the policies put into action by the Procurator Fiscal. They did not appear in statistics that related to court proceedings as procuratorial policy and practice had determined that, as a general rule, no clear public interest would be served in the prosecution of 'stale offences'. Nor did they appear in statistics relating to offences known to the police, because the procuratorial policy had an impact upon police practice. As there was little likelihood of a prosecution going forward, the police would not waste time in pursuing inquiries into old offences (Wolfenden 1957: 50–1, paras. 137–8). Another important factor influencing the formation of the statistical picture related to differences in the forms and requirements of proof used in the two jurisdictions. In England and Wales, confessions by the accused were central to the success of most proceedings. However, the committee found that the overwhelming importance given to confessions appeared to be peculiar to England and Wales. In Scotland only one of the nine men convicted during the same period made a written admission. Another 'curious difference' that informed the representation of homosexuality and homosexual behaviour in the statistics was one related to the interpretation of the law and the resulting use of specific laws to bring proceedings against men. In particular (Wolfenden 1957: 42–4, paras. 116–25), in England and Wales large numbers of men were charged with the statutory offence of persistently soliciting or importuning (originally s. 1 of the Vagrancy Act 1898 and now s. 32 of the Sexual Offences Act 1956). Its popularity was evidenced in the fact that, in 1954, 481 men appeared before the courts in England and Wales on this charge. In 1955 the figure had increased to 521. Of these offences just over 300 related to acts detected in London. In Scotland, the corresponding provision (s. 1 of the Immoral Traffic (Scotland) Act 1902) had never been used in connection with men seeking other men for genital relations, as the same provision had never been interpreted as being applicable to male-to-male relations. In England and Wales it was used almost exclusively against men seeking genital relations with other men.

The Wolfenden Committee also documented a number of other reasons why the statistics could not be taken as a representation of either levels of homosexuality in general or homosexual behaviour in particular. First, the laws relating to 'homosexual offences', and for that matter to other sexual offences, were bound to operate unevenly. Many 'homosexual acts', especially those committed by consenting adults in private, would never come to light, so that the number of those detected and prosecuted in respect of 'homosexual acts' would always constitute but a fraction of those who from time to time would commit such acts (Wolfenden 1957: 46–8, para. 129). Second, unlike some offences (such as housebreaking), which by their nature tend to be reported to the police as they occur, many sexual offences, particularly those taking place between consenting parties (victimless crimes), become 'known to the police' only when they are detected by the police or in the rare event that the incident happened to be reported to them. Thus, in general, any figures relating to homosexual offences known to the police would not be an image of the prevalence of homosexuality and homosexual behaviour *per se*. The meaning of these statistics, they concluded, was to be found elsewhere.

2   In a memorandum by Sir John Nott-Bower, KCVO, Commissioner of Police of the Metropolis, the Commissioner commented that, 'Part of the increase shown between 1946 and 1951 . . . is undoubtedly due to increased Police activity' (PRO HO 345/7, CHP/10: para. 33). This was particularly reflected in increases in offences of importuning known to the police. Statistical evidence correlating increases in police surveillance and increases in offences of importuning known to the Metropolitan Police is to be found in Appendix C of the memorandum.

3   The report noted that the increase was substantially accounted for by a large increase in the recorded incidence of offences in the London Metropolitan Police District. The majority of the remaining cases had occurred in two other major urban areas.

4   Statistics relating to offences known to the police in Scotland suggest that the extension of the application of the 1967 reforms to Scotland in the Criminal Justice (Scotland) Act 1980, s. 80, produced similar effects. There was nearly a 400 per cent rise in the number of offences known to the police between 1980 (nineteen) and 1981 (eighty-two). There was over a 300 per cent rise in the number of convictions from 1980 (eleven) to 1981 (thirty-eight) (*Gay Scotland*, 11 November/December 1983).

5   The reference to 'private' does not refer to the Sexual Offences Act 1967 definition of that term, which defines 'private' as where there are not more than two persons. Many of the incidents catalogued here would thus remain criminal after the 1967 reforms. Therefore these descriptions of police practices still have a significance today.

6   Four per cent (nineteen of the men) had come to the attention of the police as the result of a report made to the police by one of the parties to the offence. Eleven per cent (fifty-three cases) came before the police as a result of being caught *in flagrante delicto* (in the act) by someone who intruded, accidentally or otherwise, on their privacy. The remainder came before the police by various unexplained means.

7   In most instances, the police described this other offence as being of a 'homosexual character', but in thirty-four instances it was of a different type, for example larceny (Wolfenden 1957: 46–8, para. 129).

8   Evidence of similar incidents can be found in the Wolfenden papers. See, for example, PRO HO 345/9, CHP/92.

9   The advice given by the solicitors whom the men consulted was to the effect that, contrary to what the police had told them, they were perfectly within their rights to see each other and even to continue living together, although the solicitors advised against the latter. After consulting their own solicitors and the National Council for Civil Liberties, the Homosexual Law Reform Society wrote suggesting that the men's solicitors ought to approach the Chief Constable to ascertain whether the police intended bringing any charges or not, in view of the fact that eleven weeks had elapsed since the original interrogations.

10 See Wildeblood (1957) and Moran (1991a).

11 This has been a common characteristic of investigations, and has a very long history. It was central to the first published proceedings against men who had passionate relations with other men in the eighteenth century. In the case of *R.* v. *Thomas Wright* for sodomy, April 1726, the court was told how a large number of proceedings against various men who frequented Mother Clap's Molly House had arisen out of a quarrel between two men. In revenge one of the men had spoken about the Molly House (see *Select Trials* 1742: Vol. 2, 367–9). One difference between these early examples of detection and current practice is that, until the mid-nineteenth century, the investigative role of the police was not well developed. The investigation and detection were often conducted by individuals. In the case of the molly houses much of the investigation and detection work was undertaken by individuals associated with religious organizations and with organizations dedicated to the reform of manners (see Bahlman 1957; Radzinowicz 1947; Norton 1992).

12 At the time of the Wolfenden review, this belief had been inspired by a series of incidents (see Wildeblood 1957; Moran 1991b).

13 Another example of this type of investigation occurred in Huddersfield. The Huddersfield trawl is typical. Two youths were interviewed about their sex lives; they provided names and addresses of acquaintances, who were in turn interviewed and a network established. Diaries and address books were inspected, statements demanded involving explicit 'confession' of homosexuality, details occasionally leaked to friends, families and employers. The justification was the detection of under-age offences. The time spent and extraordinary detail of the questions asked suggest a wider interest in the gay community (Galloway 1983: 114–15).

14 At his trial the judge ordered the jury to acquit him. After the case, Y was dismissed from his job but sued the police authorities for unfair dismissal, and was awarded £1,600 in compensation.

15 In 1981, during the period when these investigations were proceeding, gays in Huddersfield issued a broadsheet that read as follows:

> A CRY FOR HELP.
> 1984 has arrived at least in Huddersfield three years early.
>
> Police HARASSMENT
> A minority group – the gay community – is being hounded by members of the West Yorkshire Metropolitan Police Force.
>
> Gay men are:
> being taken from their homes and places of work
> being stopped on the street and questioned
> being forcibly medically examined
> being refused legal advice whilst in police custody
> being reported to employers for being gay
> suffering physical injury whilst in police custody
> having diaries and address books confiscated . . .
>
> (Galloway 1983: 112)

16   It is of interest to note that one of the objections made by police to gay venues where applications for a drinks licence was being made was that certain gay venues were 'too blatant'. The clientele of gay saunas and sex shops are also used by the police as an opportunity to demand that homosexuality speak its name (Galloway 1983: 114). The gay press provides evidence on a week-by-week basis that this gay venue continues to be another opportunity for the police to demand that homosexuality speak its name.

17   At the time Crane and Galloway were writing, many of these police acts were illegal. Due to reforms, such as the Police and Criminal Evidence Act 1984 and the Criminal Justice and Public Order Act 1994, many of these policing techniques are now lawful.

18   While police often assume that violence against gay men, including the murder of gay men, is perpetrated by other gay men, this is often a false assumption. It is problematic in various ways. First, it may frustrate all attempts to discover the one who is committing the acts of violence and, second, it gives a spurious legitimacy to surveillance of men who have sex with men.

19   Many different stories have been told about the origins of the investigation (see Richardson 1992). The activities of the men preceded the investigation by several years, dating from at least 1978.

20   At the time of writing (1995), they continue before the European Court of Human Rights.

21   These investigations also provide further evidence that police practices are not so much concerned with the investigation and detection of criminal acts but rather with the collection of data that relates to character, identity and otherwise lawful behaviour. This is institutionalized into police practice as is evidenced in a 1980 training manual for the police in Scotland. The manual instructed officers that:

> Apart from actually detecting an act of indecency... The movements of persons of manifestly lewd disposition should always be closely watched as many and varied are the artifacts employed by these persons to achieve their evil objects.
>
> (Quoted in Crane 1982)

22   This is not to suggest that the increase necessarily represents an increase in the incidence of either homosexuality or homosexual behaviour that gives rise to complaints. The Wolfenden Committee found that in many instances the investigation was not initiated as the result of either a complaint or evidence of a specific offence.

23   Crane gives an example of an upsurge in this type of operation that appears to be connected with personnel changes, particularly at senior level, in the police. In Manchester, in the north of England, a new Chief Constable, Sir John McKay, was appointed in 1959. Before his arrival prosecutions for importuning were virtually unknown; there was only one prosecution for male importuning in 1955, none at all in 1956 or 1957 and only two in 1958. The figures thereafter were: 30 in 1959, 105 in 1960, 135 in 1961 and 216 in 1962 (Crane 1982: 225, fn. 2). Others have drawn attention to the way in which in some instances these increases continue to be both localized and at the same time very dramatic. For example, Galloway describes an instance in the northern town of Stockport, where convictions rose 700 per cent in a year (Galloway 1983: 108). The repeated references to the use of entrapment and *agents provocateurs* in the lesbian and gay press draw attention to the continuing current importance of these practices.

24   It is interesting to note that 'A' division (Hyde Park area) had the highest rates of detection of gross indecency but almost no arrests for importuning.

25   The rest were detected in parks, streets and passages and in parked vehicles. Sir John Nott-Bower noted that the offence of gross indecency was charged most commonly in

situations where the act took place in public lavatories or public house lavatories without an attendant. It normally referred to an incident between two men who were found masturbating each other. Charges of gross indecency were also brought where the defendant was about to commit sodomy and the police stepped in before the act was completed or reached the stage where an attempt could be proved. Sometimes these offences would be charged where several men were involved.

26 In part these increases related to charges of importuning but they also reflected a new use of gross indecency charges that were, after 1967, triable in courts of summary jurisdiction. The greatest increase in prosecutions was taking place in these courts. Other attempts have been used to make convictions easier still by bringing charges not under the Sexual Offences Act 1956 but under the Public Order legislation, such as the Public Order Act 1936 (see Galloway 1983: 109).

7 THE SOMATIC TECHNIQUES OF POLICING

1 These practices are not peculiar to England and Wales. See Maynard (1994) and Desroche (1990, 1991) on Canada; Edelman (1994), Humphreys (1970) and Gallo (1966) on the USA; and Wotherspoon (1991) on Australia.

2 The efficiency of other forms of police practices may differ. For example, police raids, which may be both reactive (in response to specific complaints) and proactive (to prohibit sexual activity), may be a relatively inefficient way of securing convictions, which may depend (a) upon the success of an element of surprise and (b) upon a belief by the defendants that the speed of the raid and the design of the facility allowed the police to witness criminal actions taking place.

3 In general, the CHE report to the Royal Commission on Criminal Procedure (CHE 1979) concluded that the evidence demonstrated that these operations absorbed considerable amounts of police time and evidenced remarkable police ingenuity. The practices of investigation and detection included the installation of spy-holes, mirrors, false grids and air vents, hidden compartments in cubicles, broom-cupboards and toilet roofs – all to allow for surveillance in public conveniences. In some cases the police photographed men leaving toilets. In others they made lists of registration numbers from cars parked nearby (see also Crane 1982: 49). In some instances these investigations were of considerable duration; police had been stationed in and around lavatories for up to nine hours at a stretch.

4 The CHE report (CHE 1979) noted that, while entrapment by plain-clothes police *agents provocateurs* was a tactic officially condemned by the Home Office, these investigations rarely used uniformed officers. The CHE research suggested that the use of *agents provocateurs* was widespread. Newspaper cuttings frequently referred to plain-clothes officers operating within conveniences, and to special training given to selected young constables. Arrested men often complained of such incitement, too often for coincidence. Gay men preventing offences by warning other men of clandestine police operations had been arrested for obstructing the police in the execution of their duty. Where observation was only partially successful, the CHE research found evidence that the police had falsified evidence. For example, in one case the truth of the police evidence depended upon a policeman's ability to see round two corners. More recent evidence in the lesbian and gay press suggests that police surveillance inside public conveniences is moving from low technology to high technology with the use of video cameras and fibre optics. While lesbian and gay organizations have attempted to persuade the police that prevention is better than detection and that uniformed patrols will be more effective in curbing criminal behaviour than plain-clothed officers, there has, particularly in England and Wales, been a reluctance to abandon plain-clothes operations in public conveniences.

5 This is not to suggest that plain-clothes operations originated at this time. There is evidence that this type of surveillance has been practised in various forms over a longer period of time. For example, in the eighteenth century members of the Society for the Reformation of Manners engaged in similar activities in order to prosecute 'mollies'. For a summary of their activities, see Bray (1982) and Norton (1992). These operations differ from those described in this chapter in that they took place before the modern idea of policing had been established. These investigations and prosecutions were conducted by ordinary citizens rather than a police force. Other evidence suggests that the case of *Horton* v. *Mead* was not an isolated event. A parliamentary debate in 1912 (*Hansard*, House of Commons, Vol. 43, 1912, col. 1858) discussed plain-clothes police practices that concentrate upon public conveniences. Two official reports published in the late 1920s, the *Report of the Street Offences Committee* (1928) and the *Report of the Royal Commission on Police Powers and Procedure* (Royal Commission 1929), noted the continued, if problematic, use of plain-clothes officers in the investigation and detection of men who seek sexual relations with other men, and cautiously offered support for the continued operation of these practices. Neither report contains any detail of the police practices concerned.

6 There is also evidence in the report that suggests that this particular surveillance operation was not an isolated example. During the course of the trial, two other police officers gave evidence to the court that they had seen the appellant on many occasions during the month of May in the same neighbourhood late at night behaving in a similar manner.

7 For examples of practices of invisibility in other jurisdictions, see Maynard (1994) and Desroche (1990, 1991).

8 According to the statements obtained by the police as a result of interrogation, Preece said that he had arrived before Howells, that when he heard someone enter the other cubicle he unblocked the hole, and masturbated, hoping he would be watched. He had 'sensed' that he was being watched; he himself had watched Howells. Howells admitted masturbating but denied that he had been watching Preece. A written statement signed by him was put in evidence, which contained the following words: 'I looked through the hole in the wall between the two cubicles and saw a male adult in the other cubicle. This male adult was masturbating himself. I then started to masturbate myself and was still watching the other man.' He did deny having said that he masturbated himself while watching the other man. Both men were found guilty and their appeals were dismissed.

9 The defendant contested this evidence. He said that he was only in the public lavatory for some three minutes. During that period he urinated at one of the urinals and washed and dried his hands. Then he went and stood two or three stalls away from the police officer and looked at him 'out of sexual curiosity'. He denied the rest of the prosecution account, saying that the public lavatory was well lit and fitted (as he knew) with video cameras.

10 For example, see PRO MEPO 3/990; PRO HO 345/7, CHP/10; *Gay Times*, October 1993, p. 18.

11 While the law reports are written according to these requirements of silence, they also evidence its failure in that they document these encounters and thereby enable the wider dissemination of information. They document the lives and activities of men whose lives might otherwise be silenced. Having said that, it is also important to recognize that in turn this violates the privacy they work so hard to maintain.

12 More recent evidence of these police practices has been collected by lesbian and gay organizations. For example, various aspects of these police practices were produced as a result of a data gathering exercise undertaken by the Campaign for Homosexual Equality (CHE) and documented in a report submitted to the Royal Commission of Criminal Procedure (CHE 1979). The report suggested that covert surveillance

operations were a common police practice. In presenting data to CHE, Ivan Geffen, a solicitor, informed them that his experience of these police practices suggested that:

> the police are active in providing facilities for cottaging, including creating holes in cubicle walls and setting up positions for themselves to spy on people who are inside. I assume that cottaging is fairly widespread, so that the coincidence that certain public lavatories provide a disproportionate number of cases, suggests that senior officers at the local stations are abnormally active against gays.
>
> (Geffen to CHE, 26 March 1979, Hall Carpenter Archive)

13 Both parties were over 21 and it was implicit that the homosexual conduct would take place in private. Ford was arrested, charged and found guilty.

14 Unlike in the law report version of events, where the role of the police is represented as one of almost total passivity, in this version of the events it is difficult to conclude that the police practice in this instance was one of mere passive observation. Police practice is implicated more deeply in the production of the encounter.

15 Humphreys suggests that in attempting to undertake this project the police have to cope with a kind of double closure. One may gain entrance into the deviant enterprise only if one has had previous connection with it, but one can gain such connection only if one already has that expertise (D.J. Black, quoted in Humphreys 1970: 24).

16 During the trial, Gray denied having said anything about staying the night. He denied that his purpose had been to have homosexual relations. On the contrary, he told the court that he wanted to see if he could cheer the man up because he looked miserable, and out of place, as if he was a homosexual who was having difficulty coming to terms with his condition and who might be helped by talking to someone who had experienced the same problems. He told the court that he had for some years been a member of an organization that gave advice to homosexuals. His membership had lapsed but while still a member he had done work of this kind and had respected the rule of the organization that no sexual contact was to take place with any person who was being helped in this way.

17 While this example illustrates many features that are in common with the other recorded examples of this type of police practice, it is exceptional in that Douglas resisted the pressure to plead guilty and over seven months later at Knightsbridge Crown Court a jury took 25 minutes to reach a verdict of not guilty.

18 He appeared at Tower Bridge Police Court (a court of summary jurisdiction) the following day, before W.H.S. Oulton, Esq., Magistrate, and was remanded on bail. No evidence was given as the accused requested to be legally represented.

19 Humphreys also added the problematic suggestion that this is a participant role where the sexuality is optional.

20 Humphreys notes that being a 'watchqueen' was a particularly productive role for the purposes of surveillance: 'not only has being a watchqueen enabled me to gather data on the behavioural patterns, it has facilitated the linking of participants in homosexual acts with particular automobiles' (Humphreys 1970: 28). For an application of this in the context of policing, see also Chapter 6.

21 Its advantage for one who wishes to observe, according to Humphreys, is that it avoids 'sexual pressure'.

22 Humphreys adds that chicken (teenagers), who are not, contrary to popular wisdom, the primary object of sexual interest in these encounters, and who tend generally to cause permanent disruption to an encounter (Humphreys 1970: 80), might turn into hustlers (male prostitutes).

23 Humphreys suggests that there is only one exception to this general rule of role flexibility: the straight. This 'walk on' role is recognizable upon the exit of the actor.

24 Humphreys adds that this strategy, followed by an early departure from the premises, is all that those who wish to 'play it straight' need to know about the tearoom game. If he makes the positioning move in that manner, no man should ever be concerned about being propositioned, molested or otherwise involved in the action.

25 Humphreys suggests that this draws attention to the importance of the rule of not forcing one's intentions on another. He stated that he had observed no exceptions to this rule. He went on to declare that he doubted the veracity of any person (detective or otherwise) who claimed to have been 'molested' in such a setting without first having 'given' his consent by showing an erection.

26 Humphreys stresses the importance of this stage in the proceedings. This phase of the game is a fundamental feature of the performance reflecting the non-coercive nature of these encounters.

27 In an example referred to in the CHE report to the Royal Commission on Criminal Procedure (CHE 1979), reference is made to a surveillance operation in 1974 in the public lavatory at Piccadilly Circus Underground Station that had been in operation for three weeks. The officers involved appeared to be relatively successful in their investigations: 'every day we knock off a wanker'. On this particular occasion they made allegations against a Special Branch police officer. He denied the charge, saying that he had entered the lavatory while shadowing an IRA suspect. He had been standing with one hand on his belt, with his fly zipped up and holding a statement folder in his other hand when arrested. He was eventually charged with persistently soliciting and attempting to bribe a police officer. (He was acquitted at his trial and sued the officers.)

28 Somewhat later in the memorandum a Superintendent with the Police Force gives some information about the design of this facility:

> This urinal is of such a nature and in such a position to lend itself to acts of indecency, being an old round iron structure with small holes from which any approach from outside can be observed from within.
> The Bermondsey Borough Council have been recently considering the demolition of the urinal, and have passed a resolution to do so as soon as the local District Surveyor has obtained a suitable site in the vicinity for a new and more modern structure.

> These observations are a good example of the interrelationship between sexuality and design referred to earlier.

29 Burke's collection of interviews with lesbian and gay officers provides another account of the nature of policing in these situations, which gives an insight (albeit limited) into the contradictory responses of those who are required to perform these somatic techniques (Burke 1993: 44–55).

30 The Royal Commission commented: 'the use of a foreign phrase for which there is no exact English equivalent indicates that the practice is regarded as alien to our habits and traditions' (Royal Commission 1929: 40, para. 104).

31 Similar points were repeated in 1983 by John Alderson, a retired Chief Constable of the Devon and Cornwall Police Force, who was suggesting that:

> uniformed patrols warning people of complaints and the illegality of public sex cautions for first time offenders
> involvement of gay groups, to publicise complaints and act as referral agencies for first-time offenders.

(Galloway 1983b: 108)

32   The cases referred to by the learned magistrate were all cases brought by the officers of the London Passenger Transport Board, respecting cases in the lavatories at railway stations.

33   Only recently has there been some evidence of its decline (*Gay Times*, July 1994 and *Capital Gay*, 5 August 1994). However, the gay press continues to report regular and extensive police campaigns (see the regular 'cottage alert' column in the *Pink Paper*).

34   In the documentation of those encounters a very high proportion of the men accused claim to be the victims of fabricated evidence or entrapment by a police decoy – an *agent provocateur*.

35   Foucault suggests that there is another factor at work here: a sensualization of power and a gain of pleasure. The police investigation, examination and report may have the overall and apparent objective of saying no to all wayward or unproductive sexuality, but the fact is that they function as a mechanism with a double impetus: pleasure and power. There is the pleasure that comes from exercising a power that questions, monitors, watches, spies, searches out, palpates and brings to light, and on the other hand there is the pleasure that kindles at having to evade this power, flee from it, fool it or travesty it. There is the power that lets itself be invaded by the pleasure it is pursuing, and opposite it is the power asserting itself in the pleasure of showing off, scandalizing, or resisting. Capture and seduction, confrontation and mutual reinforcement: the police and homosexuals have played this game continually since the late nineteenth century. These attractions, these evasions, these circular incitements have traced around bodies and sexes, not boundaries not to be crossed but perpetual productive spirals of power and pleasure (Foucault 1981a: 45). Mark Burke notes the potential erotic aspect of these encounters:

> This produced a twofold effect: an impetus was given to power through its very exercise; an emotion rewarded the overseeing control and carried it further; the intensity of the confession renewed the questioner's curiosity; the pleasure discovered fed back to the power that encircled it. But so many pressing questions singularized the pleasures felt by the one who had to reply. They were fixed by a gaze, isolated and animated by the attraction; it drew out those peculiarities over which it kept watch. Pleasure spread to the power that harried it; power anchored the pleasure it uncovered.
>
> (Burke 1993: 48)

8   THE USES OF HOMOSEXUALITY: RIGHTS, VICTIMS AND PARLIAMENTARY REFORM

1   See also Goodrich (1987). Goodrich's analysis is also useful as it looks at the way this decision is incorporated into the body of law as tradition and truth.

2   The conviction based upon this second offence was quashed in the House of Lords for various reasons. Two of the Law Lords, Lord Reid and Lord Diplock, quashed the conviction on the basis that no such offence as conspiracy to outrage public decency was known to the law. The three remaining judges, concluding that the offence *was* known to English law, quashed the conviction on the basis that the summing up had been defective.

3   The limited formal use in law of the terms 'homosexual' and 'homosexuality' is not a characteristic unique to the English law. A similar pattern of usage is at least a characteristic of the other major common-law legal systems: Scotland, Northern Ireland, the Republic of Ireland, Australia, New Zealand, Canada and the United States. With the exception of the USA and the Irish Republic, all the other major common-law jurisdictions have added 'homosexual' to their legal lexicon following the incorporation of provisions based upon, if not the same as, those found in the Sexual

Offences Act 1967. Only Scotland and Northern Ireland have added 'homosexuality' as found in the Local Government Act 1988. 'Sexual orientation' is another new term in law used to represent same-sex genital relations (see Herman 1994; Wintermute 1995).

4   Article 8 reads as follows:

    1.   Everyone has the right to respect for his private and family life, his home and his correspondence.

    2.   There shall be no interference by a public authority with the exercise of his right except such as is in accordance with the law and is necessary in a democratic society in the interests of national security, public safety or the economic well-being of the country, for the prevention of disorder or crime, for the protection of health or morals, or for the protection of the rights and freedoms of others.

5   This theme is developed and explored in Gaete 1993.
6   The majority opinions in *Bowers* v. *Hardwick* take up this position.
7   Many different stories have been told about the origins of the investigation (see Richardson 1992). The activities of the men preceded the investigation by several years, dating from at least 1978.
8   Subsequent to the publication of these opinions, the English Law Commission, a statutory body created under s. 1 of the Law Commissions Act 1965, has conducted an investigation into consent and offences against the person, which is dominated by a consideration of *R.* v. *Brown*. A consultation paper has been published. At the time of writing the Law Commission is considering the responses to the consultation paper. The final report will be published in due course. At the time of writing these proceedings still haunt the English legal system. It has been accepted by the European Commission of Human Rights as an arguable case and has now gone to the European Court of Human Rights (see *Gay Times*, February 1996). *R.* v. *Brown* was distinguished in *R.* v. *Wilson* (*Times*, 29 February 1996).
9   Lord Mustill, a minority judge in the House of Lords, provides the exception to this (see note 21 below).
10 In addition to the charges relating to assault occasioning actual bodily harm and unlawful wounding, and charges of aiding and abetting these assaults upon themselves, some defendants were charged with keeping a disorderly house, aiding and abetting the same, publishing an obscene article and the taking and possession of an indecent photograph of a child.
11 The judicial opinions presented in these judgments are also of significance in other respects. First, they provide evidence of the legal practices through which the performances undertaken by the defendants are made legible within the law and thereby subject to the law. Second, they provide an opportunity to study a theme that dominates the judicial attempts to make sense and nonsense of these bodies and desires: the relationship between law and violence. Third, they provide a demonstration of the way in which the law–violence distinction is used within legal practice in order to represent the practice of law itself. Finally, they provide an opportunity to consider the way in which the body and its desires might be used to develop a critique of the law.
12 The decision by the defendants to name the acts 'homosexual' is also problematic beyond the objections raised by the police, the prosecution and the judiciary. For example, a report in the *Guardian* newspaper draws attention to the attribution of 'homosexuality' to the individuals who performed these acts. The mere fact that these particular pleasures were performed by men in the context of an all-male group does not necessarily support the application of 'homosexual' to either the acts or persons involved. The *Guardian* journalist noted that one of the accused was reported to have

concealed his 'injuries' from his wife for twenty-six years (Kershaw 1992). The judicial pronouncements, especially those by Lord Lane, also provide some further evidence of the problematic nature of this use of 'homosexual'. For example, Lord Lane noted that one of the group had 'settled into a normal heterosexual relationship' (*Brown* 1992a: 310). On the one hand this might be read as an assertion of the connection between homosexuality and sado-masochism, as it implies that with the disappearance of his homosexuality his interest in sado-masochism had disappeared suggesting a radical separation between sado-masochism and heterosexuality. However, this is not the only reading of Lord Lane's observation. It might also suggest that Lord Lane's ascription of homosexuality to this sado-masochism practitioner was premature. Sociological research (Lee 1983) draws attention to the fact that men who engage in all-male sado-masochistic rituals may not define themselves as homosexual or gay but as heterosexual. In general, this research draws attention to the fact that men who are interested in sado-masochism might perform such acts with homosexually or gay defined men for various reasons. For example there is a relative absence of a developed sado-masochistic recreational culture in a heterosexual context. Sado-masochistic recreational practices are therefore more readily accessible within a gay (same-sex) context. This can be explained in various ways. It is a reflection of the different place of recreational sex within gay and straight cultures. It points to the relatively developed and institutionalized nature of the gay recreational sex culture that facilitates encounters. It draws attention to the importance and attraction of participating in activities that are well organized, and in particular participating in a context where there is a developed etiquette of public sex that facilitates risk reduction, characteristic of gay culture, and the underdevelopment of an etiquette of risk reduction for public sex in a heterosexual context. Having regard to these factors, heterosexually defined men may join other homosexually or gay defined men in order to pursue their interests. The presence of heterosexually defined men in all-male sado-masochistic activities also problematizes another assumption: that there is any necessary connection between these desires, or pleasures, and genital contact, genital preference or sexualized identity, as is suggested by the term 'homosexual'. Pleasure may, in these situations, be derived not so much from the sex, sexuality or gender of the parties involved but from performances that have little to do with such matters. However, the judges in both the Court of Appeal and the House of Lords repeatedly asserted that these acts were the acts of homosexual sado-masochism. To assert that these participants and their acts were acts of homosexual sado-masochism required the judges to ignore and erase all these dimensions of the defendants' activities.

13· Certainly the decision to charge some of the acts of the defendants as sexual offences (keeping a disorderly house, s. 8 of the Disorderly Houses Act 1751, which makes it an offence to keep a house not regulated by the restraints of morality, including decency, the taking and possession of indecent pictures and the publication of obscene materials) draws attention to the fact that at least some of the activities were defined in the proceedings as sexual (*Brown* 1994: 256–8).

14 Acts of gross indecency are an offence by virtue of s. 13 of the Sexual Offences Act 1956. While no definition of gross indecency is provided in the Act, the courts have given it a generous interpretation. For example, in *R. v. Howells* (1976), where two men were found guilty of gross indecency having been seen by police officers masturbating in adjacent cubicles in a public lavatory, the Court of Appeal, upholding the conviction, defined gross indecency as an act that required the mere participation and co-operation of two or more men in an indecent exhibition. 'Indecency' was defined in *R. v. Court* (1987; see also Moran 1989a), where the accused was found guilty of indecent assault as a result of spanking a girl's bottom. The House of Lords, upholding the conviction,

concluded that the 'indecent' of 'indecent assault' required that the act should have some proximity to the genital area.

15 Lord Jauncey argued that acts of gross indecency usually take one of three forms: 'in which none includes violence or injury'. The acts before the court were acts of violence and as such could not be defined as acts of gross indecency (*Brown* 1994: 247 D).

16 It is not only the attribution of homosexual that is to be denied but also any sexual attribution (see *Brown* 1994: Lord Templeman 235E–G).

17 This provision arose out of a proposal put forward by the Wolfenden Committee during the course of its review of the law and practice relating to homosexual offences. The committee found that in England and Wales, in some instances, the police interrogation was not confined to investigating the particular offence that gave rise to the police action. One example is given of charges relating to an incident that had occurred thirteen years prior to the police investigation, arising out of another unconnected incident. Criminal procedure in Scotland made such practices impossible (Wolfenden 1957: para. 133–43).

18 Many of the actions would not have been protected by the terms of the 1967 Act, which only provides protection for acts performed in private. 'In private' is defined in the following terms:

1(2) An act which would otherwise be treated for the purpose of this Act as being done in private shall not be so treated if done –

(a) when more than two persons take part or are present; or
(b) in a lavatory to which the public have or are permitted to have access, whether on payment or otherwise.

19 It should be noted that these time limits only relate to the two offences named 'homosexual offences' (buggery and gross indecency) under the 1967 Act. Other 'sexual offences' are not covered by this restriction. Incidents brought in 1993 under the charge of keeping a disorderly house stretch back fourteen years to 1979 (*Brown* 1994: 256–8).

20 An example is to be found in the recent reform of the law in the Republic of Ireland, the Criminal Law (Sexual Offences) Act 1993, which seeks to reform the law in response to a decision of the European Court of Human Rights (Norris 1989). The reforms include the decriminalization of importuning, other than importuning for the purposes of prostitution.

21 The two judges who make up the minority opinions in the House of Lords adopt a different approach to the human rights argument. Lord Mustill, while criticizing the concept of privacy and the jurisprudence that surrounds it, concludes in the final instance that the general tenor of the decisions of the European Court furnishes valuable guidance on the approach that the English courts should adopt. There is clear support, he concludes, for the right of the appellants to conduct their private lives undisturbed by the criminal law. Lord Slynn, having determined that the acts of the defendants are not unlawful under existing law, concluded that it was not necessary to proceed to consider the provisions under the European Convention of Human Rights (*Brown* 1994: 281H–282C).

22 The logic of this argument also informs the recent review of this issue undertaken by the Law Commission (1994: 57–60, esp. para. 33.4).

23 Girard continues, 'but the judicial system is infinitely more effective' (Girard 1979: 23). On sacrifice and the law see Rush and Young (1995) and Haldar (forthcoming).

24 A more recent case dealing with the same point is *R.* v. *Aitken*, where the court concluded that a defence of consent was viable where, during the course of a party, the defendants poured lighter fuel over a colleague, overpowered his resistance and set light to the fuel,

causing extremely severe burns with 35 per cent of his body sustaining superficial burns (*Aitken* 1992).

25   Homosocial is a word occasionally used in history and social sciences, where it describes social bonds between persons of the same sex; it is a neologism obviously formed by analogy with 'homosexual' and just as obviously meant to be distinguished from 'homosexual'. In fact it is applied to such activities as 'male bonding' which may in our society be characterised by intense homo-phobia, fear and hatred of homosexuality.

(Sedgwick 1985: 1)

26 Various references in the judgments point to this heterosocial violence. For example, it is suggested in the definition of consent discussed in the context of 'rough horseplay' in *R. v. Jones*. It is a definition that echoes the definition of consent found in the context of another manifestation of male violence: rape (Duncan 1994). As many feminist scholars have pointed out, the law is not only tolerant of acts of violence between men but also tolerant of acts of violence by men upon women (see for example Adler 1987; Brownmiller 1975; Edwards 1981, 1989; Marsh 1982; Maloesian 1993; Tempkin 1987; Bourlet 1990; Hague 1993; Russell 1990; Dobash 1992; Kapeller 1986; Dworkin 1981; Mackinnon 1987, 1989; Young 1990). Much less has been written on violence against lesbians and gay men, and little has yet been written on the tolerance of that violence by the law (but see Comstock 1991; McMullen 1990; Mezey 1992). While the judgments in *R. v. Brown* do not deal directly with violence by men against women, there is evidence in the judgments that this is also part of the intra-community violence that finds its substitute in the body and desires of homosexual sado-masochism. Two references are made in the judgments to legal condonation of violence in a heterosocial context. The first is the case of *R. v. Clarence* (1888). In that case the accused had consensual intercourse with his wife, he knowing and she ignorant that he had gonorrhoea, with the result that she was infected. The law condoned this act of violence against the wife, accepting that the act was not actual bodily harm, grievous bodily harm or an unlawful wounding. The reason given in support of this conclusion was that this act was not an assault and therefore not unlawful. The second case referred to is *R. v. Donovan* (1934), where the accused beat a woman with a cane. While this decision appears to deny the possibility of consent to acts of violence, and thereby might be thought of as a decision that protects women, it should not be forgotten that the man who beat the woman in this instance successfully appealed against conviction on the basis of the trial judge's misdirection to the jury, and remained unconvicted.

27 The absence of victims in the context of the criminalization of genital relations between men is not peculiar to this case. In the offence of buggery, all parties to the act are guilty of an offence.

28 At the same time, the opinions of the appeal court judges reveal another side to this will to knowledge: a systematic blindness. They demonstrate a refusal to know concerning the very thing that they purport to bring to light and whose formulation has been so extravagantly solicited (Foucault 1981a: 55). See Moran (1995).

29 Another police raid was reported in *Gay Times* in July 1993: 'Herts police seize gay man's SM paraphernalia'. Another report in *Capital Gay*, 30 July 1993, 'Police step up on SM raids', referred to further police raids in north London.

30 Fifteen of the men who were the object of this police operation have recently obtained compensation, £40,000 from the police on the basis of wrongful arrest (*Pink Paper*, 10 March 1995).

31 This takes many forms: raids on bookstores selling lesbian and gay material, such as Gay's the Word in London; police surveillance of public toilets (using *agents provocateurs* and fibre-optic equipment) and of public places (sometimes with infra-red surveillance

equipment) used by gay men to meet other men; and police raids on discos, all of which are catalogued regularly in the lesbian and gay press.

32 A third incident subsequent to the *Brown* decision was the publication of a consultation paper that reviews the various judicial opinions in *R. v. Brown* in particular and the issue of consent and violence in general (Law Commission 1994; Bamforth 1994). Perhaps the most interesting feature of the Law Commission's preliminary analysis is that the structure and content of the analysis mimic that of the judicial analysis in *R. v. Brown*. The analysis proceeds on the basis that homosexual sado-masochism is violence in opposition to the law. It perpetuates the myth of guilt of the consensual sado-masochism and of the designation of the consenting participants as 'victims' of their own violence (Law Commission 1994: 1, ff. 5). It repeats the belief in legal practice as a rule-bound, rational, limiting and limited practice at the same time that it reveals its arbitrary, unruly and unlimited potential.

It differs from *R. v. Brown* in the outcome that is proposed. The consultation paper suggests that certain consensual acts that were criminalized under the *Brown* decision would no longer be criminal under the terms of earlier proposals put forward by the Commission for the reform of the criminal law (Law Commission 1993: paras 15.1–15.31). Provided the acts did not amount to 'serious injury', consent would absolve the accused. However, the decriminalization of such consensual acts is far from clear. Even in its proposals for reform, the Law Commission celebrates the arbitrary nature of law. Thus the new key concept in law, 'serious injury', is said to involve 'an element of judgment'. The Law Commission notes that, 'serious injury', '…will not give a potential injurer a conclusive answer in every case as to whether he should act on a particular consent of the victim' (Law Commission 1994: paras 10.19–10.22). In the final instance, the meaning of 'serious' is to be left to the jury and as such it can only be known *post hoc* (Law Commission 1994: para. 15.8).

While the Commission appears to be able, albeit very tentatively, to recognize boxing as an institutionalized celebration of male-to-male violence and urges that its legality be reviewed (Law Commission 1994: paras 10.19–10.22), the other forms of institutionalized violence are to be called 'healthy recreation' (Law Commission 1994: para. 44.4). Thereby the essence of sport would appear to be a violence that is conducted according to rules that are not simply made up, or alleged to have been made up, by the participant as they go along but are well established (Law Commission 1994: 6, ff. 270). As such, the violence of sport appears to disappear the further it is institutionalized, only to reappear projected onto sado-masochism, which is presented as the other to 'healthy' violence.

33 The other reforms affecting the 1967 Act relate to the expansion of its operation to include Scotland and Northern Ireland.

34 Sections 146 and 147 of the Criminal Justice and Public Order Act 1994 have reformed the law on homosexuality applicable to the Merchant Navy. The effect of this reform is to apply the provisions of the Sexual Offences Act 1967 to the Merchant Navy.

35 In the period between the Policy Advisory Committee Working Party Report and the current debate, the conjunction between age and homosexuality achieved a high profile not in the context of decriminalization debates but in the context of debates relating to municipal socialism, local democracy and the central government control of local government. The legislative effect of the debates was s. 28 of the Local Government Act 1988. A small body of literature deals with this particular debate (Thomas and Costigan 1990; Colvin 1989; Cooper 1993, 1994; Smith 1995a).

36   Unless otherwise indicated, all subsequent references to *Hansard* in this chapter and in the notes to this chapter refer to this volume and this debate, which is to be found at cols. 21/2/94, 74–123.

37   For other examples of the equality theme see cols. 81, 82, 86, 90, 104 and 110.

38   The law achieves these effects by crossing the legal boundary between public and private: 'It distorts the life of every generation of gay men as they come into adulthood.' Furthermore,

> the view that homosexuals have to live apart from society can no longer be sustained. . . .
> We now have an openly gay MP, lesbian and gay police officers, journalists, actors and pop stars, sports women and men, bankers, barristers, postmen and nurses.
> This is a profound social change. It has been made possible by thousands of individual men and women who have 'come out' and made the decision to live openly, confident of their sexuality and the integrity of their lives.
>
> (Stonewall 1993)

This also draws attention to the way in which the law fails to achieve its objective of enforced invisibility. The visibility argument is used in support of the Currie reform proposal (see *Hansard*, cols. 76, 81, 85).

39   Other pro-16 advocates developed similar arguments. On law in general see *Hansard*, cols. 82, 83, 84, 85, 89, 91, 98, 99; on the specific theme of discrimination see *Hansard*, cols. 86, 89, 97.

40   At the same time, Alison also concludes that 'it is pointless to say that the law is an inhibiting factor' (*Hansard*, col. 103).

41   *Hansard* records that Sir Nicholas Fairbairn's contribution was cut short at this point due to a disputation caused by his contribution.

42   Each of these themes can be found at various points in the debate. For example, corruption and perversion inform contributions relating to the sexual fragility of males, see Walker, cols. 79, 98, Durrant, cols. 86, 87, Howard, col. 93, Alison, cols. 101, 103, and Paisley, col. 113. Cf. Kinnock, cols. 81, 83, 85, Blair, col. 98 and Smith, col. 111, where the natural–unnatural distinction is deployed in favour of the Currie reform. Here homosexual is natural.

9   CONCLUSIONS

1   I have developed this particular with respect to the law in my own work (see Moran 1991a, 1993). Other examples might be found in the following: Dyer (1987); Watney (1987); Theweleit (1987, 1989).

2   Derrida (1992) develops the point:

> 'written communication' must . . . remain legible despite the absolute disappearance of every determined addressee in general for it to function as writing, that is for it to be legible. It must be repeatable – iterable – in the absolute absence of the addressee or of the empirically determined set of addressees. . . . The possibility of repeating, and therefore of identifying, marks is implied in every code, making of it a communicable, transmittable, decipherable grid that is iterable for a third party, and thus for any possible user in general. . . . a written sign carries with it a force of breaking with its context, that is, the set of presences which organize the moment of its inscription.
>
> (Derrida 1992: 315–17)

BIBLIOGRAPHY

Adler, Z. (1987) *Rape on Trial*, London: Routledge.

Alshuler, A.W. (1994) 'Sir William Blackstone and the shaping of American Law', *New Law Journal*, 1 July, 896–7.

Altman, D. (1971) *Homosexual Oppression and Liberation*, London: Allen Lane.

—— (1982) *The Homosexualisation of America*, Boston: Beacon Press.

Atherton, J. (1641) *The Life and Death of John Atherton Lord Bishop of Waterford and Lysmore*, London.

Audley, Lord Mervyn (1642) *The Arraignment and Conviction of Mervyn Lord Audley, Earl of Castlehaven*, London.

—— (1679) *The Trial of the Lord Audley, Earl of Castlehaven, for Inhumanely Causing his Own Wife to be Ravished, and for Buggery*, London.

—— (1699) *The Tryal and Condemnation of Mervin Lord Audley, Earl of Castlehaven at Westminster, April the 5th 1631*, London.

—— (1708) *The Case of Sodomy, in the Tryal of Mervin Lord Audley, Earl of Castlehaven*, London: John Morphew.

—— (1710) *The Case of Sodomy, in the Tryal of Mervin Lord Audley, Earl of Castlehaven* (2nd edn), London: John Morphew.

Bahlman, D.W.R. (1957) *The Moral Revolution of 1688*, Newhaven: Yale University Press.

Baker, J.H. (1972) 'Coke's Note-books and the sources of his reports', *Cambridge Law Journal* 59: 59–86.

—— (1979) *An Introduction to English Legal History*, 2nd edn, London: Butterworth.

Bamforth, N. (1994) 'Sado-masochism and consent', *Criminal Law Review*, pp. 661–4.

Barthes, R. (1977) *Roland Barthes* (trans. by R. Wang), New York: Hill & Wang.

—— (1990) *S/Z* (trans. R. Miller), Oxford: Blackwell.

Bartlett, N. (1988) *Who Was That Man?: A Present for Oscar Wilde*, London: Serpent's Tail.

Bates, A.P. (1979) *The System of Criminal Law*, Chatswood: Butterworth.

Bell, V. (1993) *Interrogating Incest: Feminism, Foucault and the Law*, London: Routledge.

Bellamy, J.G. (1970) *The Law of Treason in England in the Later Middle Ages*, Cambridge: Cambridge University Press.

—— (1979) *The Tudor Law of Treason: An Introduction*, London: Routledge & Kegan Paul.

Bersani, L. (1987) 'Is the rectum a grave?' *October* 43 (Winter): 197–222.

Bingham, C. (1971) 'Seventeenth-century attitudes towards deviant sex', *Journal of Interdisciplinary History* 1: 447.

Blackstone, W. (1769) *Commentaries on the Laws of England: Volume 4, Of Public Wrongs*, reprinted 1979, London: University of Chicago Press.

Blumenfeld, W.J. (1992) *Homophobia: How We All Pay the Price*, Boston: Beacon Press.

Boswell, J. (1980) *Christianity, Social Tolerance and Homosexuality*, Chicago: University of Chicago Press.

Bourlet, A. (1990) *Police Intervention in Marital Violence*, Oxford: Oxford University Press.

Bray, A. (1982) *Homosexuality in Renaissance England*, London: Gay Men's Press.

Bristow, J. (1990) 'Introduction: texts, contexts', *Textual Practice* 4 (2): 1.

Britton (1865) *Britton (on the laws of England)*, trans. F.M. Nichols (the original French text c. 1290), Oxford: Clarendon.

Brown, B. (1993) 'Troubled vision: legal understandings of obscenity', *New Formations* 19 (Spring): 29.

Brownmiller, S. (1975) *Against Our Will: Men Women and Rape*, London: Secker & Warburg.

Brundage, J.A. (1987) *Law, Sex, and Christian Society in Mediaeval Europe*, Chicago: University of Chicago Press.

Burke, M. (1993) *Coming Out of the Blue*, London: Cassell.

Butler, J. (1990) *Gender Trouble: Feminism and the Subversion of Identity*, New York: Routledge.

—— (1991) 'Imitation and gender insubordination', in D. Fuss (ed.) *Inside/Out*, London: Routledge, pp. 13–31.

—— (1993) 'Critically Queer', *GLQ, A Journal of Lesbian and Gay Studies* 1 (1): 17.

Cain, P.A. (1993) 'Litigating for lesbian and gay rights: A legal history', *Virginia Law Review* 79: 1551–1643.

Califia, P. (1994) *Public Sex: The Culture of Radical Sex*, Pittsburgh: Cleis Press.

Cant, B. and Hemmings, S. (1988) *Radical Records: Thirty Years of Lesbian and Gay History*, London: Routledge.

Chappell, D. and Wilson, P.R. (1968) 'Public attitudes to the reform of the law relating to abortion and homosexuality', *The Australian Law Journal* 42: 175–180.

CHE (1979) Evidence to the Royal Commission of Criminal Procedure (photocopied document), London: Campaign for Homosexual Equality.

Cohen, E. (1993) *Talk on the Wilde Side*, London: Routledge.

Cohen, M. (1982) 'Soliciting by men', *Criminal Law Review*, pp. 349–62.

Coke, Sir E. (1614) *A Booke of Entries: Containing Perfect and Approved Presidents*, London.

—— (1628) *The Third Part of the Institutes of the Laws of England*, 1979 reprint, London: Garland.

Colvin, M. (1989) *Section 28: A Practical Guide to the Law and its Implications*, London: National Council For Civil Liberties.

Comstock, G.D. (1991) *Violence Against Lesbians and Gay Men*, New York: Columbia University Press.

Cooper, D. (1993) 'An engaged State: sexuality, governance and the potential for change', *Journal of Law and Society* 20: 3.

—— (1994) *Sexing the City: Lesbian and Gay Politics within the Activist State*, London: Rivers Oram Press.

Copley, A. (1989) *Sexual Morality in France 1780–1980*, London: Routledge.

Crane, P. (1982) *Gays and the Law*, London: Pluto Press.

Criminal Law Revision Committee (1966) Eighth Report: *Theft and Related Offences*, Cmnd 2977, London: HMSO.

—— (1984) Fifteenth Report: *Sexual Offences*, Cmnd 9213, London: HMSO.

Crompton, L. (1980) 'The myth of lesbian impunity', *Journal of Homosexuality* 6 (1–2): 11.

Curran, Dr. D. and Parr, Dr. D. (1957) 'Homosexuality: an analysis of 100 male cases seen in private practice', *British Medical Journal* 1: 797–801.

Deleuze, G. (1989) 'Coldness and cruelty', in *Masochism*, trans. from the French by J. McNeil, New York: Zone Books, pp. 15–138.

Derrida, J. (1977) 'Signature event context', in *Margins of Philosophy*, trans. A. Bass (originally published in French in 1972), Hemel Hempstead: Harvester, pp. 307–30.

—— (1987) 'Devant le loi', in A. Udoff (ed.) *Kafka and the Contemporary Critical Performance: Centenary Readings*, Bloomington: Indiana University Press.

—— (1992) 'Force of law: the "mystical foundations of authority"', in D. Cornell, M.

Rosenfeld and D. Gray Carlson (eds) *Deconstruction and the Possibility of Justice*, London: Routledge, pp. 3–67.

Desroche, F.J. (1990) 'Tearoom trade: a research update', *Qualitative Sociology* 13 (1): 39–61.

—— (1991) 'Tearoom trade: a law enforcement problem', *Canadian Journal of Criminology* 1: 1–21.

Devlin, P. (1965) *The Enforcement of Morals*, Oxford: Oxford University Press.

Dobash, R. (1992) *Women, Violence and Social Change*, London: Routledge.

Dollimore, J. (1991) *Sexual Dissidence: Augustine to Wilde, Freud to Foucault*, Oxford: Clarendon Press.

Douzinas, C. and Warrington, R. (1994) *Justice Miscarried: Ethics, Aesthetics and the Law*, London: Harvester Wheatsheaf.

Duncan, S. (1994) 'Law as literature: deconstructing the legal text', *Law and Critique* V (I): 3–29.

Dworkin, A. (1981) *Pornography: Men Possessing Women*, London: Women's Press.

Dyer, R. (1987) *Heavenly Bodies: Film Stars and Society*, London: Macmillan.

East, Sir E.H. (1803) *Pleas of the Crown*, Volume 1, 1972 reprint, London: Professional Books.

Edelman, L. (1994) 'Tearooms and sympathy, or the epistemology of the water closet', in *Homographesis*, London: Routledge, pp. 148–72.

Edinburgh (1992) *Edinburgh Gay Switchboard Violence Survey.*

Edwards, S. (1981) *Female Sexuality and the Law*, Oxford: Robertson.

—— (1989) *Policing Domestic Violence: Women, the Law and the State*, London: Sage.

Elias, N. (1978) *The History of Manners*, New York: Pantheon Books.

Ellis, A. (1954) 'Interrogation of sex offenders', *Journal of Criminal Law, Criminology and Police Science* 45: 41–7.

Ellis, H. (1897) *Studies in the Psychology of Sex: Vol. 1 Sexual Inversion*, London: The University Press.

—— (1900) *Studies in the Psychology of Sex: Vol. 2 The Evolution of Modesty, The Phenomena of Sexual Periodicity, Auto-erotism*, Leipzig: The University Press.

Elwood, J.P. (1992) 'Outing, privacy, and the first amendment', *Yale Law Journal* 102: 747.

Evans, D.T. (1993) *Sexual Citizenship: The Material Construction of Sexualities*, London: Routledge.

Farshae, K. (1993) *Countdown on Spanner Information Pack*, London: Countdown on Spanner.

Fernbach, D. (1980) 'Ten years of gay liberation', in D. Adlam *et al.* (eds) *Politics and Power*, Vol. 2, London: Routledge & Kegan Paul, pp. 169–88.

Fleta (1955) *Fleta, seu commentarius juris Anglicani sic nuncupatus*, edited by H.G. Richards and G.O. Sayles (original c. 1290), London: Selden Society.

Foot, P. (1990) *Who Framed Colin Wallace*, London: Pan Books.

Foucault, M. (1970*) The Order of Things: An Archaeology of the Human Sciences*, trans. A. Sheridan (first published in French 1966), London: Tavistock.

—— (1977) 'Nietzsche, genealogy, history', in D.F. Bouchard (ed.) *Language, Counter-memory, Practice*, Ithaca, NY: Cornell University Press.

—— (1979) *Discipline and Punish: The Birth of the Prison*, London: Peregrine Books.

—— (1980) *Power/Knowledge: Selected Interviews and Other Writings 1972–1977*, Brighton: Harvester Press.

—— (1981a) *The History of Sexuality, Vol. 1: An Introduction*, London: Penguin.

—— (1981b) 'The order of discourse', in R. Young (ed.) *Untying the Text*, London: Routledge & Kegan Paul, pp. 48–78.

—— (1982) 'Afterword: the subject and power', in H.L. Dreyfus and P.R. Abinow (eds), *Michel Foucault: Beyond Structuralism and Hermeneutics*, Brighton: Harvester Press, p. 208.

—— (1989) 'Introduction', in G. Canguilhem, *The Normal and the Pathological*, New York: Zone Books.

French, R. (1993) *Camping by a Billabong*, Leichhardt, Queensland: Black Wattle Press.

Fuss, D. (1989) *Essentially Speaking: Feminism, Nature and Difference*, London: Routledge.

—— (1991) 'Inside/out', in D. Fuss (ed.) *Inside/Out*, London: Routledge, pp. 1–12.

Gaete, R. (1993) *Human Rights and the Limits of Critical Reason*, Aldershot: Dartmouth Publishing.

Gallo, J.J. (1966) 'The consenting adult homosexual and the law', *UCLA Law Review* (March) 668.

Galloway, B. (ed.) (1983a) *Prejudice and Pride: Discrimination Against Gay People in Modern Britain*, London: Routledge & Kegan Paul.

—— (1983b) 'The police and the courts', in B. Galloway (ed.) *Prejudice and Pride: Discrimination Against Gay People in Modern Britain*, London: Routledge & Kegan Paul, pp. 102–5.

GALOP (1984) *1st Annual Report*, London: Gay London Police Monitoring Group.

—— (1985) *2nd Annual Report*, London: Gay London Police Monitoring Group.

Garland, D. (1985) *Punishment and Welfare: A History of Penal Strategies*, Aldershot: Gower.

Gay Left Collective (1980) *Homosexuality: Power and Politics*, London: Allison & Busby.

Gilbert, A.N. (1978) 'Sodomy and the law in eighteenth century Britain', *Societas* 8: 251.

Girard, R. (1979) *Violence and the Sacred* (trans. from the French by P. Gregory), Baltimore: Johns Hopkins University Press.

—— (1986) *The Scapegoat* (trans. from the French by Y. Freccero), Baltimore: Johns Hopkins University Press.

Glazebrook, P.R. (1971) 'Introduction', in Sir Matthew Hale, *Historia Placitorum Coronae*, Volume 1, London: Professional Books.

GLF (1971) *Gay Liberation Manifesto*, London: Gay Liberation Front.

Goldstein, A.B. (1988) 'History, homosexuality, and political values: searching for the hidden determinants of *Bowers* v *Harwick*', *Yale Law Journal*, p. 1073.

—— (1993) 'Commentaries', *Virginia Law Review* 79 (7): 1781.

Goodich, M. (1979) *The Unmentionable Vice: Homosexuality in the Later Medieval Period*, Santa Barbara, Calif.: Ross-Erikson.

Gooding, C. (1992) *Trouble with the Law? A Legal Handbook for Lesbians and Gay Men*, London: Gay Men's Press.

Goodman, J. (1995) *The Oscar Wilde File* (1st edn 1988), London: Allison and Busby.

Goodrich, P. (1987) *Legal Discourse: Studies in Linguistics, Rhetoric and Legal Analysis*, Basingstoke: Macmillan Press.

—— (1990) *Languages of Law*, London: Weidenfeld.

—— (1992) 'Poor illiterate reason: history, nationalism and common law', *Social and Legal Studies* 1: 7.

Gordon, G.H. (1978) *The Criminal Law of Scotland*, Edinburgh: Green & Son.

Gough, J. and MacNair, M. (1985) *Gay Liberation in the Eighties*, London: Pluto Press.

Grant, J.E. (1991) ' "Outing" and freedom of press: sexual orientation's challenge to the Supreme Court's categorical jurisprudence', *Cornell Law Review* 77: 103–14.

Green, J. and McCormick, J. (1961) *Victim* (unpublished final shooting film script), British Film Institute Library.

Greenberg, D.F. (1988) *The Construction of Homosexuality*, Chicago: University of Chicago Press.

Grey, A. (1992) *Quest for Justice: Towards Homosexual Emancipation*, London: Sinclair-Stevenson.

Griew, E. (1990) *The Theft Act 1968 and 1978*, 6th edn, London: Sweet & Maxwell.

Gross, L. (1993) *Contested Closets: The Politics and Ethics of Outing*, Minneapolis: University of Minnesota Press.

Habermas, J. (1990) *The Philosophical Discourse of Modernity*, Cambridge: Polity Press.

Hague, G. (1993) *Domestic Violence: Action for Change*, Cheltenham: New Clarion Press.

Haldar P. (forthcoming) 'Words with the Shaman', in S. McVeigh, P. Rush and A. Young (eds) *Criminal Legal Practices*, Oxford: Oxford University Press.

Hale, Sir M. (1678) *Pleas of the Crown, A Methodical Summary of the Principle Matters Relating to the Subject*, 1982 reprint, London: Professional Books.

—— (1736) *Historia Placitorum Coronae*, Volume 1, 1971 reprint, London: Professional Books.

Hall, S. (1980) 'Reformism and the legislation of consent', in National Deviancy Conference (ed.) *Permissiveness and Control: the Fate of the 60's Legislation*, London: Macmillan Press.

Hallam, P. (1993) *The Book of Sodom*, London: Verso.

Halley, J.E. (1991) 'Misreading sodomy: a critique of the classification of "homosexuals" in Federal Equal Protection Law', in J. Epstein and K. Straub (eds) *Body Guards: The Cultural Politics of Gender Ambiguity*, London: Routledge.

—— (1993a) 'The construction of heterosexuality', in M. Warner (ed.) *Fear of a Queer Planet: Queer Politics and Social Theory*, Minneapolis: University of Minnesota Press.

—— (1993b) 'Reasoning about sodomy: act and identity in and after *Bowers* v *Hardwick*', *Virginia Law Review* 79: 1721–80.

—— (1994) '*Bowers* v *Hardwick* in the Renaissance', in J. Goldberg (ed.) *Queering the Renaissance*, Durham, NC: Duke University Press.

Hansard (1912) Official Reports, 5th Series, *Parliamentary Debates, House of Commons, Vol. 43*.

—— (1953–4) Official Reports, 5th Series, *Parliamentary Debates, House of Lords, Vol. 187*.

—— (1955–6) Official Reports, 5th Series, *Parliamentary Debates, House of Commons, Vol. 526*.

—— (1993–4) Official Reports, 6th Series, *Parliamentary Debates, House of Commons, Vol. 238*.

—— (1994) Official Reports, 6th Series, *Parliamentary Debates, House of Commons, Vol. 255, 21 February*.

Hart, L. (1994) *Fatal Women*, Princeton: Princeton University Press.

Hawkins, W. (1716–21) *Pleas of the Crown*, Volume 1, 1973 reprint, London: Professional Books.

Herek, G.M. and Berrill, K.T. (1992) *Hate Crimes: Confronting Violence Against Lesbians and Gay Men*, London: Sage.

Herman, D. (1994a) *Rights of Passage: Struggles for Lesbian and Gay Legal Equality*, Toronto: University of Toronto Press.

—— (1994b) 'Law and morality revisited', paper presented to the Canadian Learned's Law and Society Conference, June 1994, and to the American Law and Society Conference, June 1994.

Hume, D. (1986) *Commentaries on the Law of Scotland*, Vol. 1: *Respecting Crimes*, Edinburgh: Law Society of Scotland.

Humphreys, L. (1970) *Tearoom Trade*, London: Duckworth.

Hunt, A and Wickham, G. (1994) *Foucault and Law*, London: Pluto Press.

Hyde, H.M. (1964) *Famous Trials 9: Roger Casement*, Harmondsworth: Penguin.

—— (1970) *The Other Love*, London: William Heinemann.

—— (1973) *The Trials of Oscar Wilde*, New York: Dover.

—— (1976) *The Cleveland Street Scandal*, New York: Cowards, McCann & Geoghegan.

Isenbergh, J. (1993) 'Blackmail for A to C', *University of Pennsylvania Law Review* 141: 1905.

Jeffrey-Poulter, S. (1991) *Peers, Queers and Commons*, London: Routledge.

Jeffreys, S. (1994) *The Lesbian Heresy*, London: Women's Press.

Johansson, W. and Percy, W.A. (1994) *Outing: Shattering the Conspiracy of Silence*, Binghampton, NY: Harrington Park Press.

Kapeller, S. (1986) *The Pornography of Representation*, Cambridge: Polity Press.

Katz, J. (1993) 'Blackmail and other forms of arm twisting', *University of Pennsylvania Law Review* 141: 1567–1616.

Katz, J.N. (1983) *Gay/Lesbian Almanac*, New York: Harper & Row.

—— (1992) *Gay American History: Lesbians and Gay Men in the U.S.A.*, New York: Meridian.

Kershaw, A. (1992) 'Love', *Weekend Guardian*, 28th November: 6–12.

Kinsman, G. (1987) *The Regulation of Desire*, Montreal: Black Rose Books.

Krafft-Ebing, R. (1947) *Psychopathia Sexualis* (originally published in 1876), trans. F.J. Rebman, New York: Pioneer Publications.

Kristeva, J. (1982) *Powers of Horror*, trans. L.S. Roudiez (first published in French 1980), New York: Columbia University Press.

Laplanche, J. and Pontalis, J.B. (1988) *The Language of Psychoanalysis*, London: Karnac Books.

Lauritsen, J. and Thorstad, D. (1974) *The Early Homosexual Rights Movement (1864–1935)*, New York: Times Change Press.

Law Commission (1993) *Legislating the Criminal Code: Offences Against the Person and General Principles*, Report No. 218, London: HMSO.

—— (1994) *Criminal Law: Consent and Offences Against the Person*, Consultation Paper No. 134, London: HMSO.

Lee, J.A. (1983) 'The social organization of sexual risk', in T.S. Weinberg and G.W. Levi Kamel (eds) *S and M: Studies in Sadomasochism*, Buffalo, NY: Prometheus Books, pp. 175–93.

Leinen, S. (1993) *Gay Cops*, New Brunswick, NJ: Rutgers University Press.

Lewin, R. (1990) 'A few minutes with Fractious Fran', *Advocate*, July 3: 63.

Lindgren, J. (1984) 'Unraveling the paradox of Blackmail', *Columbia Law Review* 84: 670–717.

MacKenzie, Sir G. (1688) *The Institutes of the Law of Scotland*, Edinburgh: John Reid.

Mackinnon, C. (1987) *Feminism Unmodified: Discourses on Life and Law*, Boston: Harvard University Press.

—— (1989) *Towards a Feminist Theory of the State*, Boston: Harvard University Press.

McIntosh, M. (1968) 'The homosexual role', in K. Plummer (ed.) (1981) *The Making of the Modern Homosexual*, London: Hutchinson, pp. 30–43.

McMullen, R.J. (1990) *Male Rape: Breaking the Silence on the Last Taboo*, London: Gay Men's Press.

Majury, D. (1994) 'Refashioning the unfashionable: claiming lesbian identities in the legal context', *Canadian Journal of Women and the Law* 7 (2): 286.

Maloesian, G. (1993) *Reproducing Rape: Domination Through Talk in the Court Room*, Cambridge: Polity Press.

Marsh, J.C. (1982) *Rape and the Limits of Law Reform*, Boston: Auburn House.

Maynard, S. (1994) 'Through the hole in the lavatory wall: homosexual subcultures, police surveillance and the dialectics of discovery, Toronto, 1890–1930', *Journal of the History of Sexuality* 5 (2): 207.

Mezey, G.C. and King, M.B. (1992) *Male Victims of Sexual Assault*, Oxford: Oxford University Press.

Mirror (1893) *Mirror of the Justices*, Vol. 7, edited by W.J. Whittaker, London: Selden Society.

Mohr, R.D. (1988) *Gays/Justice: A Study of Ethics, Society and Law*, New York: Columbia University Press.

—— (1992) *Gay Ideas: Outing and Other Controversies*, Boston: Beacon Press.

Moran, L.J. (1989a) 'Sexual fix, sexual surveillance', in S. Shephaerd and M. Wallis (eds) *Coming on Strong: Gay Politics and Culture*, London: Unwin Hyman, pp. 180–98.

—— (1989b) 'What is indecency?', *Liverpool Law Review* XI (1): 99.

—— (1991a) 'Justice and its vicissitudes', *Modern Law Review* 54: 146.

—— (1991b) 'The uses of homosexuality: homosexuality for national security', *International Journal of the Sociology of Law* 19: 149–70.

—— (1993) 'Buggery and the tradition of law', *New Formations* 19: 110.

—— (1995) 'Violence and the law: the case of sado-masochism', *Social and Legal Studies* 4 (2): 225.

—— (1996) 'The homosexualisation of human rights' in C. Geasty and A. Tomkins (eds) *Understanding Human Rights*, London: Mansell, pp. 313–35.

Newburn, T. (1992) *Permission and Regulation: Law and Morals in Post-war Britain*, London: Routledge.

Norton, R. (1992) *Mother Clap's Molly House: The Gay Subculture in England 1700–1830*, London: Gay Men's Press.

Ortiz, D.R. (1993) 'Creating controversy: essentialism and constructivism and the politics of gay identity', *Virginia Law Review* 79 (7): 1833.

Plucknett, T.F.T. (1942) 'The genesis of Coke's Reports', *Cornell Law Review* 27: 190.

Policy Advisory Committee on Sexual Offences (1980) Working Paper, London: HMSO.
—— (1991) *Report on the Age of Consent in Relation to Sexual Offences*, Cmnd 8216, London: HMSO.
PRO HO 345/2, Wolfenden Committee Correspondence.
PRO HO 345/3, Buggery: Points for abolitionism as a separate offence, Dr D Curran and Dr J. Whitby.
PRO HO 345/4, Note by the Secretary, September 1955.
PRO HO 345/7, CHP/2, Memorandum submitted by the Home Office, 2, Homosexual Offences.
PRO HO 345/7, CHP/4, Memorandum submitted by the Scottish Home Department, Homosexual Offences.
PRO HO 345/7, CHP/10, Memorandum by Sir John Nott-Bower, KCVO, Commissioner of Police of the Metropolis, 22 November 1954.
PRO HO 345/7, CHP/21, Memorandum from the Admiralty for the Departmental Committee on Homosexual Offences and Prostitution.
PRO HO 345/7, CHP 26, Memorandum of the Church of England Moral Welfare Council.
PRO HO 345/7, CHP/30, Royal College of Physicians, Evidence presented to the Departmental Committee.
PRO HO 345/7, CHP/36, Evidence submitted by Dr Winifred Rushworth, Honorary Medical Director of Davidson Clinic Edinburgh.
PRO HO 345/7, CHP/37, Memorandum from Paddington Green Children's Hospital Psychological Department on Homosexuality and the Law.
PRO HO 345/8, CHP/42, Memorandum of the Institute of Psycho-Analysis.
PRO HO 345/8, CHP/51, Statement submitted by Mr Peter Wildeblood.
PRO HO 345/8, CHP/57, Memorandum submitted by the Institute of Psychiatry.
PRO HO 345/8, CHP/59, Memorandum prepared for submission to the Departmental Committee on Homosexual Offences and Prostitution.
PRO HO 345/8, CHP/67, Memorandum submitted by Dr Eustace Chesser, Harley Street.
PRO HO 345/8, CHP/68, Memorandum submitted by the Foundation International Committee for Sexual Equality, Amsterdam.
PRO HO 345/8, CHP/69, Memorandum submitted by one of the witnesses to be heard on at 2.15 p.m. on Thursday 28 July.
PRO HO 345/8, CHP/76, Memorandum submitted by the Roman Catholic Advisory Committee.
PRO HO 345/8, CHP/84, Comment on fifty cases of homosexual personalities submitted by Dr R. Sessions Hodge.
PRO HO 345/9, CHP/86, Note by the Prison Commissioners for England and Wales.
PRO HO 345/9, CHP/90, Memorandum presented to the Departmental Committee on Homosexuality and Prostitution by a Joint Committee representing the Institute for the Study and Treatment of Delinquency and the Portman Clinic, London.
PRO HO345/9, CHP/92, Letter to the Chairman by Mr Richard Elwes, OBE., TD, QC, Recorder of Northampton and Chairman of Derbyshire Quarter Sessions.
PRO HO 345/9, CHP/93, Note by the secretary of a meeting between members of the Committee and Professor Alfred C. Kinsey.
PRO HO 345/9, CHP/95, Memorandum of Evidence prepared by a special committee of the Council of the British Medical Association for submission to the Departmental Committee, November 1955.
PRO HO 345/9, CHP/100, Federal Republic of Germany.
PRO HO 345/9, CHP/101, Netherlands.
PRO HO 345/9, CHP/102, Sweden.
PRO HO 345/9, CHP/103, Notes on the Law in New York.
PRO HO 345/9, CHP/104, Note by the Secretary on Recidivism.

PRO HO 345/9, CHP/107, Memorandum from Drs Curran and Whitby.
PRO HO 345/9, CHP/109, Denmark.
PRO HO/345/10, CHP/MISC/2, Note by the Chairman.
PRO HO 345/11, CHP/DR/3.
PRO HO 345/17, Part II Homosexual Offences, Chapter III.
PRO HO 345/18, CHP/DR/11 (Replacing CHP/DR/3).
PRO MEPO 3/987, Police Report, Metropolitan Police, 16 October 1935.
PRO MEPO 3/990, Police Report, Metropolitan Police.
Radzinowicz, L. (1947) *A History of Criminal Law and its Administration*, London: Stevens.
—— (1957) *Sexual Offences*, London: Macmillan.
Rank (1961) *'Victim' Press Book*, London: Rank.
Richardson, C. (1992) 'Myths, half truths and fantasies', *Gay Times*, February: 14.
Ricoeur, P. (1991) 'Narrated time', in M.J. Valdes (ed.) *A Ricoeur Reader: Reflection and Imagination*, London: Harvester Wheatsheaf, p. 340.
Rights of Women (1984) *Lesbian Mothers on Trial*, London: Rights of Women.
—— (1986) *Lesbian Mothers' Legal Handbook*, London: Women's Press.
Robson, R. (1992) *Lesbian (Out)law*, Ithaca: Firebrand.
—— (1995) 'Convictions: theorizing lesbians and criminal justice' in D. Herman and C. Stychin (eds) *Legal Inversians*, Philadelphia: Temple University Press, pp. 180–94.
Royal Commission (1929) *Report of the Royal Commission on Police Powers and Procedure*, Cmd 3297, London: HMSO.
Rush, P. and Young, A. (1995) In D. Nelken, *The Future of Criminology*, Sage, London.
Russell, D. (1990) *Rape in Marriage*, Bloomington: Indiana University Press.
Sarat, A. and Kearns, T.R. (1991) 'A journey through forgetting: towards a jurisprudence of violence', in A. Sarat and T.R. Kearns (eds) *The Fate of Law*, Ann Arbour: University of Michigan Press, p. 208.
(1992) 'Making peace with violence', in A. Sarat and T.R. Kearns (eds) *Law's Violence*, Ann Arbour: University of Michigan Press, p. 211.
Sedgwick, E. Kosovsky (1985) *Between Men*, New York: Columbia University Press.
—— (1991) *Epistemology of the Closet*, Hemel Hempstead: Harvester Wheatsheaf.
—— (1993) 'Queer performativity', *GLQ, A Journal of Lesbian and Gay Studies* 1 (1): 1.
Select Trials for Murder Robberies, Rape (1742) 4 volumes.
Signorile, M. (1993) *Queer in America*, New York: Random House.
Simpson, C., Chester, L. and Leitch, D. (1976) *The Cleveland Street Affair*, Boston: Little Brown.
Sinfield, A. (1994) *The Wilde Century*, London: Cassell.
Smart, C. (1989) *Feminism and the Power of Law*, London: Routledge.
Smith, A.M. (1990) 'A symptomology of an authoritarian discourse', *New Formations* 10 (Summer): 41–65.
—— (1995) *New Right Discourse on Race and Sexuality*, Cambridge: Cambridge University Press.
Smith, B.R. (1991) *Homosexual Desire in Shakespeare's England: A Cultural Poetics*, Chicago: University of Chicago Press.
Smith, F.B. (1976) 'Labouchère's amendment to the Criminal Law Amendment Bill', *Historical Studies* 17: 165.
Smith, J.C. (1989) *The Law of Theft*, 6th edn, London: Butterworths.
Smith, J.C. and Hogan, B. (1992) *Criminal Law*, 7th edn, London: Butterworths.
Smyth, C. (1992) *Lesbians Talk Queer Notions*, London: Scarlet Press.
Staunford, Sir W. (1557) *Les Plees Del Coron*, 1971 reprint, London: Professional Books.
Stephen, H.J. (1845) *New Commentaries on the Laws of England*, London: Butterworth.
Stephen, Sir James Fitzjames (1883) *A History of the Criminal Law of England*, London: Macmillan.
—— (1894) *A Digest of the Criminal Law*, 5th edn (1st edn 1877), London: Macmillan.
Stonewall (1993) *The Case for Change*, London: Stonewall.

Street Offences Committee (1928) *Report of the Street Offences Committee*, Cmd 3231, London: HMSO.

Stychin, C. (1995) *Law's Desire: Sexuality and the Limits of Justice*, London: Routledge.

Symonds, J.A. (1928) *Sexual Inversion*, 1984 reprint, New York: Bell Publishing.

Tatchell, P. (1992) *Europe in the Pink*, London: Gay Men's Press.

Taylor, F.H. (1947) 'Homosexual offences and their relation to psychotherapy', *British Medical Journal* II: 525–9.

Tempkin, J. (1987) *Rape and the Legal Process*, London: Sweet & Maxwell.

Theweleit, K. (1987) *Male Fantasies*, Vol. 1, trans. from German by S. Conway, E. Carter, and C. Turner, Cambridge: Polity Press.

—— (1989) *Male Fantasies*, Vol. 2, trans. from German by C. Turner, E. Carter and S. Conway, Cambridge: Polity Press.

Thomas, K. (1992) 'Beyond the privacy principle', *Columbia Law Review* 92: 1431.

—— (1993) 'corpus juris (hetero)sexualis: doctrine, discourse, and desire in *Bowers* v *Hardwick*', *GLQ, A Journal of Lesbian and Gay Studies* 1 (1): 33.

Thomas, P. and Costigan, R. (1990) *Promoting Homosexuality: s.28 of the Local Government Act 1988*, Cardiff: Cardiff Law School.

Thompson, B. (1994) *Soft Core*, London: Cassell.

—— (1995) *Sadomasochism*, London: Cassell.

Truman, C. (1994) *Lesbians' and Gay Men's Experiences of Crime and Policing: An Exploratory Study*, Manchester: Manchester Metropolitan University Department of Applied Community Studies.

Trumbach, R. (1977) 'London's sodomites: homosexual behaviour and Western culture in the 18th century', *Journal of Social History* 11: 1.

—— (1986) *Marriage, Sex and the Family in England 1660–1800: Sodomy Trials*, London: Garland.

Ulrich, K.H. (1975) *Forschungen über das Rätsel der mannmännlichen Liebe*, New York: Arno Press.

Vassall Tribunal (1963) *Report of the Tribunal Appointed to Inquire into the Vassall Case and Related Matters*, Cmnd 2009, London: HMSO.

Waaldijk, K. (1993) *Homosexuality: A European Community Issue*, Dordtrecht: Nijhoff.

Walkowitz, J.R. (1992) *City of Dreadful Delight*, London: Virago.

Walmsley, R. (1978) 'Indecency between males and the Sexual Offences Act 1967', *Criminal Law Review*, pp. 400–7.

Warner, M. (1993) *Fear of a Queer Planet*, Minneapolis: University of Minnesota Press.

Watney, S. (1980) 'The ideology of GLF', in Gay Left Collective (eds) *Homosexuality: Power and Politics*, London: Allison & Busby, pp. 64–73.

—— (1981) 'On gay liberation: a response to David Fernbach', in D. Adlam (ed.) *Politics and Power*, Vol. 3, London, pp. 295–308.

—— (1987) *Policing Desire: Pornography, AIDS and the Media*, London: Methuen.

Weeks, J. (1977) *Coming Out*, London: Quartet.

—— (1981) *Sex, Politics and Society: The Regulation of Sexuality Since 1800*, London: Longman.

West, D.J. (1970) 'Foreword', in L. Humphreys, *Tearoom Trade*, London: Duckworth.

—— (1985) *Sexual Victimisation: Two Recent Researches into Sex Problems and their Social Effects*, London: Gower.

Westwood, G. (1960) *A Minority: A Report on the Life of the Male Homosexual in Great Britain*, London: Longmans.

Wick, R.F. (1991) 'Out of the Closet and into the headlines', *Georgetown Law Journal* 80: 413.

Wilde, O. (1891) *The Picture of Dorian Gray*, London: Ward, Lock.

—— (1894) 'Phrases and philosophies for the use of the young', *Chameleon*, December; reprinted 1987, in *The Works of Oscar Wilde*, Leicester: Galley Press.

—— (1905) *De Profundis*, London; reprinted 1972 in *Selected Letters of Oscar Wilde*, edited by R. Hart-Davis, Oxford: Oxford University Press.

242

Wildeblood, P. (1957) *Against the Law,* Harmondsworth: Penguin.

Williams, P.J. (1991) *The Alchemy of Race and Rights,* Cambridge, Mass.: Harvard University Press.

Wintermute, R. (1995) *Sexual Orientation and Human Rights,* Oxford: Clarendon Press.

Wolfenden, J. (1957) *Report of the Departmental Committee on Homosexual Offences and Prostitution,* Cmnd 247, London: HMSO.

—— (1976) *Turning Points: The Memoirs of Lord Wolfenden,* London: Bodley Head.

Wotherspoon, G. (1991) *City of the Plain: History of a Gay Sub-Culture,* Sydney: Hale & Iremonger.

Young, A. (1990) *Femininity in Dissent,* London: Routledge.

Young, I. (1995) *The Stonewall Experiment: A Gay Psychohistory,* London: Cassell.

Zizek, S. (1991) *Looking Awry: An introduction of Jacques Lacan through Popular Culture,* London: MIT Press.

INDEX